The Presidency of
JAMES
BUCHANAN

AMERICAN PRESIDENCY SERIES

Donald R. McCoy,
Clifford S. Griffin,
Homer E. Socolofsky,
General Editors

James Buchanan

The Presidency of
JAMES
BUCHANAN

by

Elbert B. Smith

THE UNIVERSITY PRESS OF KANSAS
Lawrence / Manhattan / Wichita

© Copyright 1975 by The University Press of Kansas
Printed in the United States of America

Library of Congress Cataloging in Publication Data

Smith, Elbert B.
The Presidency of James Buchanan.

(American Presidency series)
Bibliography: p.
Includes index.
1. United States—Politics and government—1857-1861.
I. Title. II. Series.
E436.S6   320.9'73'068   74-31220
ISBN 0-7006-0132-5

To
Avery Craven
from a grateful student

Editors' Preface

The aim of the American Presidency Series is to present historians and the general reading public with interesting, scholarly assessments of the various presidential administrations. These interpretive surveys are intended to cover the broad ground between biographies, specialized monographs, and journalistic accounts. As such, each will be a comprehensive, synthetic work which will draw upon the best in pertinent secondary literature, yet leave room for the author's own analysis and interpretation.

Each volume in the series will deal with a separate presidential administration and will present the data essential to understanding the administration under consideration. Particularly, each book will treat the then current problems facing the United States and its people and how the president and his associates felt about, thought about, and worked to cope with these problems. Attention will be given to how the office developed and operated during the president's tenure. Equally important will be consideration of the vital relationships between the president, his staff, the executive officers, Congress, foreign representatives, the judiciary, state officials, the public, political parties, the press, and influential private citizens. The series will also be concerned with how this unique American institution—the presidency—was viewed by the presidents, and with what results.

All this will be set, insofar as possible, in the context not only of contemporary politics but also of economics, international relations, law, morals, public administration, religion, and thought. Such a broad approach is necessary to understanding, for a presidential administration is more than the elected and appointed officers composing it, since its work so often reflects the major problems, anxieties, and glories of the nation. In short, the authors in the series will strive to recount and evaluate the record of each administration and to identify its distinctiveness and relationships to the past, its own time, and the future.

Donald R. McCoy
Clifford S. Griffin
Homer E. Socolofsky

Preface

Expecting the president to be chosen by an elite group of electors or by the House of Representatives, the American founding fathers gave him immense power, particularly for dealing with matters related to peace and war. In domestic affairs he is more limited by the authority of Congress and the courts, but in dealing with the public he has both responsibilities and opportunities for personal influence far beyond his constitutional duties and powers. Having rid themselves of a British king, the often unruly American people quickly turned to the presidency for the fulfillment of deep-seated psychological and emotional needs formerly met by the monarchy. Americans have always demanded a role in determining the national goals and direction, but they have usually felt more secure and contented with the image of a strong and trustworthy hand in the White House and most often restive and troubled when they doubted either his strength or his dedication. Indeed, they have often considered the office even more powerful than it is. In times of national calamity the president is condemned. When the nation is relatively serene, he receives the praise. His words and actions are closely watched and disseminated to anyone and everyone willing to read or listen, and regardless of what he can or cannot do, he is held responsible for the state of the nation.

Depending upon the national problems, crises, or mood, a president may become immensely popular by leading a whirlwind of activity or by doing almost nothing. Americans have occasionally idolized the mediocre and rejected the wise, but surprisingly often this has affected the national destiny very little. Fortunately, not every period in American history has needed a president whose personality, principles, and talents can change the direction of an entire society. The great challenge to the system by which Americans choose their high priest and political pilot is the matching of the man with his times. Obviously, every president is subject to the momentum or inertia and the direction of his immediate predecessors and to powerful social, economic, and psychological forces and trends that he did not create and cannot change. On occasion, however, the particular beliefs, philosophy, temperament, strength of purpose, understanding of political processes, and rhetorical talents of certain presidents have in fact determined which of quite different alternative directions the United States would take.

In the 1850s the United States desperately needed strong, eloquent presidents who could understand the ambitions, feelings, sensitivities, and fears of both North and South and who could communicate his views of each to the other. Each section was slowly but inexorably developing a highly inaccurate image of the other's objectives and intentions, and only the president had the national platform from which a more balanced and realistic appraisal could emanate. People in both North and South were looking to the White House for comfort, support, and guidance; and supplying these commodities to either section without alienating the other beyond recall would require great wisdom as well as good intentions. It was an extraordinarily difficult but not entirely impossible challenge.

No one can say with certainty that a different president in the years 1857–61 might have turned the United States away from the path to war. It can be strongly argued, however, that James Buchanan might have prevented the key event that triggered the Southern secession. The election of Abraham Lincoln in 1860 was made certain by vigorous political policies that stemmed directly from the White House, and the origins and impact of these policies are a major theme of this book.

Aside from the president's direct role, the national events and situations of the Buchanan years remain highly controversial. James Buchanan had firm convictions about his America, and his views cannot be tested without studying and evaluating a vast amount of research and literature often unrelated to Buchanan himself. This book, therefore, often digresses from the president and admittedly expresses my own biases and convictions about the period in general. If I claim a knowledge and insight superior to that of the president, it is with humble sympathy for a man who lacked our access to more than a century of historical research. If I occasionally disagree with the convictions of fellow historians who read the evidence differently, it is with gratitude, respect, and admiration for their efforts and a willingness to admit that on rare occasions even I might be mistaken.

Acknowledgments

In the preparation of this book I have acquired many debts, particularly to:

The University of Maryland for summer research grants and a teaching program highly conducive to scholarly productivity.

Yong Chong, Mona Stockham, and Vera Blenkiron for typing and patience, and Dorothy Lukens, Ann Mechalek, and Wanda Cutright for making other tasks easier.

Yvonne Willingham for careful editing.

Colleagues like Donald Gordon, Keith Olson, Walter Rundell, and Wayne Cole for listening.

Several generations of historians from whom I have borrowed both facts and ideas.

My dear wife, Jean, for everything she is.

Contents

Contents

1

★★★★★

THE UNEASY REPUBLIC

The America that elected James Buchanan president in November, 1856, was already painfully divided by sectional differences, animosities, and fears, but the people also had much in common. They spoke the same language, granted homage to the same flag and other symbols of national loyalty, and thrilled to the same historical events and legends. They worshiped essentially the same God through churches national in scope, even though some of these had recently divided over the question of slavery. They shared a mutual pride in the vast size and varied geography of their homeland. With but one recent glaring exception they also expressed their self-interest and indulged their highly competitive instincts through support and work for nationwide political parties. Most Americans of every section were highly materialistic as befitting a people endowed with a continent of matchless resources and a religious philosophy that equated hard work and economic achievement with godliness. Most also shared the American dream of a land in which each generation would inevitably enjoy greater benefits than the last and in which every man had an equal chance to succeed on his own merits. Such hopes, of course, were not for Indians and Negroes, and already many citizens resented any further intrusions by immigrants from the Europe of their own recent origins; but among the white majority the dream came true at least often enough to maintain a robust vitality.

Both in groups and as individuals, Americans also shared an aggressive sense of their own superiority. If not everyone agreed

1

with contemporary historian George Bancroft on the glories of Jacksonian Democracy, few would have questioned his view of the nation as a uniquely blessed favorite of the Almighty. Abraham Lincoln was not the only American to consider his country a worldwide experiment in self-government whose success or failure might well determine the future of mankind.

The pride and arrogance of the average American did not lack for solid nourishment. Population, wealth, and power were increasing at an astonishing rate, and the rising living standards were being shared by more and more people. Millions of new acres were being cultivated each decade, and the outlines of a continental empire had already taken clear shape. As the covered wagons and river boats carried adventurous Americans farther and farther west, new towns and cities to consume their crops, process their resources, and supply the amenities of civilization were springing up in their tracks and growing at a geometric rate. Meanwhile, the older cities to the east were building factories, trading overseas, controlling the money markets, and receiving immigrants fast enough to cause the serious growing pains usually associated with too-rapid urban growth. Northern wheat and Southern cotton had become vital to the economies of various European nations. If American scientific technology was still only a robust child, it was daily outgrowing its ideological clothing and was clearly marked for gianthood. Americans could be justly proud of their achievements and attribute them at least in part to the nobility of their philosophical objectives.

By modern standards, of course, this claim to supernatural favor was seriously flawed by the refusal of most Americans, whether in the North or the South, to accept either Indians or Negroes as members of the human race. By 1857, however, a significant number of Americans, whatever their views on race, did see the institution of slavery as a glaring negation of the Declaration of Independence and the Christian Bible. Almost all of these lived safely in Northern states, which had long since outlawed slavery, and all but a few were quite ready to tolerate indefinitely this sin of their Southern brethren as long as it was no threat to their own well-being or self-interest. Indeed, Southerners quite correctly derided the hypocrisy of those ready to condemn Southern slavery while carefully ignoring the cruel discriminations and oppressions inflicted upon free blacks in their own Northern states.[1]

As long as the slavery question applied only to the South, the abolitionists remained unpopular, weak, and divided, with almost no visible public support. The annexation of Texas and the Mexican War, however, created an entirely new question. Abolishing slavery in the South meant the risk of a bloody war and the possible inundation of the North by free blacks. Keeping slavery out of new territories, however, could be accomplished merely by electing the right people to high office, and regardless of their attitudes toward slavery in the South, most Northerners objected strongly to even the possibility of having the institution in territories where they might someday wish to go. Strong racial prejudices were an integral part of the free-soil sentiment, and apparently most free-soilers were entirely happy to see slavery continued in the South as long as it did not spill over into territories they wished for themselves. Just as millions of nonslaveholding Southerners defended slavery in desperate fear of the social consequences of abolition, a great many free-soilers wanted all blacks, whether slave or free, kept from the new territories.[2]

Southern leaders, however, either could not or would not recognize the wide gulf between free-soilism, which did not threaten Southern slavery, and abolition, which was impotent through lack of popular support. The Southern white population pictured every effort to deny slavery full rights in the new territories as a blow against the existence of Southern slavery itself. The angry congressional debates of 1850 took the nation to the brink of disunion; but wiser heads prevailed, and the compromise brought at least a temporary peace.

In 1850 the struggle was still essentially a politicians' quarrel, and people in the North and the South generally accepted the compromise with enthusiasm. Northern and Southern radicals, however, remained ready to take advantage of new events and situations that were almost certain to occur. Northerners refused to obey the Fugitive Slave Law of 1850. While only a relative handful of slaves actually escaped, each act of assistance to a slave by Northerners was considered by Southerners to be a mortal insult and proof that the Constitution no longer offered adequate protection. The vast sale and popularity of Harriet Beecher Stowe's *Uncle Tom's Cabin* lacerated Southern feelings still further. Then, in 1854, the South won a nominal victory that stirred up a rage in the North. Trying to keep the Northern and Southern wings of the Democratic party united, Senator Stephen A. Douglas of Illinois put into action a formula that he thought would soothe Southern sensibilities without resulting in any new slave territories or states to rouse the North. He would admit Kansas and Nebraska as territories with the question of slavery to be left up to the future inhabitants. Since slavery was already illegal in both Kansas and Nebraska because of the Missouri Compromise, which since 1820 had barred slavery from all territory north of 36° 30', Douglas was further persuaded to call for the repeal of the Missouri Compromise.

To Northerners stirred up by their own ambitious politicians this meant the opening of a vast new area to slavery and the violation of a sacred trust that had existed for thirty-four years. Aided by the all-out efforts of the Pierce administration, Douglas got the bill passed, but Northern sentiment was heavily against it. The ensuing efforts by Northern and Southern organizations to get Kansas settled first by their own people were far less significant than the horde of greedy land-seekers who flooded into Kansas on their own, without urging or support from anyone. The settlers did tend to line up on one side or the other according to their origins, but by 1857 there were fewer than two hundred slaves in Kansas and the number was declining.

The violence and political frauds in Kansas differed little from those in other frontier areas—Nebraska for example—but the politicians, editors, clergymen, and free-lance propagandists quickly created a national image of Bleeding Kansas as a battleground between slavery and freedom. By 1856, Kansas had a legal but minority-chosen proslavery government at Lecompton, and an illegal but heavily supported antislave government at Topeka, each claiming to represent the true will of the Kansas people, most of whom probably wished only to be left alone.

The collapse of the Whig party after the election of 1852 and the Northern crusade against slavery in Kansas produced a new line-up in American politics. By 1856 former Whigs seeking a new political home, Northwestern Democrats angry over Kansas, Northeastern Democrats and Whigs who had bolted once before to the Free-Soil party in 1848, abolitionists, and other people discontented for various reasons had found a common bond in a new free-soilism dedicated to saving the West from slavery. Calling themselves Republicans, they nominated for president John C. Fremont, the dashing pathfinder and assistant conqueror of California who had been semi-martyred by the army in a well-deserved court-martial during the Polk administration. With an economic platform immensely attractive to both Western and industrial interests, they stood squarely against any further expansion of slavery and thereby eliminated themselves from any consideration in the South. The new party was thus entirely Northern, and while it neither enunciated or offered any real threat to slavery in the South its very existence was a mortal affront to Southern sensibilities. Southern radicals filled the air with appeals to Southern fear and pride for secession if Fremont should win.

At the Democratic convention in Cincinnati, the author of the Kansas-Nebraska bill, Stephen A. Douglas, could not capitalize on his efforts to find a common ground for Northern and Southern Democrats. The party wanted a winner, and both the incumbent, Pierce, and Douglas had too many enemies. On the seventeenth ballot the convention chose the sixty-five-year-old former Senator, Secretary of State, and diplomat James Buchanan of Pennsylvania. Buchanan had been minister to England throughout the fateful struggles over Kansas, and was unconnected in the public mind with the sectional struggle. Many Southern leaders knew him as a personal friend. Most Northerners found him at least acceptable on the basis of his earlier record. "Never a leading man in any high sense," said the elderly ex-Senator Thomas Hart Benton, "but eminently a man of peace."[3] Benton probably spoke for many Americans in finding Buchanan totally uninspiring but at least preferable to the dangers of a victory by Fremont and a party centered entirely in the North. Fremont was the husband of Benton's favorite daughter, but in 1856 the old man made twenty speeches in twenty-two days urging the voters to reject a sectional candidate and support Buchanan as the one hope for keeping the Union together.

The Democratic platform called for the right of the people of all territories acting through the "legally and fairly expressed will of the majority of the actual residents . . . to form a constitution with or without domestic slavery, and be admitted into the Union."[4] This seemed to imply that the territories could deal with the slavery question only when ready to become a state, which meant that during the entire territorial stage the advocates of slavery would have at least a legal chance to win the future state. In fact, however, this question of timing would depend on the president and the Congress when and if the issue arose. The platform also included a firm support for the Compromise of 1850 and strong opposition to any further agitation of the slave question. It was an honest effort to unite the party and relax the sectional tensions.

The Republican platform, however, made no concessions to the cause of national unity. Alongside its promises to promote a Pacific railroad and finance river and harbor improvements was an indictment of the previous administration for murder, confiscation of private property, false imprisonment, and tyrannical subversion of the Constitution in Kansas. President Pierce and his advisers, agents, supporters, apologists, and accessories were declared guilty of crimes against humanity and promised a "sure and condign punishment hereafter" if Fremont should win. Having thereby promised to jail and perhaps execute all leaders who disagreed with them on Kansas, the Republicans proceeded to stage an exciting, highly moralistic campaign that almost elected their candidate.

Small wonder that President Pierce responded with bitter counteraccusations or that Buchanan staged his own campaign as the savior of the Union against the divisive schemes of the Black Republicans. *"The Union is in danger and the people everywhere begin to know it,"* Buchanan wrote. "The Black Republicans must be, as they can be with justice, boldly assailed as disunionists, and this charge must be reiterated again and again." The ancient issues of bank and tariff were dead, but Democrats everywhere must publicize the treasonable sentiments of "the abolitionists, free soilers and infidels against the Union. . . . This race ought to be run on the question of Union or disunion." Buchanan made no speeches, but carried on a vast correspondence that both reiterated and strengthened his convictions with regard to Republican wickedness.[5]

If the Republican platform, like most of its kind, was largely empty rhetoric, the Democratic editors and politicians would not accept it as such. They constantly quoted the threats in the platform, and usually cited only the most radical of the Republican spokesmen. By quoting out of context they could make even these gentlemen sound much more radical and violent than most of them really were, and Buchanan himself was completely captured by this theme. The constant repetition of an accusation does help convince those who hear it, and the process is usually even more effective on the person making the charge. To the end of his days, James Buchanan believed with an almost religious conviction that the only real disunionists and the only people actually responsible for the Civil War were the Republicans, all of whom he classified as abolitionist fanatics poised to strike a mortal blow against the South, if not against all reasonable men everywhere.

The 1856 election was complicated still further by the American or Know-Nothing party, which ran former president Millard Fillmore on a platform calling for the exclusion of Catholic immigrants. At least some of this party's leaders hoped to reunite North and South in a common crusade against foreigners and aliens, and which major party this exercise in lunacy hurt most is difficult to determine. In the end, however, James Buchanan was elected president and the Union was given another chance.

Whether or not the American Civil War was already inevitable by 1857 historians will probably debate forever. Whatever hopes for peace did exist, however, rested squarely upon the shoulders of the new president-elect. The major forces driving the nation toward catastrophe were fear and pride. Northeasterners and Northwesterners alike genuinely feared that slavery might spread into the new territories in defiance of morality, Christianity, and their own best economic and social interests. They also desperately wanted and felt entitled to tariffs, liberal land-policies, river and harbor improvements, and western railroads, and they bitterly resented the role of Southerners and Southern sympathizers in blocking these programs. They were tired of Southern or pro-Southern presidents, and each national election had deepened their frustrations. Since 1828 Presidents Jackson, Tyler, Polk, and Taylor had all been slaveholding Southerners, and Van Buren, Fillmore, and Pierce had been strongly identified with Southern principles. The one possible exception, Harrison, had died after only a month in office. Van Buren had turned Free-Soiler in 1848, but as vice-president and president he had supported both the efforts to censor antislavery literature from the mails and the "gag" laws against Northern petitions for abolition in the District of Columbia. This Southern control of the White House had been reflected in cabinet appointments and political patronage in general, agrarian suppression of cherished Northern economic policies, and the acquisition of a vast territorial empire under Southern auspices in a war widely denounced as immoral throughout the North. True, only Texas had joined the Union as a slave state, but in Congress the South had fought bitterly for the other areas, and the questioned remained far from settled. Legally, Texas could still be subdivided into five states and send ten instead of two senators to Washington, and the recent repeal of the sacred Missouri Compromise was ominous evidence for many that the "Slave Power" was real enough. Legally, the heart of the continent from Missouri to the western mountains had been thrown open to slavery, and the uselessness to the South of this favor was not at all clear to the average Northerner.

Actually, as Webster had pointed out in his magnificent plea for Northern compassion in 1850, time was all on the side of the Northerners, but they needed to hear this over and over from politicians who, unfortunately, were instead more intent upon stirring up their fears. Southern control of the national destiny was in fact declining at the very moment when millions of Northerners feared it was growing. Words of assurance and corresponding deeds by a

7

trusted president who understood their feelings were essential if Northern attitudes toward the South were to move back toward reality.

Southerners' fears were even more irrational, in part because their grievances involved a serious threat to their own self-esteem. Whether or not, as some historians believe, many Southern leaders were afflicted by deep inner doubts about the righteousness of slavery, they did resent bitterly the Northern and growing worldwide view that slavery was evil, immoral, cruel, un-Christian, and undemocratic. While John C. Calhoun, their self appointed spokesman until his death in 1850, had achieved consistency by attacking both the Declaration of Independence and the concept of mass democracy, most thoughtful Southerners were still trying to make slavery fit into the system of democratic and libertarian values they shared with the rest of the country. The constant implication that Southerners themselves were cruel, immoral, un-Christian, and undemocratic was like a splinter under the skin, always present and impossible to ignore or forget.

Aside from such subtle considerations, the fear of slave insurrections, particularly in isolated rural areas, was both real and simple. Tales of the horrible race war in Haiti, the alleged Denmark Vesey conspiracy in South Carolina, and the Nat Turner rebellion in Virginia, as well as numerous lesser incidents both real and imagined, kept large numbers of white Southerners constantly uneasy. And since the happiness of slaves and the advantages of slavery to the slave himself were articles of faith, Southerners had to believe that the dangers stemmed primarily from the evil efforts of Northern agitators who through pamphlets and in person stirred up the rebellion with dishonest and impossible promises. More than three-fourths of all Southern whites had no direct relation with slavery at all, but most of these accepted without question the warning that emancipation would mean social equality, inbreeding, and amalgamation of the races into a mulatto society. Slavery made all white men equal, argued slavery defenders, because their white skins kept them superior to the Negroes. Those who had no other distinction were not prepared to surrender it lightly.

Most Northerners were ready to grant tolerance for slavery and leave it undisturbed in the South, but they would not grant it their moral approval in the form of equal rights in the new territories. Southerners, on the other hand, had a powerful psychological need for approval as well as tolerance, and easily identified disapproval with a nonexistent Northern threat to slavery in the South. The

United States desperately needed a president who understood this need and would try to convince Southerners that the impossibility of its attainment did not mean either a physical danger to Southern slavery or a valid reflection upon their integrity and character. Ironically enough, Abraham Lincoln did recognize and sympathize with the South's moral, psychological, and sociological problems, and if he had been elected in 1856 instead of 1860 the Union might have survived his election. Southerners needed a president who would spell out the realities in firm but sympathetic language, strive to assuage their fears and wounded feelings, and carefully avoid intensifying their paranoia by rousing false hopes doomed to failure.

It was a tall order, but a great many people hoped James Buchanan could fill it.

2

★★★★★

THE PRESIDENT

"Whatever may have been the effect of Mr. Buchanan's elevation to the Presidency and of the possession of its overshadowing
powers upon himself, he was, assuredly, before that occurrence, a
cautious, circumspect and sagacious man, amply endowed with
those clear perceptions of self-interest and of duties connected with
it that are almost inseparable from the Scotch character."[1] Thus
wrote Martin Van Buren, who probably recognized most of his
own characteristics in Buchanan.

For more than a century the most common adjectives applied
by historians to James Buchanan have been "indecisive" and "weak."
All too often, however, such words mean essentially that the person
so designated did not make the same decisions the historians know
they themselves would have quickly made in the same circumstances. In most of his actions during a long lifetime, however,
James Buchanan was neither indecisive nor weak. He was occasionally inconsistent and erratic, but his decisions and actions usually served a purpose that he clearly had in mind.

In 1824 Buchanan was strongly identified with Henry Clay,
but even after contradicting Andrew Jackson publicly he was on
Old Hickory's winning side by 1828. As a representative and
senator he was regularly elected first as a Federalist and then as a
Democrat in a state in which his own party was usually divided
bitterly on both issues and personalities. As secretary of state to
James K. Polk, he opposed the president's demand for 54° 40′ as the
boundary of Oregon, prepared a brilliant argument for 54° 40′, re-

fused to support his own argument and advocated a compromise, and finally, on the grounds that 54° 40′ was correct, refused to help prepare the message submitting 49° to the Senate. During the Mexican War he advocated only limited annexations, opposed Polk's effort to send a high-level peace commission for fear it would not demand enough territory, and finally opposed submission of the actual treaty to the Senate because it did not annex enough of Mexico to the United States. Indecisive? Perhaps, but the indecisiveness resulted from some very shrewd decisions. Almost alone among the members of the bitterly controversial Polk administration, he escaped with no serious political scars or handicaps.

Even Buchanan's appearance, through no conscious fault of his own, occasionally led others to consider him deceitful. He was tall, heavy, and imposing looking, with a large head, white hair that had once been blond, blue eyes, and rather handsome fine features. He had a defect in one eye, however, and to compensate for it he would tilt his head forward and sideways. Thus he always appeared to be listening intently with great concern. In the words of his most perceptive biographer: "The mere appearance conveyed so definite an impression of assent and probation that many people, on early acquaintance, sincerely believed that they had completely captivated James Buchanan and reciprocated by attentions to him which he attributed to traits more complimentary to him than a wry neck. . . . Difficulties often arose when those who thought they were close to him realized that they had been reading his looks rather than his mind, and such persons would break off with a sense of personal injury."[2]

Born in 1791 to relatively humble parents in rural Pennsylvania, Buchanan ultimately amassed a large fortune—some $300,000—through intelligence and talent, hard work, thrift, and shrewd management. In 1819, while still a struggling young lawyer, he became engaged to a Lancaster belle whose father was one of America's first millionaires. A combination of the father's objections, gossip that Buchanan was interested chiefly in her fortune, and the young swain's apparent neglect of his fiancée in favor of clients led to a broken engagement, followed by the young lady's sudden death. Whether or not the tragic event had been affected by her grief, her parents forbade Buchanan to attend the funeral, and he resolved to honor her memory by remaining a bachelor. Eighteen years later he almost broke this vow, but with no apparent struggle he abandoned his suit because of self-imposed obligations to a large crew of orphaned nephews and nieces. Finally, at the age of sixty-seven he expressed interest in a nineteen-year-old charmer, but he let his judgment rule his heart and wrote her a poem explaining all this. During the intervening years he had expressed much platonic affection for various handsome ladies, but invariably selected those who were already safely and happily married to someone else. All available evidence indicates that he remained celibate as well as unmarried, without ever expressing any sense of deprivation or loss.

Those who study such matters often correlate bachelorhood and celibacy with certain physical and psychological characteristics, although whether these are the cause or the result may be open to question. At the age of sixty-six the new president was in fact meticulous and fussy about trivial matters; excessively inquisitive about the personal affairs of his cabinet, younger family members, and friends; reluctant to delegate authority free from his own personal supervision; and extremely sensitive to personal slights both real and imagined. He did not make friends easily; but he had a strong need for personal affection and companionship, and he was highly receptive to the influence of those willing to grant it.

Whatever the effects of bachelorhood upon his personality, the lack of a wife and family obviously affected his personal associations and emotional attitudes. For thirty years in Washington Buchanan's closest friends were Southerners who during the congressional sessions tended to dominate the male society of Washington's hotels and rooming houses. Without proof it may be speculated that the Southern representatives and senators were more prone to leave their wives at home on the plantations, and perhaps the Southern wives who did come to Washington may have showed more interest in the well-being of a lonely bachelor. For many years Buchanan's roommate and closest friend was Senator and later Vice-President William R. King of Alabama, and in a letter to Mrs. James K. Polk, Representative Aaron V. Brown of Tennessee once referred to the two men as "Buchanan & his wife."[3] At the time King was expected to be Polk's chief rival for the 1844 vice-presidential nomination, and Brown was supporting Polk. In short, Buchanan apparently found most of his deeper friendships among the numerous, gregarious, and sympathetic Southerners in the Washington community.

Meanwhile, his entourage of nephews, nieces, and family-type servants continued to increase, and the elderly uncle gloried in the role of patriarch. By 1852, he had some twenty-two nieces and nephews and thirteen grandnephews and grandnieces. Seven of these were orphans in his full care, several others were half-orphans whom he was helping to support, and he was perpetually concerned with the personal affairs of most of them. This self-imposed family responsibility may also have helped Buchanan appreciate the paternalistic aspects of both slavery and the Southern upper-class life-style. When Howell Cobb complained about owning a thousand slaves who were an economic burden but could not be sold because Cobb would not separate their families, Buchanan probably recognized a kindred soul.

During his first four terms in Congress, Buchanan was a Federalist, and many of the Jacksonians whom he joined in 1828 always suspected the sincerity of his conversion. Perhaps in response to this, Buchanan as he grew older became more and more committed to Jacksonian laissez-faire agrarian economics at the very time when such principles were becoming more and more obsolete, even among the Democrats. In keeping with the views of his Southern friends, he adamantly opposed such government programs as homesteads, river and harbor improvements, and land grants for schools; and despite the tariff needs of his own state, he even lost any taste he might have ever had for this form of protection. Wheatlands, his magnificent home on a farm near Lancaster, was his idealization of the good life, and it symbolized the rural values and principles for which the South claimed exclusive guardianship. The owner of a manorial farm valuable more for its psychic rewards than its economic production could appreciate a plantation society whose advocates stressed order, harmony, and pleasant living rather than mere profits.

While Buchanan occasionally expressed regret that slavery existed, and called it wrong in his final memoir, there is no evidence that he ever felt any moral indignation against it or sympathy for the slaves. More than once he defended the right of post-masters to censor abolition literature. In the struggle over Northern petitions for abolition in the District of Columbia he took the popular view that the petitions should be accepted but immediately tabled without consideration. In 1844 and 1845 he supported the annexation of Texas on the grounds first expressed by Robert J. Walker that various border states were slowly abandoning slavery and that Texas was needed to become a new home for border-state slaves who might otherwise be liberated to inundate the North. When he opposed the war-ending Treaty of Guadalupe-Hidalgo

14

because he wanted more Mexican territory, he fully expected any such territory to be open to slavery. In 1847 he announced that the question had been solved by the Missouri Compromise and that the 36° 30' line should apply to any new areas to be taken from Mexico.

In 1850 Buchanan prophesied that within four years there would be two independent republics, but he saw no reason for war between them. In the debates of that year he argued that Congress had the right and duty to define the status of slavery in the territories. He felt that Congress could grant the South equal rights in the territories without actually extending slavery because economics would keep slavery out of the west anyhow. This, he insisted, would prove that slavery could not be extended and thereby help confine it to the South. Congressional abdication of control, he warned prophetically, would be a disaster because it would create fighting zones where people would fight over slavery during the territorial stage. After passage of the 1850 compromise, Buchanan urged obedience to the Fugitive Slave Act, and deplored its violation as angrily as any Southerner.

In 1853 Pierce awarded Buchanan the mission to London, where he performed creditably, but again displayed his affinity for Southern interests. In the famous Ostend Manifesto, which he signed with Pierre Soulé, the American minister to Spain, and Virginian John Mason, the minister to France, the three diplomats advocated the purchase of Cuba from Spain and recommended seizing it by force if the sale could not be arranged. Stressing the danger that the Spanish might abolish slavery in Cuba, they insisted that this must be prevented because of its danger to slavery in the United States. Buchanan's biographers have insisted that he tried to tone the message down and and that the version publicized was stronger than the one actually signed, but his approval of the basic idea and its justification cannot be denied.[4]

Buchanan ran for president as the savior of the nation from the disunionist radical Republicans, and he never ceased to believe that they and they alone were responsible for the Civil War. He vehemently opposed the Emancipation Proclamation, and as late as November, 1864, he suggested that "a frank and manly offer to the Confederates that they might return to the Union just as they were before they left it, leaving the slavery question to settle itself, might possibly be accepted."[5] In his 1866 memoir he insisted that slavery would have been peacefully extinguished "if rashly." It should have been tolerated, he wrote, for the same reason that

Christians were not using force to destroy Islam and Catholics and Protestants were no longer making war on each other: different beliefs and ways of life should be viewed tolerantly. Denouncing every Republican policy, he was perhaps most angry about the fears of slave insurrection caused by the Northern glorification of John Brown.[6]

James Buchanan's greatest handicap in the White House was neither indecisiveness nor weakness. It was his profound emotional attachment to the South. He could not understand either the true character or the strength of the Free-Soil movement, because he felt no repugnance himself against the establishment of plantation slavery in any new territories where it could survive. Fearful Southerners needed to know the difference between free-soilers and abolitionists, but Buchanan could not teach them this because he did not understand it either. Equally excited Northerners needed to understand the actual relative weakness of the South. If, however, the President tried to favor the South without an adequate sensitivity to Northern feelings, he would instead magnify enormously the North's fears of an evil Slave Power threatening to make the West into a slavery-cursed economic and social desert.

3

★★★★★

THE ADMINISTRATION

"Disunion is a word which ought not to be breathed amongst us even in a whisper," wrote James Buchanan during the 1856 election campaign. "Our children ought to be taught that it is a sacrilege to pronounce it. . . . There is nothing stable but Heaven and the Constitution." In the first flush of victory, the president-elect announced his major goal: "to arrest, if possible, the agitation of the slavery question at the North, and to destroy sectional parties. Should a kind Providence enable me to succeed in my efforts to restore harmony to the Union, I shall feel that I have not lived in vain."[1]

Clearly, in Buchanan's eyes, the fault lay with the North, and Senator Alexander H. Stephens of Georgia spoke the confidence of many Southerners when he assured a friend: "My word for it you need have no apprehensions for the Wilmot Proviso hereafter if Buchanan should be elected. . . . I do verily believe if in the approaching contest we shall succeed, there will never be another sectional or slavery struggle in the United States, at least in our day."[2]

The first step was the selection of a cabinet. No president picks his immediate subordinates lightly, and the men chosen by James Buchanan would help make decisions of national life-and-death significance. Obviously, no one expected him to appoint any Republicans to high office, but if the Democratic party were to triumph or even survive as a national party he would need a balance among its major factions. A solidly Democratic South might be a worthy political objective, but alone it would not be enough to keep a Democrat in the White House or to control Congress. This would require the additional votes of several hundred thousand Northerners who were still loyal to the Democratic party and willing to accept its popular sovereignty formula, but were also anxious to keep the West free from slavery.

After a long and successful career of balancing the warring factions in his own state of Pennsylvania, Buchanan now abandoned the practice. His closest friends and advisers during the critical process of cabinet selection were Howell Cobb, owner of a thousand slaves but still a Unionist; John Slidell, wheeler-dealer politician from Louisiana; Indiana Senator Jesse Bright, who owned a large slave-worked plantation in Kentucky; and Henry Wise, the often erratic former congressman and governor from Virginia who once had threatened to shoot a witness at a congressional hearing. In 1844 Wise had made an irreversible offer of the State Department to John C. Calhoun without bothering to first consult President Tyler, who had had no such intention.[3] Buchanan offered cabinet posts to all four, but Wise, Slidell, and Bright felt their talents could be more useful elsewhere and preferred influence without responsibility. Cobb ultimately became secretary of the treasury.

For State, Buchanan had considered Robert J. Walker of Mississippi, a former senator and secretary of the treasury under Polk, but Southerners considered him lukewarm on slavery and Northerners remembered that he had once urged the annexation of all of Mexico. Also, the proud Cobb would not serve in a post subordinate to Walker. This problem was solved by appointing the aged, fat, and senile Lewis Cass of Michigan, the party's presidential candidate in 1848, with the understanding that the able John B. Appleton would be assistant secretary and actually run the department. Cass, just defeated for reelection to the Senate, would not have to go home with his tail between his legs, and none of the factions objected.

Since Cobb had supported the Compromise of 1850, Buchanan sought balance by appointing an opponent of the Compromise, Jacob Thompson of Mississippi. Thompson was a Southern radical who had attracted less attention than some by remaining quieter. He had left North Carolina a poor boy, but had accumulated a great fortune in land and slaves in Mississippi. In 1840 he had married a poor girl of fourteen and sent her off to Paris for four years of education before consummating the union. At thirty-one she was a gay, beautiful woman, and one of Buchanan's favorites. Thompson became secretary of the interior.

For secretary of the navy Buchanan selected Isaac Toucey of Connecticut, who had close family ties in the South and like Buchanan had usually sided with the South on most issues. Ultimately, in the early secession period, Toucey would be accused of treason and the Connecticut legislature would remove his picture from its gallery of ex-governors. Toucey would be proven innocent of wrong-doing, but the very fact of suspicion of treason indicated his pro-Southern reputation.

The Democratic factions in New York were so irreconcilable that Buchanan decided to ignore that state altogether. Pennsylvania was almost as bad, but here he finally settled upon Jeremiah S. Black for attorney general. Black was an able, well-read, humorless, self-righteous, former chief justice of the Pennsylvania Supreme Court. He was not pro-Southern as such, but he ardently disliked any kind of radicalism, which included free-soilism, and he believed firmly in party discipline and solutions based upon legality, whether or not they fit the existing political or social realities. More like Jackson and Polk than like his fellow Scotch-Irishman Buchanan, Black was a tough fighter on any side he chose to support.

The president and his advisers finally settled upon former Governor John B. Floyd of Virginia for secretary of war and former Congressman and Governor Aaron V. Brown of Tennessee for postmaster general. Floyd, whose prominence had been inherited from his father, was thoroughly incompetent. Brown was a better administrator, but neither could be expected to act or advise impartially on matters related to the South and slavery.

It was a relatively homogeneous cabinet composed of four essentially orthodox, slaveholding Southerners and three Northerners, one of whom was useless, one of whom was ideologically pro-Southern, and one of whom would be pro-Southern on legal grounds until the actual advent of secession. Conspicuously, the big city politicians, the growing forces of commerce and industry, the free-soil Democrats, and the popular-sovereignty Democrats of the Douglas persuasion had been completely ignored. As Buchanan's able biographer Philip Klein has pointed out, the president was surrounded by rural politicians and lawyers still wedded to the America of Andrew Jackson, and from them he received only a partial and highly antiquated view of the realities in 1857. For eight years he had been out of office or out of the country, and he was strangely oblivious to the changes that had occurred. New cities had sprung up and old cities had grown much larger, and their needs could no longer be met with mere Jeffersonian rhetoric. Throughout most of the North the political principles and habits of Jacksonian democracy had long since been taken for granted by both political parties, and the Northwesterners' demands for an expanded currency, homesteads, and federal subsidies for internal improvements, including railroads, could not safely be opposed by either party. Perhaps most important, the quarrels over the Mexican War annexations and the recent Kansas imbroglio had generated a conscious, powerful, and widespread Northern antipathy to the spread of slavery and genuine fears of a Southern Slave Power.

Buchanan's most serious blunder was the omission of any friend or supporter of Stephen A. Douglas. Douglas was the party's most popular senator and the idol of much of the Northwest, and he had contributed much to the nomination of Buchanan by withdrawing his own name at the strategic moment. He was enormously influential with the rank and file of Democrats in several states. He could be a powerful ally or a dangerous enemy. He would obviously be a leading presidential contender in 1860, but Buchanan had already stated his own aversion to a second term. If the president did not wish to strengthen Douglas, he might at least have sought to neutralize him with a minimum of recognition. Jesse Bright, however, saw himself as the great patronage broker of the Northwest, and was determined to displace the Little Giant as the area's political leader. Bright and Douglas despised each other personally, and Bright constantly had the ear of James Buchanan. The president, after all, was human; and, while Douglas had withdrawn from the contest at Cincinnati in time to prevent the convention from turning to a third candidate, he had nonetheless been Buchanan's chief rival. Bright, on the other hand, had labored long and hard both before and during the convention for Buchanan's nomination. The obligation to repay debts is not unique to Scotch-Irish Presbyterianism; but it is a basic article of faith, and Buchanan was meticulous in his religious duties. He could not satisfy both Douglas and Bright; and Douglas, therefore, had to be disappointed.

Bright's task of defamation, furthermore, was probably not too difficult, because Buchanan already held Douglas responsible for reopening the slavery quarrel with the Kansas-Nebraska Act. Also, Douglas was by nature cast in a perfect mold for the enmity of James Buchanan. He was daring, exciting, aggressive, bold, impulsive, and bumptious. Gifted with great charisma, he roused the love and enthusiasm of supporters in a way Buchanan could never do, and at the age of forty-four Douglas already had a position in the Senate that Buchanan had never attained. Buchanan had once complained bitterly that the party newspaper edited by Francis P. Blair did not give his speeches their proper attention, and Blair's denial implied that on the contrary the speeches got all the space they merited.[4] When Douglas spoke, however, the galleries were full and his speeches received good national newspaper coverage. Buchanan even appeared to resent the marriage of Douglas, a widower, to the beautiful Adele Cutts, whom he himself had admired for years. Against the unanimous advice of his cabinet and despite the written opposition of Douglas, who feared charges of nepotism at home, Buchanan gave the father of Mrs. Douglas a high office in his administration. Buchanan declared, "Should I make the appointment, . . . it will be my own regard for Mr. Cutts and his family, and not because Senator Douglas has had the good fortune to become his son-in-law."[5]

Douglas had campaigned vigorously for Buchanan, and later claimed that the canvass had cost him $42,000. By so doing, of course, he had advanced his own popularity and future prospects, but he still had reason to expect at least some gratitude. Buchanan did write Douglas a letter of thanks, but, almost incredibly, he addressed it to "The Hon. Samuel A. Douglas."[6] Thus informed that the president-elect was perhaps less than fully concerned about the name and reputation of his donor, the proud senator called to present the claims of his friends for political patronage. The Little Giant came away in a fury—Slidell soon reported that Douglas was "ready to run amok like a maddened Malay." Douglas after all had proposed the formula on territorial slavery that had been the chief plank in the platform, and he had fought the party's battles while Buchanan rested in London. A Douglas man was appointed postmaster in Chicago, but all other state appointments in Illinois were made without even consulting the state's one Democratic senator.

The hundreds of subordinate appointments throughout the country reflected the same bias. The general rule was that the men appointed by Pierce should serve out their terms if they had performed well, but it was soon altered in the case of those who did not go along with the administration's policies. The result was a party machine that gave the external appearance of great power, but one which could control the actions of Congress only if the presidential goals coincided at least reasonably well with the feelings of the general public. In short, the president felt strong enough to impose his will on Congress through political pressures, but he might be disappointed. If he thereby led the South to expect certain advantages that in fact he could not deliver, the result would be a serious exacerbation of the sectional conflict.

Buchanan's cabinet selections were of enormous importance for a man of his particular temperament and background. While he was not averse to making decisions, he always preferred sharing the responsibility for them with others. Also, of course, becoming president reduced the time he could spend with the friends and cronies of earlier years. The presidency is a lonely office at best, even for a man with a wife and family, and Buchanan was never a lover of solitude. Except for Cass, his cabinet was selected largely on the basis of compatibility with his own views and outlook, and until secession it was a uniquely harmonious group upon which he imposed social obligations as well as the role of counsellors on most important issues. Regular cabinet meetings were supplemented by equally regular dinners and family-type gatherings. No crises were met without long, special cabinet sessions in which the president and his advisers convened as allies against adversaries usually considered enemies as well as opponents on principle.[7]

The unanimity of the cabinet and the president on virtually every issue until secession led both contemporaries and later historians to call his administration a directory in which the cabinet members seemed to possess coequal powers with the president. The members themselves, however, always insisted that despite the attention their views invariably received, the president himself was always in command. The administration was a directory because the president shared fully the basic precepts and emotional attachments of his ministers. He can be faulted for selecting such a cabinet, but the national issues soon became so polarized that any cabinet dissenters would probably have felt morally bound to resign anyhow. James Buchanan did not want a quarrelsome family. He was therefore often shielded from information and advice superior to that which he was receiving. More facts and different counsel might have made him uncomfortable, but they probably would have changed his policies only rarely if at all.

4

★★★★★

ALLIES: THE PRESIDENT
AND THE COURT

As the Congress awaited the inauguration of a new president, Franklin Pierce, still smarting from the insults and threats of the Republican platform, delivered his own farewell address. It was a bitter denunciation of the Republicans for reviving the sectional quarrel, and the accused members of Congress responded in kind. The Republicans taunted the Democrats for being divided among themselves, and the rancorous debate did show that the party was sharply divided over the meaning of popular sovereignty. Northern Democrats, represented by men like Douglas and Cass, argued that a territorial legislature could decide whether or not slavery was to be allowed. Most of the Southerners, however, insisted that the decision could not be made until the territory was ready for statehood.

Preparing his inaugural address, Buchanan felt that he must deal with this question. He personally agreed with the Southern view, but hoped to avoid alienating the Northerners if possible. His judgment during these weeks may or may not have been impaired by a severe attack of dysentery, which he suffered in common with a large number of patrons of the National Hotel in Washington. The pipes had frozen there, and while some suggested that rats had fallen into the water supply, others believed that the frozen pipes had backed sewage up into the kitchen. Whatever the cause, several dozen people were severely affected, and one of Buchanan's favorite nephews, Eskridge Lane, actually died from it. The president suffered terribly for several weeks but recovered;

then, because of loyalty to the proprietor, he defied his doctor's orders and returned there just before the inauguration. The disease returned and again lasted for many painful weeks.

As he struggled to write an inaugural speech that would pacify rather than irritate, the president-elect suddenly saw a glimmer of hope in a case being argued before the Supreme Court. The issue concerned a sixty-two-year-old slave, Dred Scott, who had spent the years 1834–1838 with his army-officer master in free territories before being returned to Missouri. When the master died, his widow had found Scott and his family a burden rather than an asset. The son of Scott's former owner, who was helping to support Scott, financed a suit for freedom on the grounds that residence in free territories had made Scott a free man. A Missouri circuit court agreed but the Missouri Supreme Court reversed the lower court with an obviously political ruling that earlier precedents were no longer applicable because "since then not only individuals, but States, have been possessed by a dark and fell spirit in relation to slavery, whose gratification is sought in the pursuit of measures whose inevitable consequences must be the overthrow and destruction of our government. Under such circumstances, it does not behoove the State of Missouri to show the least countenance to any measures which might gratify this spirit."[1] Ultimately, the case was brought before the Supreme Court for the deliberate purpose of getting a ruling on the constitutional aspect of the case. Scott's owner, Mrs. Emerson, had by this time married an abolitionist, and her brother had assumed full control of their controversial ward. All agreed that whatever the decision of the Court, Scott would in fact go free.

The defense attorneys, George Ticknor Curtis and Montgomery Blair, argued brilliantly on the grounds of constitutionality and precedent. The opposing lawyers, Reverdy Johnson and Henry S. Geyer, dramatically stressed the rights and needs of the slaveholding states. Johnson, particularly, made insulting remarks about Negroes in general and infuriated free-soilers and abolitionists alike with the view that slavery would exist for all time and must be expanded as the only way to preserve the constitutional freedom of the nation.

The Supreme Court of 1857 was led by an ancient Marylander, Chief Justice Roger B. Taney. Though he had freed his own slaves years before, Taney was in fact an angry Southern partisan who felt the South was in grave danger. The other judges were John A. Campbell of Alabama, James Wayne of Georgia, John Catron of

Tennessee, Peter B. Daniel of Virginia, Samuel Nelson of New York, Robert C. Grier of Pennsylvania, Benjamin R. Curtis of Massachusetts, and John McLean of Ohio. The Southerners were all strongly partisan, although both Wayne and Catron would stay with the Union in 1861. Nelson was a conservative Democrat who had been appointed by Tyler. Grier had been a strong defender of the Fugitive Slave Act. Obviously, only McLean and Curtis were likely to see merit in Scott's claim; and if the Court chose to leap from the confines of the specific case into the broader area of general principles, the result was almost certain to uphold or expand the territorial rights of slaveholders.

Facing the question of when territorial citizens could make their decision on slavery, James Buchanan looked for a way to avoid a stand that might alienate the Northern Democrats. In early February he wrote his friend Judge Catron. Could he safely say in his inaugural address that the Court would soon decide the question? Catron answered that all depended upon Taney. A conference had been delayed by the tragic death of Justice Daniel's beautiful young wife, who had burned to death when her clothes caught fire while she was dressing for a party. He would keep the president-elect informed. On February 10 Catron wrote Buchanan that the case would be settled the following Saturday. He doubted, however, that the decision would help Buchanan in preparing his speech because some of the judges would not deal with the question of federal power in the territories. No opinions would be announced until the end of the month.

Within the Court, meanwhile, a majority had decided to accept the ruling of the Missouri Supreme Court without delving into broad principles. Curtis and McLean, however, were determined to publish a minority dissent supporting Scott and stressing the right of Congress to restrict slavery. Some historians believe the majority changed their minds and reviewed the entire constitutional question only because of the obstinacy of McLean and Curtis. In fact, however, Justice Wayne had been urging his colleagues to take this action even before the disagreement erupted. Justice Daniel was also anxious to express his views in full, and Wayne, under pressure from various Southern friends, including Alexander H. Stephens, had already begun writing a broad opinion. Following the original plan, Justice Nelson prepared a brief opinion limited to Dred Scott, but then the judges agreed to a motion by Wayne that Taney should write a majority opinion with each member to dissent where he wished. Obviously strengthened

25

by the opposition views of the two Northerners, Wayne persuaded Catron and Campbell as well as Taney that this plan should be followed.[2]

As a Northern Justice, however, James Grier was reluctant to take an overt Southern stand, and the others did not wish to deliver such an important majority opinion restricted to five slave-state judges. If Grier had kept his resolve, the others might have returned to their original plan, but at this point Catron again wrote his old friend James Buchanan. If he wished to pass the responsibility to the Supreme Court in his inaugural the president-elect should "drop Grier a line, saying how necessary it is—& how good the opportunity is, to settle the agitation by an affirmative decision of the Supreme Court, the one way or the other . . . He has no doubt about the question on the main contest, but has been persuaded to take the smooth handle for the sake of repose."[3]

Buchanan immediately wrote Grier a strong plea to join the other justices in stopping the slave agitation. This letter has been lost, but its content is plain from Grier's answer. He had showed Buchanan's letter to Taney and Wayne, and they agreed with Buchanan's view that the time was ripe for "an expression of the opinion of the Court on this troublesome question." Grier's letter continued with a full summary of the court's deliberations and blamed the need for a broad decision on Curtis and McLean. Grier, however, was probably trying to show his fellow Pennsylvanian that he had always been on the right side, and Buchanan's pressure on Grier may well have been just as important as the opposing views of Curtis and McLean in producing the final decision.[4] Grier, of course, was not difficult to persuade. He was strongly pro-Southern, and his son-in-law would later fight as a Confederate officer. Later, however, Grier would denounce secession and ecome a judicial bulwark for the Union.

Aside from the impropriety of the communications between Catron, Buchanan, and Grier, the president-elect demonstrated an appalling ignorance in assuming that a judicial opinion denying either the Congress or a territorial legislature the right to exclude slavery would be acceptable to the North. Ignoring the enormous popular and electoral support in the North for the Republicans and Fremont, whose Northern votes had far exceeded his own, Buchanan acted as though the free-soilers really were just a small group of misguided fanatics whose efforts could be stopped by a Supreme Court decision. Perhaps the illness he had contracted at the National Hotel was affecting his judgment. A more astute politician would have stuck to the vague pledge of the Cincinnati platform and would have avoided even a hint of association with any decision the Supreme Court might make.

On March 4, after a colorful parade, Buchanan stood before a huge crowd and took the oath of office from Chief Justice Taney. He then almost eagerly identified himself with an as yet unannounced Court decision that in theory would nullify the Republican party's reason for existence and destroy the version of popular sovereignty presented by most Northern Democrats to their constituents. The question of when territorial settlers could approve or reject slavery, he said, legitimately belonged "to the Supreme Court of the United States, before whom it is now pending, and will, it is understood, be speedily and finally settled. To their decision, in common with all good citizens, I shall cheerfully submit, whatever this may be, though it has ever been my individual opinion that, under the Nebraska-Kansas Act, the appropriate period will be when the number of actual residents in the Territory shall justify the formation of a constitution with a view to its admission as a State . . . ."[5]

Thus the new president lit a fuse. Two days later, while his supporters were still recovering from eating five hundred gallons of oysters, eight hundred chickens, a hundred gallons of ice cream, and uncalculated quantities of venison, beef, turkey, pheasants, ham, and lobster served at the inaugural ball, the Supreme Court announced its expected decision. Several judges disagreed with various minor points and explained their positions in different ways, but all but Nelson, Curtis, and McLean agreed with or acquiesced in the two main contentions. Dred Scott had no right to sue in the Court because no Negro, slave or free, could be an American citizen. The due-process clause in the Constitution concerned with the protection of property applied to territories as well as to states, and therefore neither the federal government nor a territorial legislature had the right to bar slavery from any territory. The Missouri Compromise, still regarded as a sacred pact by millions of Northerners angry over its repeal, had been unconstitutional from the beginning. Judge Catron based his view on the acceptance of slavery in the Louisiana Purchase rather than on a constitutional principle, but the effect was the same.

It was an explosive decision couched in angry words. Negroes, said Taney, had always been considered "unfit to associate with the White race . . . and so far inferior that they had no rights which the white man was bound to respect."[6] In fact, however, many

27

freedmen had fought in the nation's revolution and wars, had owned property, had voted for years in several states, and were often highly respected. Even though only three judges actually supported the principle of noncitizenship for all blacks, it quickly became the official law of the land. Free blacks had often been denied such government privileges as preemption rights to western lands, access to minor government employment, and passports, but there had always been exceptions. The secretary of the interior had only recently decided that a New York black had preemption rights in Minnesota, and the Pierce administration's recent ruling against passports would have been tested in the courts. The Dred Scott decision, however, meant an immediate total denial of any further such efforts. Ironically, Taney cited examples of privileges denied to blacks as legal justification for a decision officially denying them all such privileges.[7]

The red flag to Northern whites, however, was the ruling on the territories. The realistic argument of Douglas and others that slavery probably could not survive in any of the remaining territories anyhow now fell on deaf ears. Five Southern judges and a compliant Pennsylvanian, ruling against all earlier precedents, in theory opened the entire West to slavery, regardless of what the opinion of the popular majority in the territories might be. To Northerners it was a crushing violation of democratic principle by the Slave Power with the open support and connivance of the president.

Editorials, speeches, and mass meetings fanned the reaction. The dissenting opinions of McLean and Curtis, which did have the earlier precedents on their side, were circulated by the tens of thousands in pamphlet form. The aged Thomas Hart Benton quickly wrote a book which disappointed his hope that it would become a household necessity, but did furnish many angry editors and orators with 192 pages of precedents and logical arguments against the decision.[8] Many more thousands of Northern Democrats now crossed the line to the Republicans, and in Illinois an aspiring politician named Abraham Lincoln gained a new and powerful issue. The decision had cut the ground from under popular sovereignty, and Stephen A. Douglas must now find some way to reconcile his doctrine with a legal principle that denied territorial settlers the right to reject slavery until the moment of statehood.

Southerners, like most people engaged in controversy, now looked ahead for a new vantage to be gained. The decision had not called for positive federal protection of slavery in the territories, but it made a demand for this seem logical. Northerners, having lost a vital point through what they considered chicanery and false reasoning, were equally determined to reject the decision and any Southern efforts for legislation to implement or expand it would meet total resistance. Northern radicals could not have asked for an incident better calculated to benefit their cause. It was hardly an auspicious beginning for a president whose stated goal was to quiet the Northern fanaticism against slavery.

5

★★★★★

KANSAS

James Buchanan had always shown a talent for shifting positions under political stress, and the balancing of issues had been a major part of his success. He had opposed both protective tariffs and free trade, had opposed both unregulated state banking and state control of banks, and had advocated hard money for payment of wages while calling for a more elastic currency. As secretary of state he had jumped back and forth with almost unique agility on the Mexican War aims and the Oregon problem. In 1857 he had a glorious opportunity to soothe the ruffled feelings and calm the fears of the North with no real change of policy at all. Northerners needed proof that the Dred Scott decision was not really going to sweep the western territories for slavery, and the obvious test case was Kansas.

Kansas was still afflicted with two territorial governments—a proslavery legislature at Lecompton working in conjunction with the governor and other officials legally appointed by the president, and the Free-State establishment at Topeka led by its chosen Governor Charles Robinson. The Free-State government had been briefly abolished by troops ordered from Fort Leavenworth by President Pierce, but it had recovered quickly. The earlier violence had subsided, but a permanent peace obviously required the creation and acceptance of a single government to replace the two still in conflict.[1] Topeka, incidentally, still has no Pierce Street or Avenue to go with its numerous other presidential thoroughfares.

Governor John W. Geary, appointed by Pierce in late 1856,

was a thirty-seven-year-old Mexican War hero who had served as the first mayor of San Francisco and had played a leading role in making California a free state. He hoped that Kansas would become a free state, and he could see that this was inevitable because of the huge influx of Midwesterners who wanted neither slaves nor free blacks in Kansas. Using federal troops to suppress violence and strike a balance between the warring groups, Geary accomplished an uneasy peace without winning the trust or support of either side. The Free-State leaders were strongly influenced by Republican politicians in the East who recognized the political advantages of a Kansas still endangered by slaveholders. The proslavery leaders saw their prospects dwindling with each new wagonload of immigrants and were anxious for a last-ditch effort to win the state. There were less than two hundred slaves in all of Kansas and the number was shrinking, but the proslavery leaders in control of the legislature, post offices, land offices, judgeships, and other positions of influence were desperately anxious to keep their power. Surveyor-General John Calhoun, the leader of this group, managed several hundred employees in the various land offices, where settlers had to have their preemptions confirmed. With this nucleus, he and his friends were determined to expel Geary and form a constitutional convention to make Kansas a slave state. They knew the president's cabinet was pro-Southern and had reason to believe he too would be sympathetic. Obviously the time was now or never.

Geary had already quarreled with the legislature over laws prescribing inhuman penalties for writing, printing, or speaking against slavery. On February 14, 1857, the legislature sent him a bill authorizing the election of delegates to a state constitutional convention in September. In March the county sheriffs and their deputies, predominantly proslavery, were to list all white, free males under twenty-one as qualified voters to choose delegates on the third Monday in June. Only those resident on March 15 could vote, and any suggestion for submitting the finished product to the people was conspicuously absent.

During the debate over this the governor was viciously insulted by a reckless county sheriff, who was himself killed in a shooting affray at the mass meeting called to protest the insult to Geary. The governor courageously vetoed the bill on the grounds that Kansas—with only 25,000 to 30,000 people, heavy debts, unfinished buildings, questionable land titles, and a severe shortage of schools, courthouses, and jails—still needed the federal government. The legislature promptly passed it over his veto amid loud boasts that he would be assassinated within forty days. Geary asked for two additional companies of soldiers for protection, but General Persifor Smith, supported by Pierce, refused. Geary resigned on March 4.

Back in Washington the ex-governor was ignored by Buchanan but lionized by the Republicans and numerous Northern Democrats. In several speeches he insisted that the great majority of Kansans were conservative and peaceful, but that unscrupulous men were fomenting disorder to create a sectional quarrel. Geary was obviously referring to proslavery leaders, although in fact various Free-State newspapermen were equally hopeful that the Kansas conflict might become national in scope.

Buchanan apparently believed that Kansas would finally be a free state, but he wanted his Southern friends to feel they had been fairly treated, and he hoped the state would at least be Democratic in its voting habits. To achieve a Democratic Kansas he appointed as governor his former colleague in the Polk cabinet, Robert J. Walker of Mississippi. Walker was a skilled manipulator who had played a major role in the annexation of Texas and the nomination of Polk, and had worked for even greater annexations. He had been an effective senator and a successful secretary of the treasury, and had authored the well-designed tariff of 1846. Though not much more than five feet tall and slightly built, he had a lion's heart and had more than once offered to settle quarrels by duels. In 1857, at the age of fifty-six, he remained energetic and ambitious. Several years later he would serve Abraham Lincoln by flying over London in a balloon to distribute leaflets urging Englishmen to buy bonds and support the Union.

Walker knew that Kansas had ruined three governors already, that he could earn more than the salary with a single law case, and that his wife was very unwilling to have him go to Kansas, but Buchanan was persuasive. Walker, he argued, would probably return as a senator from Kansas with a reputation that would make him president. Being both optimistic and self-confident, Walker accepted the challenge on condition that his friend Frederick P. Stanton, a former congressman from Tennessee, should be his territorial secretary. He also believed the president was pledged to a fair and free popular referendum on any constitution to be written for Kansas. Although he had once owned slaves, Walker already believed that Kansas would and must become a free state.

Stanton, who was both proslave and dedicated to an honest

33

choice for Kansas, proceeded to Kansas ahead of Walker. The free-state citadel, Lawrence, was on the road to Lecompton, and Stanton stopped there long enough to deliver a conciliatory speech and enjoy a banquet. Before a considerable crowd he recited from *The Song of Hiawatha* the Great Manitou speech exhorting the Indians to stop fighting and live together as brothers. His audience was impressed, even if not entirely convinced.

In Lecompton, meanwhile, Calhoun and his assistant, L. A. Maclean, had just returned from Washington and conferences with Walker, Secretary Thompson, and Jefferson Davis. They were prepared to create a slave state regardless of the consequences.

From Lecompton, Stanton continued to urge the free-soilers to register and vote in the coming election for constitutional delegates. The free-state leaders, however, insisted that the census and registry taken by the Lecompton government had already left out large numbers of free-state settlers, had included numerous nonresidents, and therefore could not possibly be fair. They would participate only if their own representatives could help correct the registry. Stanton of course lacked the authority to grant this. The registration in fact was highly improper. No census was taken in nineteen of the thirty-eight counties, and in fifteen counties no voters were registered. These included some of the oldest organized counties in Kansas, and no voting precinct at all was established in Lawrence, whose citizens would have to go twelve miles by horse or foot to vote. Part of this was the fault of free-staters reluctant to be registered, but the government had made no effort to perform its duties in the areas in question. Perhaps for the sake of a national political issue the free-staters might have refused to cooperate in any case, but the proslavers did give them strong grounds for such action.

In New York City, meanwhile, Walker announced that after a fair census of the inhabitants at the time, Kansas would have a full, free, and solemn referendum on any constitution that might be written. A few weeks later he arrived in Kansas, by coincidence on the same boat with Massachusetts Senator Henry Wilson, the poet and clergyman John Pierpont, and the abolitionist Samuel Gridley Howe. At Leavenworth Walker stopped long enough to order champagne and brandy for all drinkers. The city fathers insisted on assuming their guest's bill, but after his departure they refused to "open the city treasury for the encouragement of intemperance, the mother of crime," and the $210 liquor tab went unpaid. At Lawrence, Wilson, Pierpont, and Howe addressed some 2,000 people, and Walker appeared briefly on the same platform.

Preceded by news of his associations with the hated New Englanders, Walker arrived in Lecompton and delivered his inaugural address. It was conciliatory and realistic, but unwise at a critical point. He promised that the laws of the regular legislature would be enforced, and urged everyone on both sides to vote for delegates to the constitutional convention. He also warned that Congress would never admit Kansas "as a slave state or free state, unless a majority of the people shall first have fairly and freely decided this question for themselves by a direct vote on the adoption of the Constitution, excluding all fraud or violence." Walker should have stopped with this pledge, but he then infuriated Southerners both inside Kansas and out by indicating that he had prejudged the issue. The question of slavery, he declared, would be decided by climatic law, and an "isothermal line" regulating labor and production had already made Kansas unsuitable for slavery.[2]

The response of the proslavery leaders was immediate. At a banquet the following evening, Calhoun's assistant, Maclean, a huge red-haired bully who had been drinking heavily, gave the diminutive Walker the word: "And do you come here to rule over us?—you, a miserable pigmy like you? You come here with ears erect, but you will leave with your tail between your legs. Walker, we have unmade governors before; and by God, I tell you, sir, we can unmake them again!"[3] As for Buchanan, added Maclean, the president should be instructed to mind his own business.

Walker, however, could not be intimidated. He believed the voters were divided among some 9,000 Free-State Democrats, 6,500 proslave Democrats, 8,000 Republicans, and 500 proslave Know-Nothings. If he could win and hold the Free-State Democrats without losing all of the proslave Democrats, who obviously would not vote Republican, Kansas would become a new star in the Democratic crown.

On June 6 Walker launched his effort to persuade the free-soilers to cooperate with legitimate legal processes. Amid threats of violence Walker delivered a threat and a promise. If the legislature enacted and tried to enforce laws, he would crush it with federal troops. If, however, the free-staters acted sensibly he would guarantee that Kansas would be governed by its actual residents. If the constitutional convention tried to evade a popular referendum, both he and the president would join the free-staters in opposition. In response the Topeka legislature passed resolutions against the approaching convention and adjourned.

Proslave reporters were estimating the free-soil edge among the new immigrants at fifteen to one, and the proslave leaders acted accordingly. On June 11, a deputation served Walker an ultimatum—there would be no popular vote on the pending constitution, and he had better stop talking about it. The fearless little governor answered in no uncertain terms that he would not be coerced.

The proslave faction was running short on population but long on determination. The thousands of free-soilers pouring into Kansas all spring and summer could not vote because March 15 was the cut-off date. A land association from Missouri had preempted large tracts of empty land in the Shawnee Reserve and assigned them to 2,700 men, most of whom simply drove stakes and left. Most of these would return to register and vote. The allocation of delegates gave three proslavery counties next to Missouri 24 of the 60 seats. The Shawnee Reserve with less than 50 actual inhabitants got 3 delegates. In all, 6 proslave counties got 37 of the 60 seats, while 30 counties, including the populous free-soil areas, got only 23. Voters had to prove three months' residence and show a receipt for payment of a territorial tax. Some people thought the census takers were checking land claims and drove them away; others did not register because avoiding taxes was obviously easier for the unlisted. The census takers deliberately avoided some counties. Large numbers of free-soilers felt, correctly, that registering would imply recognition of the Lecompton government, and Republicans knew that a minimal registration would enhance the appearance of foul play and injustice.

The June 15 election for delegates to the constitutional convention at Lecompton proved only that Kansas still lacked the machinery for an accurate expression of the public will. Half of the free-soilers could not vote and, unfortunately but understandably, the other half would not. Of the area's some 20,000 adult white males, only 9,251 were registered, and only some 2,200 of these bothered to vote. The result, naturally enough, was a strongly proslave convention that represented only a small fraction of the people of Kansas.

Most Southern politicians and editors everywhere considered Walker a traitor whose "isothermal" speech and insistence upon a popular referendum were aimed at giving Kansas to the North.

Obviously, a proslave constitution could be written but it would be defeated by a vote of the whole people. Speeches, editorials, and public meetings demanded Walker's recall, and the president's cabinet and friends assured him that the Democratic party would lose the South and thereby its chief strength if he did not act immediately.

Buchanan's position was painful. He had promised Walker that when a constitution was completed the people "must be protected in the exercise of their right of voting for or against that instrument." Biographers have insisted that he was committed only to submission of the slavery question rather than the entire constitution, but some of his written words to Walker can be interpreted otherwise.[4] Senator Bigler of Pennsylvania assured him that the Southern anger stemmed from a misunderstanding of Kansas. It could not become a slave state, and allowing 2,000 out of 20,000 men to make a constitution would be outrageous. Bigler urged the president to stand by Walker and thereby make Kansas a Democratic state. From Kansas came other reports to the White House that the convention would probably submit a constitution without mention of slavery to the voters and then submit the slavery question separately.

In mid-July Buchanan wrote Walker that he himself would be willing to stand or fall "on the question of submitting the constitution to the bona fide residents of Kansas." If this principle were applied, he assured Walker, the recent condemnations of Walker by conventions in Georgia and Mississippi would be quickly forgotten.[5] If Buchanan thought a submission to the bona fide residents would make Georgia and Mississippi happy, he must have also thought that the result would be an acceptance of the constitution. The key to this sentiment probably lay in Buchanan's definition of bona fide citizens, whom he would later limit to those defined as such by the Lecompton government, willing to vote under the supervision of that government, and ready to accept its judgment of the results.

Unfortunately for Walker's goals, James Buchanan was human, and the people whose love, friendship, and respect he wanted most were Southerners. His cabinet was more than a group of department heads and advisers. It was his family. In addition to frequent state dinners, which the cabinet attended as a matter of course, the president held small weekly dinners just for his inner circle. During long periods when Mrs. Cobb remained in Georgia to produce new children or care for her already large brood,

Buchanan insisted that Cobb live in the White House on constant call for either work or companionship. Cobb, like Buchanan, had once been expelled from college for drinking, and Buchanan loved to swap exaggerated stories with Cobb about their earlier misdeeds. Kate Thompson was his favorite among the cabinet wives, and he spent so much time with her, including evening visits when her husband was away, that probably only his age and reputation prevented gossip. In 1845, by a deceptive act, Walker had kept Jacob Thompson from becoming his appointed successor in the Senate, and Thompson still remembered the deed and hated Walker. Both Cobb and Thompson could report accurately that conventions in their states were threatening rebellion if Walker should be upheld, and other Southerners in the cabinet were not inclined to argue. For no discernible reason, Cass was also won over; and Black, while he held no brief for slavery, considered free-soilers and abolitionists identical, hated both, and wanted to arrest the members of the Topeka government as traitors.[6]

While the cabinet developed its case against Walker, both factions in Kansas remained irresponsible. The free-staters created their own municipal government for Lawrence. Walker issued a proclamation against it and led a force of dragoons to the town. Fearing an armed conflict between the two groups, he asked Buchanan for an additional 2,000 troops. The request was refused, but the free-soilers backed down.

On October 5 and 6 Kansas elected a new legislature and a congressional delegate. For the first time the Free Staters voted, and their candidate for delegate won by a majority of 4,000 votes. Incomprehensibly, the legislature went proslavery, but Walker and Stanton quickly found an explanation. McGee County had fewer than a hundred qualified voters, but had reported 1,266 proslave ballots. Johnson County, with about the same population, had returned 1,628 votes. In Lawrence, Walker showed off the Oxford returns. On a roll of paper fifty-four feet long were listed 1,601 names all in the same handwriting, and 1,500 of them had been copied in consecutive order from the Cincinnati directory. The angry governor threw out the fraudulent votes and declared the legal election of a Free-State legislature.

The pro-slave Democrats held an angry mass meeting, a judge issued a futile writ of mandamus, and one sheriff tried to get accredited as a legislator through threats of violence. Hearing of this, the furious Walker marched with a pistol through all the ramshackle saloons and gambling dens along Lecompton's single, dilapidated street and stopped in each to denounce the proslavers with every oath and obscenity he could muster.

On October 19 the Lecompton convention finally met. The sixty delegates were for the most part ignorant and semi-illiterate, and their deliberations were often spiced with large amounts of whiskey. Chosen by a small minority, they faced the angry opposition of most of the territory. They were American frontiersmen, however, and whether or not they were the filthy, whiskey-sodden, tobacco-squirting, blasphemous ruffians pictured by Republican newspapers, they were not short on nerve and determination.[7] Most of them were ready to send a proslave constitution directly to Congress without any nonsense about letting Kansans vote first. A few, however, led by Calhoun and Henry L. Martin, an agent sent by Cobb and Thompson, knew that Congress would require at least a limited submission. The result was a constitution that forbade the legislature to emancipate any slaves already in Kansas without consent of the owner and compensation, denied any right of amendment before 1864, called for stringent enforcement of the Fugitive Slave Law, required twenty years' citizenship for Kansas governors, limited the state to only one bank with not more than two branches, created an inefficient tax system that had already failed in Illinois, and excluded all free Negroes. In a referendum scheduled for December 21 the people could vote for the constitution with slavery or for the constitution without slavery. Those who opposed its provisions related to existing slaves, banks, taxes, or any other matters were thus disfranchised.

The convention also enacted a schedule that ousted Walker and other federal officers as of December 1, 1857, and created a new provisional government to be headed by John Calhoun. He was to order new elections for state officers and legislators, appoint all judges of elections, count the votes, and convene the new legislature by proclamation. For the constitutional referendum he was to appoint three election commissioners for each county, who in turn would name three judges to establish precincts and open the polls. The referendum clearly was to be managed by proslavers. If the voters rejected slavery, the 200 slaves already there would remain and no provision was made for their descendants. Only the entry of new slaves would be forbidden, and the smuggling of new ones into the state was at least theoretically possible. If the vote was for slavery, it could not be amended until 1864 and then only if two-thirds of each house submitted an amendment to the people and a majority of "qualified voters" supported

39

it. If approved in this vote, therefore, slavery in Kansas could be preserved by one more than one-third of the legislature.

Only one of twenty newspapers in Kansas supported the new constitution, but the Southern press and the administration organ, the *Washington Union*, immediately began praising it to the skies. With equal fervor, newspapers throughout the North denounced it as a plot to deprive Kansans of their democratic rights.

James Buchanan was not only under the inexorable pressure of his cabinet family and his friends; he also honestly believed they were right, although he probably disagreed with their hope for a proslave vote in the referendum. If the people of Kansas voted for the constitution without slavery, his obligations to both sections would be met, and perhaps the agitation would cease. Unfortunately, however, his annual address was scheduled for December 8, while the referendum would not occur until December 21. If he staked his position with the North on the hope of an antislavery vote, he would have to wait for confirmation of his judgment.

On November 26 Walker spent two hours at the White House arguing unsuccessfully that he and the people of Kansas were being betrayed and that the vote would mean slavery regardless of its outcome.

Fully briefed by Walker, Stephen A. Douglas also reached a decision. Buchanan expected his support, however reluctant, but fifty-five of fifty-six papers in Illinois were in opposition, Douglas faced a reelection battle in 1858, and on principle he really was furious over events in Kansas. Douglas went to the White House to support Walker's demand for the calling of a new constitutional convention for Kansas. The chemistry between Buchanan and Douglas was volatile as always. The president argued that the Lecompton convention and constitution had fulfilled the law, and that by refusing to vote the free-soilers alone were responsible for its defects. Only the immediate admission of Kansas would keep it from remaining a hornet's nest and from electing a Republican president in 1860, which in turn would cause a civil war. Douglas answered that he would have to oppose it as a dirty fraud that made popular sovereignty a joke. Referring to Democrats banished by President Jackson, Buchanan warned: "Mr. Douglas, I desire you to remember that no Democrat ever yet differed from an Administration of his own choice without being crushed. Beware of the fate of Tallmadge and Rives."

" 'Mr. President,' replied Douglas, 'I wish you to remember that General Jackson is dead.' "[8]

Addressing Congress on December 8, 1857, Buchanan upheld the Lecompton Constitution and urged Kansans to vote for or against slavery. He insisted that his promise of a fair expression by the voters had referred only to slavery and not to the entire constitution, and that he would be duty-bound to submit the document to Congress regardless of the vote. The peace and quiet of the nation was, he said, "of greater importance than the mere temporary triumph of either of the political parties in Kansas."[9]

On the following day, Douglas launched his attack in the Senate. On December 15 Walker resigned with a warning that the constitution represented no more than 10 percent of the people and that its imposition might cause a civil war throughout the Union. Territorial Secretary Frederick P. Stanton, who had just been replaced for calling a special session of the newly elected Kansas legislature, added his voice.

On December 21 Kansas voted. As the recent legislative election had shown, there were more than enough eligible voters to vote down slavery for the future if they had also been willing to accept the rest of the constitution. Also, Buchanan was probably correct in his belief that the arguments over the fate of the existing slaves if the state went free-soil were splitting hairs. A free state of Kansas would easily find a way to end the remaining fragments of slavery among the numerous precedents created when the Northeastern states were eliminating the institution. Slavery, in fact, was already declining steadily in the neighboring state of Missouri. The president also reasoned accurately that the immediate admission of a free Kansas would weaken the Republican party, while a continuation of the struggle would make it ultimately supreme.

The question of allowing a vote on the entire constitution was at stake, however, and Buchanan should have realized that neither his Republican enemies nor the Free-Soil Democrats would surrender the principle. The Republican party thrived on turmoil, and the ideals of its members were therefore doubly reinforced by self-interest. Buchanan's able defender Philip Klein has pointed out that thirty-three of the sixty-three state constitutions written between 1776 and 1858 were enacted without a popular vote. He admits further, however, that by 1858 only nine of the thirty-three states still lived under charters never ratified by the people and eight of these were Southern.[10] Northerners and Westerners, at least, had long since made the right to vote on a constitution into a sacred precept.

Republicans and Free-Soil Democrats alike were also still angry over the recent election frauds and feared their repetition with no Walker or Stanton to stand in the breach. Actually, Walker's replacement as governor, General James W. Denver, was equally honest and objective, but Kansans had not yet learned this.

Too much blood had flowed and too many animosities had been inflamed. If Kansans could not vote for or against the entire constitution they would not vote at all. The result was 6,143 votes for slavery and 569 against it, and opponents claimed that some 2,700 of the proslave votes were fraudulent. Meanwhile, the session of the newly elected legislature called by the departed Stanton met and organized a referendum on the whole constitution. On January 4, 1858, this vote went 10,336 against the constitution, 138 for it with slavery, and 24 for it without slavery.

The January 4 vote gave Buchanan a strong excuse to change his mind. Southerners would be angry, but probably less than they would be if he continued to raise hopes that could not be realized. His new acting governor, General Denver, soon wrote that the people of Kansas would not accept the constitution. Denver urged a new enabling act and a fresh convention, but the president ignored both Denver and the recent referendum. On February 2 he asked the Congress to accept Kansas as a slave state under the Lecompton Constitution. It was, he said, "at this moment as much a slave State as Georgia or South Carolina."[11] The constitution and the proslave referendum met every legal test and nothing else mattered. If Kansas did not really want slavery, he argued, it could change its mind as soon as statehood was conferred. Privately, he was now convinced that any new constitution would be filled with abominations offensive to the South, while the later abolition of slavery in Kansas by a state constitutional amendment would have no such effect.

The president's oft-expressed view that the immediate admission of a proslave Kansas would weaken the Republican party was roughly akin to his belief that the Dred Scott decision would stop the slavery quarrel. He was either totally blind to Northern sentiment, or his stated ambition for sectional peace was merely a self-deceiving rationalization. True, his cabinet did relay various Southern threats of secession, but a Kansas lost in a fairly elected state constitutional convention and an honest referendum would have fallen far short of the provocation needed by Southern radicals to bring their people to the point of disunion in 1858. The real crisis would come if the Republicans should win the presidency. Instead of doing everything possible to avoid this, however, Buchanan's policies were enabling the Republicans to become the defenders of democracy itself, and were thereby driving Democrats by the thousands into the Republican camp.

Stephen A. Douglas understood all this. The survival of his party, his own career, and the Union required the defeat of the Lecompton Constitution, and he was ready for the battle. For Northern congressional Democrats, who were under constant pressures, threats, and temptations because of the administration's control and flagrant use of patronage and other favors, there was Buchanan's argument that Kansas once admitted could quickly abolish slavery. Not so, answered Douglas: the constitution could not be amended before 1864, more slaves could enter legally during the interval, and constitutions could be changed without bloodshed only when public opinion approached unanimity. The Calhoun gang, he charged, would never permit a two-thirds vote for amending the constitution when they could use the federal army to keep down domestic violence. Would Southerners submit, he asked, if the free-soilers had prevented their voting against a free-soil constitution and then had forced it on them if a majority clearly did not want it? Without forgiving him for past sins, the Republicans accepted the leadership of Douglas; and a handful of Democratic senators were also willing to brave the wrath of the president, or were perhaps more fearful of their constituents at home.

The anti-Lecompton members of Congress may have been helped enormously by a flamboyant speech by Senator Hammond of South Carolina. He was for Lecompton or separation and seemed to prefer the latter. With 850,000 square miles, rich natural resources, a million brave warriors, and cotton commanding the fate of the world, said Hammond, the South could become a great independent power. He favored secession "if we can do no better, with South Carolina, Georgia, Florida, Alabama, and Mississippi—three and a half million people and two and a half million cotton bales. . . . You dare not make war on cotton . . . . Cotton is king." With supreme arrogance Hammond attributed Southern power to its possession of a permanent menial class. Every society, he said, required a mudsill, and the South had the ideal race for it. The North had abolished "the *name* slavery, but not the *thing* itself."[12]

With some boasting of their own humble origins, various Northern senators, led by Henry Wilson of Massachusetts, delivered scathing rebuttals to Hammond's speech, and both the speech and the answers spread quickly through the Northern press. Simultaneously, thousands of copies of the senator's flight of fancy were being circulated in pamphlet-form throughout the South. For those who might believe its assurances, it offered some dangerous arguments.

With the cabinet lobbying directly, firing opposing postmasters and other officeholders right and left, and using both threats and promises wholesale, eight Northern Democrats finally joined with the twenty-five Southerners to pass the bill in the Senate by thirty-three to twenty-five. The measure stressed the immediate right of amendment and cut the huge original land-grant request from 16,000,000 acres to the more normal 4,000,000.

The House, however, facing reelection every two years by the public rather than by state legislatures, was a different matter. Despite Southern control of the parliamentary leadership and machinery and despite administration pressures that came close to bribery, the bill never had a chance. At one point in the fierce debate, Lawrence Keitt of South Carolina and Galusha Grow of Pennsylviana exchanged insults and blows. After Grow knocked Keitt down, more than fifty congressmen engaged in a free-for-all, with the damage limited only by the age and poor physical condition of the combatants. Representative John Covode of Pennsylvania was threatening any and all potential attackers with a heavy spittoon when someone knocked the wig off Representative Barksdale of Mississippi. Chagrined that his secret baldness had been revealed, Barksdale rescued his wig from the trampling feet and clapped it on backward. The resulting peals of laughter ended what could have developed into serious violence.[13]

Among Democrats even the social life of the city was part of the struggle. At the White House Buchanan's niece, Harriet Lane, presided over countless dinners and less formal gatherings, at which wine flowed freely but dancing was forbidden. Described by Hawthorne as being "of stronger outline than most of our young ladies," Harriet was a skilled and gracious hostess. Winsome Southern wives and unattached ladies alike at her parties did not hesitate to talk strong politics to wavering or uncommitted congressmen. Several blocks away, the beautiful Mrs. Douglas competed with equally generous hospitality aimed at reinforcing her husband's position as a national leader. Numerous people enjoyed the advantages of invitations from both, but after the Lecompton battle the president's closer friends were rarely if ever seen at the Douglas home, and the anti-Lecompton Democrats were not very welcome at the White House, even though Walker himself ultimately came to dinner and tried to reconcile the factions.

The opponents of the constitution even received unexpected help from John Calhoun, who came to Washington without certifying the results of the January 4 election for officers in Kansas. The evidence of an overwhelming Free-State victory was clear, and Calhoun's delay only served the Republicans and Douglas Democrats. Finally, after a committee had found a cache of votes under a woodpile, Calhoun announced a Free-State victory, which alienated the South without mollifying the North. Southern papers denounced Calhoun as a traitor and Buchanan promptly discharged him. Calhoun insisted that he would have been reappointed if he had certified a proslave victory; whatever the causes for his removal, Buchanan was again cast for Northerners in the role of agent for Southern vengeance against an official who had only done his duty.

The Republicans swept the spring elections of 1858 in several Northern states and carried former Democratic strongholds like Chicago, Toledo, Cincinnati, and St. Louis. Northern Democratic representatives had to choose between loyalty to the administration and political suicide. In the Senate the aged Kentuckian John J. Crittenden had proposed that the constitution be submitted to the people of Kansas; if they rejected it the people should choose another convention to write a new constitution. This plan was introduced in the House by Democrat William Montgomery of Pennsylvania, and on April 1 it passed by 120 to 112, despite Buchanan's threat to veto it. The president was now willing to have the constitution submitted, but remained adamant against any new convention. The Senate rejected the House bill, but the administration now sought to avoid a total defeat by seeking a compromise. Persuading the House to accept a conference committee required another round of administration favors, threats, and promises, but Representative William H. English, an anti-Lecompton Democrat from Indiana, finally sponsored a new bill actually suggested in large part by the administration. Kansas should hold a referendum on the land grant. If the people voted to accept the 4,000,000 acres provided in the Senate bill plus 5 percent of the proceeds from 2,000,000 acres to be sold in July, the state would be immediately admitted under the Lecompton Constitution. If they rejected this offer, they could not apply for statehood again until the population had increased significantly. This would be a clear-cut submission of the constitution to the people of Kansas, and realistic observers knew that it would be overwhelmingly rejected regardless of the land provisions.

Walker and Stanton endorsed the bill and, with others, tried to reunite the Democrats by getting Douglas to vote for it. The few Democratic senators who had stood with him through the battle were furious, however, and his Illinois mail was overwhelmingly against it. In the end he announced that while he wished no personal triumph over the administration he could not support a bill that based admission on unfair conditions and offered only an indirect choice to the voters. The English bill passed the House by 112 to 103 and the Senate by 31 to 22. Three months later, on August 2, 1858, the people of Kansas rejected the land grant and thereby the Lecompton Constitution by 11,812 to 1,926. Slavery was dead in Kansas.

Southerners, led to believe by their politicians and newspapers and by the Senate vote that Kansas had been won in a fair contest, were now convinced that it had been stolen by a Yankee conspiracy led by their traitorous former friend Stephen A. Douglas. In Kansas the most flagrant abusers of the democratic process were men concerned with slavery only as a political tool, and they did not represent either the Southern people or its leadership. Northerners everywhere, however, could hardly help identifying the president, his cabinet, and the Southern leadership with a brutal and fraudulent attempt to impose slavery on an unwilling majority. The Slave Power now loomed ever larger in their imaginations, and James Buchanan was chiefly responsible. From beginning to end the harassed president had done almost everything possible to thwart his own most cherished goal—to destroy the appeal of the Republican party in the North. Primarily through his efforts the Republicans had enhanced their image as the defenders of the most sacred democratic precepts against efforts by the so-called Slave Power to enslave a territory through violence and fraud. In the South he had gained sympathy, and perhaps a limited affection, but little respect. He had assumed the role of protector of Southern interests, but had succeeded only in emphasizing the weakness of his office when opposed by the Northern people.

6

★★★★★

SEQUEL TO KANSAS: DOUGLAS VERSUS LINCOLN

With Bleeding Kansas about to run dry as a political resource because of the free-soil triumph, the Republican party needed new leadership and a broader appeal. Thinking people could now see that neither Dred Scott nor popular sovereignty was going to spread slavery throughout the West, but the politicians could still find hope in the animosities already generated.

Historians disagree as to which man was more responsible for continuing the Buchanan-Douglas feud, but the question is irrelevant. To be reelected senator in Illinois, Douglas had to remain the enemy of those who had supported the Lecompton Constitution, and he found this position entirely compatible with his personal feelings. Likewise, hatred for Douglas had become an integral part of Buchanan's daily life. If the president had possessed enough self-assurance and inner strength to endure Douglas painlessly, he might have taken a more objective view of his enemy's problems. Without pretending to forgive Douglas, he should have preferred the reelection of a Democratic senator to the selection of a Republican. Without trying to help Douglas he could at least have remained neutral. Had he been able to read the future of Douglas's opponent, he would certainly have acted differently.

With Douglas excommunicated by the president, various eastern Republican leaders began suggesting and arguing that he should be recruited into their own ranks. Illinois Republicans, however, had fought the Little Giant for too many years, and could rightly show that he was not a free-soiler by profession. They were not prepared to accept him, and they had a candidate of their own.

The choice of the Illinois Republicans had actually joined their ranks reluctantly because he did not agree with the party's more radical members. He was a former Whig and a free-soiler, however, and on principle no other party was available. Unlike both Douglas and Buchanan he did have strong moral feelings against slavery, and despite his upbringing in Southern Indiana and Illinois he was remarkably unafflicted with the dislike, fear, and hatred usually defined as racism. In his rise from the humblest origins to considerable success as a talented attorney he had acquired an inner self-confidence and personal security that made him quite immune to emotional prejudice and bigotry. He was prone to expressions of humility, which were genuine enough when he considered the limitations of mankind generally and his own place in the cosmos. In dealing with other men, however, he showed a self-confidence bordering on arrogance, which enabled him to accept insult, mistreatment, betrayal, and flattery alike with no observable pain or rancor. He was intensely ambitious for both himself and his principles, and he had no time or emotional energy to waste on the petty emotions that stem from a bruised ego. The judgments of Abraham Lincoln would rarely be affected by hurt pride, hatred, or a desire for personal vengeance.

He was also a realist. Both Illinois and Indiana barred the immigration of free Negroes, and cruel discrimination characterized the entire Northwest. Because of white attitudes and white power, the social, economic, and political inferiority of American blacks was simply an existing reality that every aspiring politician had to consider. With his roots among the poorer Southern element of the old Northwest, he understood that people could simultaneously fear and hate slavery, free blacks, and abolitionists because of a confusion of motives compounded from moral and ideological principle, racial prejudice, self-interest, and faith in the progress of a free and democratic America.

Lincoln recognized slavery as a tragedy for black and white alike, and he offered no immediate solution. "I hate it [slavery]," he avowed in 1854, "because of the monstrous injustice of slavery itself. I hate it because it deprives our republican examples of its just influence in the world—enables the enemies of free institutions, with plausibility, to taunt us as hypocrites—causes the real friends of freedom to doubt our sincerity, and especially because it forces so many really good men among ourselves into an open war with the very fundamental principles of civil liberty. . . ." He added, however, that Southerners should not be blamed, because they were just what Northerners would be in the same situation. If slavery did not exist the Southerners would not introduce it. If Northerners had it they would not know what to do with the existing situation. He would send the slaves to Liberia but this would be physically impossible. Freeing them and keeping them as underlings would be no real improvement. As for making them political and social equals: "My own feelings will not admit of this; and if mine would, we well know that those of the great mass of white people will not. Whether this feeling accords with justice and sound judgment, is not the sole question, if indeed, it is any part of it. A universal feeling, whether well or ill-founded, can not be safely disregarded."[1]

Popular sovereignty had already created a free Kansas, but Lincoln was prepared for this. From the first introduction of the Kansas-Nebraska Act, Lincoln had argued that popular sovereignty was wrong regardless of its practical results because it implied that slavery was a moral and acceptable institution that Southerners had a legal right to expand if they could. The founding fathers, argued Lincoln, had thought otherwise and had expressed their disapproval by ending the African slave trade. The Northwest Ordinance and the Missouri Compromise had continued this policy of containment. Throughout the North as well as in much of the South it had been taken for granted that slavery was an evil, even though an evil which defied any immediate solution. Now, however, the Democratic party had passed a bill that removed the moral stigma from slavery and legally opened the great West to its expansion. This, concluded Lincoln, could mark the beginning of a process that might very well weaken the Northern repugnance against slavery and thereby give the institution a dangerous new lease on life. Thus, popular sovereignty had to be defeated as the dangerous symbol of a newly tolerant national attitude toward slavery. A man who could eloquently preach high principle to anti-slavery listeners without offending those who wished only to keep blacks out of new territories, and whose words inspired moral comfort without imposing any disturbing sense of obligation, was a natural Republican choice for senator in the Illinois of 1858.

With the Dred Scott decision and the Kansas fiasco on everyone's mind, Lincoln accepted the nomination for senator at Springfield on June 16, 1858, with a masterly political oration. "A house divided against itself," he warned, could not stand. "Either the opponents of slavery, will arrest the further spread of it, and place it where the public mind shall rest in the belief that it is in the course of ultimate extinction; or its advocates will push it forward, till it shall become alike lawful in all the States. . . ."[2] His suggestion that slavery if unchecked by federal laws against territorial expansion would take over the free states was nonsense but it was skillful politics. The house-divided argument was politically risky and later cost him votes. The phrase "ultimate extinction," however, was sheer political genius. It could mean tomorrow or a thousand years hence. Ultimate extinction, to begin with containment, was a doctrine that inspired moral contentment without requiring any sacrifice by those who believed in it.

In the remainder of this speech and throughout his ensuing debates with Douglas, Lincoln continued to expound views which brought comfort without alienation to thousands of voters.[3] Slavery extension must be forbidden by law so that Americans would not be allowed to forget its evil character. Because Douglas refused to admit that slavery was wrong, said Lincoln, Douglas should not be trusted with a place in the United States Senate. And finally, Lincoln argued, his own position was the true road to sectional peace, because the North would stop agitating only when assured that slavery could not expand. And, in turn, the South would stop threatening the Union only when the North would stop denouncing slavery. Thus, sectional peace could be attained only by convincing both sections that slavery was indeed contained. In the candidate's own words: "I believe if we could arrest the spread, and place it where Washington, and Jefferson, and Madison placed it, it *would be* in the course of ultimate extinction and, the public *would*, as for eighty years past, believe that it was in the course of ultimate extinction. The crisis would be past and the institution might be let alone for a hundred years, if it should live so long, in the States where it exists, yet it would be going out of existence in the way best for both the black and white races."[4]

In addition to citizens who found this sophisticated yet simple argument appealing, there were also those thousands who objected to slavery, if at all, only because they feared the presence of Negroes. Before such voters Douglas appealed shamelessly to racial prejudice and accused Lincoln of seeking full social and political racial equality. In reply Lincoln, the ambitious candidate, denied the charges with statements that have been quoted by both racists and his liberal critics ever since:

. . . I have no purpose directly or indirectly to interfere with the institution of slavery in the States where it exists. I believe I have no lawful right to do so, and I have no inclination to do so. I have no purpose to introduce political and social equality between the white and the black races. There is a physical difference between the two, which in my judgment will probably forever forbid their living together upon the footing of perfect equality, and inasmuch as it becomes a necessity that there must be a difference, I, as well as Judge Douglas, am in favor of the race to which I belong . . . but I hold that notwithstanding all this, there is no reason in the world why the negro is not entitled to all the natural rights enumerated in the Declaration of Independence, the right to life, liberty and the pursuit of happiness. I hold that he is as much entitled to these as the white man. I agree with Judge Douglas he is not my equal in many respects—certainly not in color, perhaps not in moral or intellectual endowment. But in the right to eat the bread, without leave of anyone else, which his own hand earns, *he is my equal and the equal of Judge Douglas, and the equal of every living man.*[5]

The words of Lincoln are important because they probably reflected the thinking of most Northerners in 1858. His speech showed a clear-cut moral antipathy to slavery as a negation of both Christian ethics and the national ideology, and expressed an uncompromisable objection to its expansion. It indicated sympathy for the Southern people and a strong unwillingness to disturb the status quo; a vague hope that the Creator, having produced America and its divine mission, would eventually solve the problem; a profound uneasiness about the racial attitudes of others; and a confused inner conflict between his conscience and his need for the approval of Illinois voters with Southern origins and ties. It was a speech designed to keep a prejudiced audience happy, but it was carefully loaded with conscience-easing qualifications. The physical difference, he said, "will" (not "should") "probably" (not "certainly") forbid living together in "perfect" equality. "Inasmuch as it becomes a necessity," which means "*if*" it becomes necessary to have a difference, he favors the white race. "Perhaps" the Negro is not his moral or intellectual equal, but in the right to keep and enjoy whatever he can earn, the Negro is the "equal of every living man."

In Chicago, and even in Alton, in southern Illinois, Lincoln lashed out at the paternalistic defense of slavery and took a daring stand for the Illinois of 1858. The argument that slavery was for the benefit of the slaves, he said, was the same one always used by kings to justify riding the necks of their people. This, he warned, was:

> . . . the same old serpent that says you work and I eat, you toil and I will enjoy the fruits of it . . . whether it come from the mouth of a King, an excuse for enslaving the people of his country, or from the mouth of men of one race as a reason for enslaving the men of another race, it is all the same old serpent, and I hold if that course of argumentation . . . should be granted, it does not stop with the negro. . . .
> . . . let us discard all this quibbling about this man and the other man—this race and that race being inferior, and therefore they must be placed in an inferior position —discarding our standard that we have left us. Let us discard all these things, and unite as one people throughout this land, until we shall once more stand up declaring that all men are created equal."[6]

Douglas, of course, fought back with all the skills of a brilliant orator and tireless campaigner. Over and over he stressed the illogic of the "House-Divided" speech, and accused Lincoln of promoting disunion. In reply Lincoln insisted that his meaning and actual words were different, and here perhaps Lincoln was weakest. Popular sovereignty, Douglas repeated over and over, would give the South justice and bring sectional peace without spreading slavery another foot, but Lincoln's policy would give aid and comfort to the abolitionists, spread free Negroes throughout the Northwest, and drive the South ever closer to disunion. More than once Douglas compelled Lincoln to admit that if a territory qualified for statehood and asked for admission as a slave state, the request would have to be honored.

The most serious dilemma for Douglas was the Dred Scott decision, which denied territorial settlers the right to exercise popular sovereignty against slavery, and Lincoln demanded an answer to this inconsistency. At Freeport, Illinois, Douglas gave an answer that quickly reached national prominence as his "Freeport Doctrine," even though he had said the same thing earlier and would continue to repeat it. The Supreme Court, said Douglas, had forbidden territorial governments to pass laws barring the entry of slaveholders with slaves. The Court, however, did not require any territorial government to pass laws defining slaves as property and protecting the master's rights of ownership. Thus, if a territorial government did not provide for the legal enforcement of slavery, no slaveholder would dare bring his slaves to that territory. A territorial government, therefore, could in fact exclude slavery without violating the Dred Scott decision.

This argument was not new; and various Southerners, including Jefferson Davis, had also expounded it. Following his opposition to the Lecompton Constitution, however, the Freeport Doctrine gave Southern radicals and moderates a heavy club against Douglas in their own states. He had not only cheated them out of Kansas; he was now opposing their constitutional rights as defined by the Supreme Court.

Kansas and Freeport all but destroyed Douglas's chances for Southern support in the 1860 presidential election. In the North, however, they made him stronger. The Northern presidential vote in 1860 would depend in large part upon the Republican party's choice of a candidate. The most likely aspirant was William H. Seward, generally considered a dangerous radical in both sections. If Douglas had beaten Abraham Lincoln soundly in the senatorial election of 1858, Seward or some lesser candidate might well have been nominated. The Illinois election, however, established Lincoln as an able vote-getter untainted with radicalism and thoroughly identified with a position upon which abolitionists, free-soilers, and ordinary people with no feelings toward the slaves except prejudice could fully agree. While Douglas supporters won a majority in the Illinois legislature, Lincoln candidates won a bare majority of the popular vote. The Rail-splitter was defeated only by the gerrymandered division of the legislative districts.

At least some of the responsibility for this new Republican hope rested upon the shoulders of James Buchanan. Throughout the campaign the administration did everything possible to destroy Douglas. Democratic newspapers had to oppose him or lose the public printing. Postmasters, other officeholders, and those hoping to be officeholders dared not speak a word in his favor. In some districts administration candidates competed with Douglas candidates for Democratic votes. These vindictive efforts failed, but they probably cost Douglas a substantial number of votes. Buchanan legislative candidates received 5,071 votes while the difference between Lincoln and Douglas candidates was 4,185 (125,275 to 121,090). This of course does not measure the number who may have voted for Lincoln or may have stayed home because of the

President's attacks on Douglas. In 1858 citizens still cast their clearly marked ballots in full view of their fellow voters.

Having won more popular votes than the famed Douglas, Lincoln would have to be reckoned with in 1860. Buchanan would not be the last chief executive to learn the hard way that a president cannot afford the luxury of a personal vendetta.

7

★★★★★

ECONOMICS AND IDEOLOGY

Unfortunately, the Dred Scott and Lecompton explosions were accompanied by economic circumstances that did much to spread the shock waves. Until late July, 1857, prosperity and economic growth abounded. Responding to the needs of an energetic and acquisitive people, the nation's banks had doubled their number between 1853 and 1857, and had loaned out some $7.50 in paper notes for every dollar in specie actually in their vaults. The credit expansion was stimulated enormously by gold from California and Australia and by the rising demand for American products caused by the Crimean War. As prices went up, however, Americans actually imported more goods than they exported and thereby helped drain away the incoming gold. Some $1,250,000,000 in railroad securities were sold between 1850 and 1860, but many of the new lines were built in uncrowded areas where profits would not be made for several years. Likewise, land speculators were mortgaged to the hilt for unsettled lands not yet ready to pay for themselves. In August, 1857, the Ohio Life Insurance and Trust Company, which had $5,000,000 lent to the railroad builders, failed with huge debts owed to Eastern banks. Overnight the notes of 1,400 state banks became worthless, most western railroads went bankrupt, and more than 5,000 businesses failed. Soon the major cities had long lines of hungry workers chanting "bread or blood."

The basic problem was the lack of a flexible money and credit system able to grow in step with the ambitions and imaginations of those busily converting the matchless resources of a rich continent into usable wealth. James Buchanan, however, was a dedicated even if late-blooming disciple of Andrew Jackson. Old Hickory had always blamed every economic catastrophe on easy money, and Buchanan was prepared to contract the currency at the very moment when Northern banks and businesses were crying for more rather than less capital and credit. Actually, Treasury Secretary Cobb immediately concentrated a large stock of the government's gold supply in New York and won temporary gratitude from businesses there. Other federal departments, however, had to curtail their public works, and alongside his recommendations for Kansas the president came down hard on the bankers and speculators in his annual message of December, 1857. The government, he promised, would not stop public works in progress, but would start no new ones. Congress, he recommended, should provide for the immediate recision of the charter of any bank that suspended specie payments. States should require banks to reserve one dollar in specie for every three issued as paper, and prohibit banknotes of less than $20 so employers would have to pay all wages in coin. He would oppose the use of federal or state bonds as security for banknotes. In Buchanan's view the speculators deserved their punishment, and the rugged individualism of the innocent victims would eventually triumph over adversity.[1]

The message offered small comfort to the thousands suffering hunger and despair, and the leaders of American finance were appalled. Actually, within two years a substantial recovery occurred, but it won no new friends for the president. Looking for a simple explanation, Northern business blamed the panic on the extremely low tariff passed by the Southern-dominated Congress the day before Buchanan took office. Western farmers and settlers losing their land to high interest payments and high freight rates blamed Eastern jobbers and speculators, and were already creating the Wall Street mystique so important in Populist politics later in the century. Western cities complained bitterly about the 10 percent to 15 percent rate of exchange with New York. For decades Westerners had considered cheaper land prices and federal support for roads, canals, and river and harbor improvements to be their natural right and just reward for enduring the hardship involved in carrying civilization westward. Unfortunately, congressional Southerners opposed to faster expansion of free territories and congenitally averse to federal spending stood squarely in the path of the West's most cherished goals. And looming behind them was a president prepared to veto any such measures that might accidentally clear Congress. The concept of a Southern Slave Power blocking the nation's God-given right to progress was strongest in the old Northwest, but Republican editors rarely gave their readers anywhere a chance to forget it.

Even more significant, however, was the reaction of the South. Like the Northwesterners, Southerners blamed the depression on Northern bankers and speculators. The South suffered less and recovered more quickly, and this led to widespread public gloating about Southern superiority over the unstable free-labor capitalism of the North.

The Southern response to Northern suffering was conditioned in part by two new antislavery books with greater claims to authenticity than the fiction of Harriet Beecher Stowe. In 1856, after a leisurely trip through the Southern back roads and byways, Frederick Law Olmsted published *A Journey in the Seaboard Slave States*. In this book and in two sequels he described much that was admirable, but he also found both whites and blacks far worse off than he had expected. With nothing but sympathy for his erstwhile hosts, he attacked slavery as a terrible economic burden to everyone. From slavery, he wrote, came ignorance, the misuse of labor, poverty for the less-fortunate whites, and wasted resources. It banished free white labor, kept the blacks far below their potential, restricted education for everyone, and worked against democracy by breeding an aristocracy contemptuous of the rights of others. Olmsted's *Journey* did not inspire fear, but it must have been particularly galling to those who could recognize truth in his words.[2]

Hinton Rowan Helper, formerly of North Carolina, went much further than Olmsted. He felt little sympathy for the slaves and nothing but prejudice for blacks in general, but as a child of the Southern lower-middle class he had developed a burning hatred for the slaveholding aristocracy. He saw the North and Northwest outstripping the South in economic progress and blamed it all on the backwardness of slavery and the resulting stagnant poverty of Southern nonslaveholders. To the small-farmers, merchants, clerks, mechanics, and white laborers of the lower middle class he addressed *The Impending Crisis of the South and How to Meet It*. Like Mrs. Stowe he found several publishers unwilling to alienate their Southern customers, but by guaranteeing the costs he finally got the 420-page book on the market in the summer of 1857. Abolitionists and free-soil politicians were immediately excited, and a group eventually subsidized an abridged paperback edition of

100,000 copies, which sold for only sixteen cents per copy. After a hundred pages of moral and humanitarian antislavery arguments, supported by statements from Washington, Jefferson, Madison, Marshall, Randolph, and Monroe, Helper paraded statistics to show the vast Northern superiority in wealth, libraries, education, churches, and literature. By enslaving the blacks, he argued, the slaveholders had also enslaved the nonslaveholding whites. Unlike Olmsted, Helper viciously attacked the slaveholders and issued a clarion call to action. He called upon the nonslaveholding whites to recognize that "the arrant demagogues whom you have elected to offices of honor and profit, have . . . used you as mere tools for the consummation of their wicked designs. They have purposely kept you in ignorance, and have, by moulding your passions and prejudices to suit themselves, induced you to act in direct opposition to your dearest rights and interests." To the slaveholders Helper offered a fearsome warning: "Do you aspire to become the victims of white non-slaveholding vengeance by day, and of barbarous massacre by the negroes at night? Would you be instrumental in bringing upon yourselves, your wives, and your children, a fate too horrible to contemplate?"[3]

Skillfully dealing with the racial prejudice responsible for the poorer whites' acceptance of slavery, Helper proposed that all slaves should be emancipated and sent back to Africa. Thus the lower and lower-middle classes could get rid of both slavery and the blacks. Helper proposed an eleven-point program, calling for exclusion of slaveholders from public office; boycotts against slaveholding merchants, hotels, professional men, and proslavery newspapers; and a tax of sixty dollars per slave on each slaveholder, with the money to be used for transporting the slaves to Africa, Latin America, or some distant part of the United States.[4]

While the poorer nonslaveholders rarely saw a copy of the book, the slaveholders were both angry and frightened, particularly after the subsidized cheap edition. Among those most indignant was President James Buchanan, who considered Helper both an instigator of bloody revolution and an agent of the Republican party. In 1866 Buchanan still considered *The Impending Crisis* a major cause of the Civil War and ranked it alongside John Brown's raid as a justification for Southern secession.[5]

Southerners were quick to answer. Samuel M. Wolfe in *Helper's Impending Crisis Dissected* and Gilbert J. Beebe in *Review and Refutation* argued with equal fervor that poor whites were better off in the South than in the North and that the Negro was where he was happiest and most useful. George Fitzhugh had already taken the offensive in 1854 with *Sociology for the South; or the Failure of Free Society*, which glorified the humanity of slavery and attacked the cruelties of the Northern wage-slave system. In 1857, just in time to refute Helper, although not specifically so designed, Fitzhugh followed with *Cannibals All! or Slaves Without Masters*. Slavery, he argued, suited the masses best whether they were white or black. Protecting the weak always required their enslavement, and the North would be better off if it adopted slavery as a form of communism. Capitalism in the North, Fitzhugh wrote, had been proven a failure, and the North should look to the South for the proper example of a superior system. The Northern states should assign and compel people to work and give them economic security in return. Fitzhugh was confident that the North would ultimately substitute the Southern system for its own.[6]

For those whose fears were not eased by Fitzhugh's confidence, fresh appeals to the racial prejudices of the Southern poor were in order. Typical was Mississippi Senator Albert G. Brown's widely circulated warning in 1860 that with emancipation the slave would "insist upon being treated as an equal—that he shall go to the white man's table and the white man to his—that he shall share the white man's bed, and the white man his—that his son shall marry the white man's daughter, and the white man's daughter his son. In short, they shall live on terms of perfect equality."[7]

The old argument that slavery made all white men equal in the color of their skins was again dusted off, and Helper probably contributed inadvertently to a new movement for the revival of the African slave trade. By federal law the trade was punishable by death, but various Southern conventions met to discuss it anyhow. Advocates invariably argued that a new supply would drive the price of slaves down until almost every white man could own one, and this would still the dissatisfaction of those whites who might be receptive to appeals such as Helper's. Fortunately, many Southern leaders on principle did not want the trade renewed and most large slaveholders in the deep South as well as those selling slaves from the border states did not really want the price to fall. Thus, the movement accomplished nothing but sound and fury, which angered Northerners far more than it influenced many Southerners.

Thomas Prentice Kettell, former editor of the *Democratic Review*, fought back with Helper's own methodology. In *Southern Wealth and Northern Profits*, he mustered 170 pages of statistics and arguments to prove that the South produced enormous wealth but then lost most of it to the greedy North. With extremely flimsy documentation and reasoning, Kettell calculated the annual Northerns profits at Southern expense to be $231,500,000. It was a good answer for disturbed Southerners. To themselves, at least, they could not deny the poverty described by Olmsted and Helper, but they could blame it on the North. For the North, Samuel Powell answered with *Notes on Southern Wealth and Northern Profits*, which disproved Kettell's conclusions to the equal satisfaction of Powell's Northern readers.[8]

Throughout 1858 and 1859 the slavery quarrels coincided in Congress with fierce debates over tariffs, homesteads, and federal subsidies for railroads, canals, roads, higher education, and other internal improvements. A Pacific railroad bill almost passed, but Southerners who would support only a road that crossed Texas defeated it with the aid of New Englanders who considered it a gigantic land swindle. A homestead bill passed the House, but got strangled in the Senate by its connection with Buchanan's request for $30,000,000 to be used in another attempt to buy Cuba. Despite the woebegone arguments of the iron rail and textile industries, the South and the Northwest continued to keep tariffs at a low level. Buchanan, meanwhile, vetoed a bill to grant lands for the support of colleges of agriculture and mechanical arts on the grounds that states should not expect gifts from the federal government. For constitutional reasons he also vetoed a bill to eliminate the dangerous shoals in the St. Clair channel connecting Lakes Huron and Erie.

The failure of these programs helped keep the Northeast and the Northwest angry at the South and at each other, but by 1859 prosperity and economic growth were again in full swing. Railroads were being built in all three sections without government aid, factories were again operating full time, wages were up, settlers were swarming westward, and the prices of cotton and slaves were rising toward a peak. Indeed, secession and war finally came in 1861 at a point of high prosperity when animosity over economic affairs should have been at a minimum. The economic achievements of each section contributed to arrogance and self-confidence as their leaders approached the crisis, but economic resentments had abated significantly.

A once-popular view that still survives in various forms attributes the Civil War to the struggle between Southern agriculture and Northern industrialism, and minimizes slavery except for its connection with agriculture.[9] The editorials, articles, books, debates, and speeches of the Buchanan years, however, invariably begin and end with slavery. The Northeast did not secede because of the tariff, and the Northwest did not secede because of homesteads or internal improvements. The South seceded, and those responsible must be at least given credit for knowing why, however irrational their reasoning may have been. The Northeast and the Northwest blamed the South's opposition to paternalistic economic policies on slavery, and identified their adversary as the Slaveocracy or the Slave Power. In turn, virtually every Southern economic argument was in the final analysis a defense of slavery, whether in answer to Olmsted, Helper, or abolitionist and free-soil politicians.

On specific economic measures neither North nor South was a monolith. Northwesterners voted against the tariff. Northeasterners voted against railroad grants. Southerners themselves were often divided on economic matters. Until the early 1850s the Southern states elected numerous legislators, representatives, senators, and governors who avowed their allegiance to the Whig party of Henry Clay and Daniel Webster, which stood for all of the capitalistic national policies the South supposedly seceded against. Confederate Vice-President Alexander H. Stephens, Confederate Secretary of State Robert Toombs, and Confederate Secretary of War (and later of State) Judah P. Benjamin were all Whigs.

Oversimplifying the economic differences into a struggle between an agricultural South and an industrial North ignores several million Northern farmers as well as a sizable Southern middle class of merchants, bankers, speculators, and professional men.[10] In the Northern cities, also, workingmen, already unhappy over what they considered excessive foreign immigration, feared that any emancipation would bring a horde of hungry blacks after their jobs. Northern businessmen and bankers often had many profitable ties with Southerners, and as always tended to be conservative on social issues. The actual question that triggered secession and war—the right of slavery to expand westward—was surely as much a struggle between Northern free agriculture and Southern slave agriculture as it was between Northern capitalism and Southern agriculture.

Without slavery the ideological differences between South and North would have been minimal. To demonstrate the evils of slavery, Northerners as well as Southerners like Helper attacked Southern civilization as backward, ignorant, illiterate, immoral, and

61

poverty-stricken. To show the glories of slavery, Southerners contrasted the open air, healthy exercise, self-sufficiency, harmony, stability, and religious and moral advantages of rural living with the labor conflicts, riots, atheism, slums, unemployment, crime, and dangerous social experiments of the urban North. The South, wrote Fitzhugh, "has been so quiet and . . . it has suffered so little from crime or extreme poverty, that its attention has not been awakened to the revolutionary tumults, uproars, mendicity, and crime of free society."[11] Slavery and slavery alone imposed the moral burden that required each section to defend itslf and attack the values of the other.

For most Southerners, of course, slavery as a system of social segregation and control far outweighed the question of economic profitability. Since three-fourths of the Southern whites had no direct connection with slavery at all except through its cheap competition with their own labor, the institution clearly offered most Southerners nothing except a solution to their racial fears and prejudices. In the 1940s and 1950s the so-called revisionist historians, who questioned the necessity for the Civil War and blamed it upon human errors rather than inevitable forces, came face to face with the modern civil-rights movement. Younger historians, rightly sensitive to injustices against the slaves' descendants, accused the revisionists of being callous and indifferent to the evils of slavery. The revisionists in turn often defended themselves in part with the view that slavery in the not-too-distant future would have died a natural death anyhow.

In recent years several historians, with no new synthesis of their own and attracted by the new mathematical and mechanical techniques available to "quantitative" historians, have devoted much energy and ability to proving that slavery was in fact quite profitable for most slaveholders.[12] The implication, of course, is that nothing short of war could have destroyed a profitable institution and that those still willing to question the war's origins and purposes are thereby condoning slavery. One basic weakness in most such studies is their failure to calculate a salary for the time and efforts of the slaveholders, who in the overwhelming majority of cases managed their own enterprises. The usual profit margin is 10 to 12 percent, but any person with a $30,000 investment who has to work full time to make it pay $3,000 a year does not really have a good investment. Also, statistical averages do not always reveal what is actually happening to most of the people who comprise the statistics. Aside from these considerations, however, is the obvious fact that for the three-fourths of the Southern whites who had no economic stake in slavery the question of profitability was largely irrelevant. They tolerated, supported, and ultimately fought and died for slavery because racial prejudice and fear made war preferable to the specter of emancipation and racial equality.

For the same reason, however, any proof that slavery was in fact unprofitable may be equally inconclusive as a guarantee for its disappearance. If a society believes an economic burden to be worth its cost for other reasons, the burden may well survive indefinitely. Post–Civil War segregation and Jim Crow have not been economic bargains for most Southern whites, but the whites most damaged by them have usually been the ones most ready to commit violence for their preservation. The warnings of Albert G. Brown still outweigh economic logic in the minds of vast numbers of white Americans. And finally, to reverse the argument, profitability alone would not have guaranteed the survival of slavery in the face of all pressures short of war. Societies do occasionally abolish profitable activities for moral, religious, and ideological reasons. Brazil and most of the Spanish-American nations, as well as Britain, France, and Russia, did not abolish slavery because it had become unprofitable.

The arguments over the economics of slavery have taken some strange new twists, as historians of equal integrity and dedication to the ideals of the Declaration of Independence continue to disagree sharply. In their zeal to prove the profitability of slavery and refute the thesis of Stanley Elkins that slavery afflicted many Afro-Americans with unfortunate behavioral characteristics, Robert W. Fogel and Stanley L. Engerman have published the strongest defense of slavery since George Fitzhugh. Using the latest quantitative methods, they argue that except for its limitations on slaves of unusual ability, the institution was in fact quite humane as well as highly efficient. Eugene Genovese, on the other hand, has painted the most devastating picture of the catastrophic economic effects of slavery since Hinton Rowan Helper. Fogel and Engerman believe the Civil War was inevitable because no other means could have destroyed such a viable and profitable institution. Genovese is equally certain that the War was inevitable because only the expansion of slavery into new territories could have saved the institution from destruction by its own weaknesses, and expansion required secession. In this view the demise of slavery through containment would have destroyed the political and social power of the planter class, and the planters seceded, therefore, to prevent an internal revolution.[13]

If Fogel and Engerman are correct, why did the Southern leaders act with such fear and irrationality in the face of the obvious racial prejudices of most Northerners and the constant insistence of the Republicans that they would not disturb slavery where it already existed? Why did they stake the continued existence of their humane, stable, prosperous, and productive society, which needed no expansion, on demands for equal rights in territories generally considered unfit for slavery? If Genovese is correct, why were so many nonslaveholding whites, as well as smaller slaveholders, so ready to fight for the interests of the 2 to 3 percent of the population that comprised the planter class?

Fogel and Engerman argue that the earlier condemnations of slavery insult the character and ability of the slaves and are responsible for many stereotypes that underlie American racism. In an earlier book, J. C. Furnas blames Harriet Beecher Stowe and the "Uncle Tom" shows based on her novel for making the same kind of contribution to the racist philosophy.[14] Are these historical and literary images, however, actually essential links in the chains of discrimination that American blacks have been struggling to shed since 1619? Was the racial prejudice that made slavery possible in the first place even remotely related to feelings that slavery was inefficient or unprofitable? Did the willingness of the nonslaveholding whites to fight for slavery in 1861 really stem from a conviction that the slaves were lazy or incompetent? How many prejudiced, white Americans have ever heard of Hinton Rowan Helper or Frederick Law Olmsted, or have ever felt the slightest curiosity as to whether ante-bellum slavery was profitable or not? Neither Elkins's comparison of slavery with the Nazi concentration camps nor *Uncle Tom's Cabin* has become recommended reading for the White Citizens Councils or the Ku Klux Klan. The achievements and potential of America's black minority can be defended with equal logic on the basis of its resistance to a tyrannical and degrading system. The work of Fogel and Engerman may do much to restore the reputation of the planters for both kindness and high intelligence, and could well start another wave of pro-Southern agrarian history. Its contribution to racial harmony, however well intentioned, may be considerably less. It most assuredly validates the image of the South held by President James Buchanan in 1860. Its historical soundness, however, is already being questioned, and will face a long period of serious testing.

8

★★★★★

LAMB, LION, OR FOX?

Historians have found it easy to compare the reactions of James Buchanan to secession with the bold strokes of Andrew Jackson during the nullification crisis of 1832–1833, and the usual result depicts a timid, indecisive appeaser and weakling, paralyzed by a fear of violence.

How Buchanan might have reacted to a threat of hand-to-hand combat or a duel was never tested. On several occasions as president, however, he indicated a firm and immediate willingness to threaten force or send men into battle. His efforts to speak the language of Jackson were not always limited to agrarian economics. "If I can be instrumental in settling the slavery question . . . , and then add Cuba to the Union," he wrote just after the election, "I shall be willing to give up the ghost." In his inaugural he added that "Our past history forbids that we shall in the future acquire territory, unless this be sanctioned by the laws of justice and honor. Acting on this principle, no nation will have a right to interfere or to complain if, in the progress of events, we shall still further extend our possessions." And in a special message to Congress on January 7, 1858, he concluded that "It is, beyond question, the destiny of our race to spread themselves over the continent of North America, and this at no distant day."[1]

Only the tact and persuasiveness of a remarkable peacemaker kept Buchanan from fighting a bloody war against his fellow Americans of the Mormon faith.[2] Persecuted without mercy all the way from New York to Missouri and back into Illinois, the members of the Church of Jesus Christ of Latter-Day Saints had finally emigrated beyond the immediate reach of their tormenters. In the faraway territory of Utah they had applied the hard work and ethics prescribed by their religion and had achieved a remarkable prosperity. In 1850 President Fillmore appointed the Mormon prophet and leader Brigham Young as governor, commander of the militia, and superintendent of Indian affairs for Utah. Young, a bearded giant with great charisma as well as practical sense, established industries, cooperative stores, banks, and transportation agencies. The population quickly grew to forty thousand, as converts by the hundreds pushed handcarts across the plains. Young announced in no uncertain terms that he would be governor until the Almighty ruled otherwise.

Twice Congress denied the Saints' petition for authority to write a state constitution. Unwilling to wait longer, they wrote a constitution and established a government anyhow, which President Pierce simply ignored. The great stumbling block was their refusal to outlaw polygamy, which neither Congress nor the president could accept in the face of overwhelming national opposition. In numerous cases, also, the Mormons had claimed and cultivated lands technically still belonging to the Indians, and the Federal Land Office refused to grant titles until the Indian titles could be extinguished. Knowing how little attention had been paid to Indian rights in earlier cases, the Mormons, many of whom had lost their property to persecutors in other states, were suspicious and angry.

In 1855, President Pierce, with his usual acumen, appointed two renegade ex-Mormons and one well-known Mormon-hater to federal judgeships in Utah. After two years of turmoil, the judges and a delegation of Mormons were back in Washington with conflicting stories. The Mormons accused the judges of conspiring to defraud them of their lands. The judges claimed they had been prevented from executing their duties, their official papers had been confiscated and burned, and they had been driven from the territory in fear of their lives. The Mormon legislature had in fact declared that no laws would be obeyed except those enacted by the governor and assembly and those passed by Congress "when applicable," which meant when approved by Brigham Young. Judge W. W. Drummond charged that his predecessor, Judge Leonidas Shaver, had been poisoned by the Mormons and that the late secretary of the territory as well as a party of eight surveyors had been killed by Indians instigated by the church. The surveyor general and his clerks also fled, leaving two Indians agents as the only federal officers in the territory. Judge Drummond's appeal to the country coincided with the publication of a lurid book called *Horrors of Mormonism*, by apostate F. G. J. Margetson. Most of Margetson's claims and probably half of the charges by the judges were untrue, but they were widely believed.

President Buchanan reacted with speed and vigor. He appointed Alfred Cumming of Georgia to replace Young as governor and added a new chief justice, two associate justices, a secretary, and a marshal. Most important, he ordered Colonel Albert Sydney Johnston and 2,500 troops to accompany Cumming to his new post. Johnston, later to be a great Confederate hero and martyr, had once killed a puma with a clubbed rifle.

The Mormons got the word and reacted. Their presses asked why the federal government didn't spend its time dealing with bloody riots in Baltimore, Washington, and New York instead of bothering the Mormons. Brigham Young announced that his people would fight "in the mountains, in the canyons, upon the plains, on the hills, along the mighty streams, and by the rivulets."[3]

The Mormons got a windfall when Governor Robert J. Walker persuaded the president to leave Johnston's cavalry in Kansas. Johnston's troops marched westward and found Mormons on horseback waiting for them. The Saints destroyed three supply trains of seventy-four wagons owned by Russell, Majors, and Waddell of Leavenworth, who were the army's provisions contractors. Thus deprived of both horses and supplies, Johnston's men struggled through cold and snow to winter quarters at Fort Bridger, which the Mormons had already gutted. One magazine compared the march to Napoleon's retreat from Moscow. Regarding all gentiles as enemies, the Mormons also decimated a party of 137 California-bound emigrants. They were clearly too strong for the expedition sent against them, and Congress promptly authorized two additional volunteer regiments.

The official letter replacing Brigham Young actually never reached him because the Pierce administration had annulled the Utah mail contract. Young knew only that his land was being invaded, and in the spring of 1858 he ordered a scorched-earth policy. All outlying lands were to be evacuated with a handful of men left to burn everything if necessary: there should "not be one building, nor one foot of lumber, not a stick, nor a tree, nor a particle of grass and hay that will burn, left in reach of our enemies."[4]

By spring, also, Johnston's tormented army was spoiling for vengeance against the "modern sodomites" responsible for all their troubles. Fortunately, however, a peacemaker appeared at the critical moment. Thomas L. Kane, brother of Elisha Kent Kane, the famous Arctic explorer, had lived with the Mormons and had written a favorable book about them. He was from Pennsylvania and he had both the ear and the trust of James Buchanan. Kane argued that the Mormons were peace-loving and would cooperate with any honest program if given the opportunity. Buchanan gave Kane a chance to prove this. Without salary or expense account, Kane soon made his way to Utah and negotiated an agreement with Young. Washington would be supreme in temporal affairs. The Mormons would remain autonomous in religious matters. Kane returned to Governor Cumming's camp and the two were soon enjoying peaceful conferences with Young while the impatient and disappointed officers and soldiers waited. On April 25, 1858, Young introduced the new governor to several thousand Mormons at the tabernacle. Cumming assured them that he would demand submission to the United States Constitution and laws, but would not station troops near their settlements and would not interfere with their religion. Invited by the new governor to comment, dozens of people then rose to deliver emotional accounts of all they had suffered in the past and repeat their determination not to be over-run by any army. On April 6 Buchanan announced pardons for all who would submit to the federal government. A brief lapse occurred when several thousand Mormons burned their buildings and crops at the appearance of Johnston's troops, but on June 2 a full agreement stipulated that the troops would stay thirty-six miles away from Salt Lake City. Peace reigned.

If Buchanan was occasionally tormented by inner conflicts between his affections for the South and a sense of national duty, he had no such problems when dealing with other nations. With Secretary of State Lewis Cass apparently unfit for either administration or crucial decisions, Buchanan ran his own Department of State. He maintained an office there, and with his old friend and associate Appleton as assistant he clearly enjoyed some of his happier moments in this role. In quarrels abroad he was reasonably certain that most Americans would prefer that their country should have its own way, and thus fortified he was often bold and decisive.

If the president really meant everything he said and wrote, and no contrary evidence exists, he wanted to eliminate all European influence in Central America and establish American control there by purchase, annexation, or intervention.[5] Both an obstacle and an excuse was the vaguely worded Clayton-Bulwer Treaty of 1850, in which the United States and Britain had agreed that neither would seize territory or establish protectorates in Central America. Americans had interpreted this to mean the British would get out of Central America, while the British insisted it meant they would take no new territory in the future. Buchanan actually took office during the final stages of an Anglo-American crisis that involved threats of war.

During the 1850s English settlers and officials in Greytown, capital of the Mosquito Kingdom in Honduras under the protection of the British, often interfered with American trade and travelers crossing from ocean to ocean enroute to California. In turn, equally quarrelsome American travelers provoked altercations with the British and their native allies. In 1852 the British seized the Bay Islands. In 1854 an American warship bombarded Greytown and burned it to the ground. Only the Crimean War prevented the British from serious retaliation. In 1856 William Walker, the little Tennessee-born filibuster actively trying to conquer Central America with only nominal objections from his own government, met strong opposition from the British. President Franklin Pierce answered by recognizing Walker's government in Nicaragua and breaking relations with Great Britain. Simultaneously, the Crimean War had ended, and the British could face the United States with a considerable force already under arms.

Fortunately, however, a number of British newspapers and statesmen, including Benjamin Disraeli, had concluded that American control of Central America might not be a bad thing after all. It would increase the efficiency, population, and productivity of the region, which could be translated into greater consumption of British products. An American canal there would surely be open to British use; and, besides, in Asia and Africa the British themselves might want to follow the example being set by their country cousins.

In July, 1858, the Earl of Malmesbury, the British foreign secretary, actually told George M. Dallas, the American minister, that he and others believed that "all the southern part of North America must ultimately come under the government of the United States." Such a development, he added, would benefit the entire world.[6]

Whether or not Buchanan fully realized how completely his apparent risks were in fact being minimized, he followed the example of his old chief, James K. Polk, and looked John Bull squarely in the eye. To work for normal relations, the British sent a special envoy, Sir William Gore Ousley, a brother-in-law of Mrs. James Roosevelt's and a personal friend of Buchanan's. In November, 1857, Ousley offered to cede the Bay Islands to Honduras, place the Mosquito Kingdom under Nicaraguan sovereignty, and define clearly the disputed boundaries. Buchanan, however, refused to accept anything that did not include the formal abrogation of the Clayton-Bulwer Treaty.[7]

The confrontation with the British over Central America was also complicated by the zeal of British efforts to stop the African slave trade. In the Webster-Ashburton Treaty of 1842, both nations agreed to maintain a squadron off Africa for suppression of the trade when carried on under their respective flags, or any claim or use of their flags, or by their citizens or subjects. This article was accompanied by a forcible statement from Webster that the American government admitted no right of visitation and search of merchant vessels in peacetime, and the Senate argued long and loud over this before ratifying the treaty. In practice, the United States made no serious efforts against the trade, while the British upheld their end of the bargain with remarkable determination. Most of the slavers were from other nations, but none hesitated to run up an American flag when approached by British men-of-war. In turn, British commanders with long experience in recognizing the slave ships would stop suspicious-looking vessels regardless of the colors at their mastheads. Naturally enough, they made some mistakes, but they also reduced the slave trade. As might be expected also, Americans, most of them from the South, began denouncing British high-handedness in rhetoric quite similar to that which had led to the War of 1812. Ship commanders, some of whom may have jettisoned their human cargo just before capture, complained of rude and offensive treatment by crews from the searching ships.

A potential crisis developed in 1858 when the British sent a small fleet of cruisers to the coast of Cuba and to the Gulf of Mexico with orders to search any merchantman suspected of slave trading. Americans North as well as South objected, and Buchanan reacted boldly. Speaking for the president, Secretary Cass lodged a vehement protest.

The British claimed no unlimited right of visit and search, but did argue for the right to inspect ships flying the American flag to determine whether they were really American. Cass admitted that no ship illegally flying the Stars and Stripes was entitled to protection, but warned that British commanders would be stopping American ships at their own risk if they made a mistake. The Senate was already on record with a unanimous resolution that the "immunity of their merchant vessels upon the high seas will be steadily maintained by the United States under all circumstances as an attribute of their sovereignty never to be abandoned, whatever sacrifices its protection may require." With this support, Buchanan ordered every available naval vessel to the Gulf of Mexico "to protect all vessels of the United States on the high seas from search or detention by the vessels of war of any other nation."[8]

Rather than risk war on such an issue, the British government ordered its naval officers to abandon any further efforts against ships flying the American flag. The British, however, did appeal to Buchanan for greater cooperation in trying to eliminate the slave trade. The president responded by increasing the United States naval patrols in the suspected areas, but this was only a fraction of the effort made to compel the British to leave all suspected American slavers alone. It was a diplomatic victory for Buchanan, who was right on principle, but serious American efforts to stifle the slave trade would have prevented the confrontation in the first place.[9]

The British had clearly opted for peaceful settlements all along the line. On November 28, 1859, the British governor signed a treaty with Honduras acknowledging that republic's ownership of the Bay Islands and recognizing also the sovereign rights of Honduras over that part of the Mosquito Kingdom that lay within its borders. Two months later the British also agreed to recognize the sovereignty of Nicaragua over that part of the Mosquito territory within its boundaries, with the natives to have home rule until they should agree to join Nicaragua. While the Clayton-Bulwer Treaty was not fully abrogated, the concessions were considerable; and Buchanan could with reason congratulate himself, as he did in his annual message of 1860.[10]

Encountering only sweet reasonableness from the British to the south, Buchanan was correspondingly aggressive in the northwest. The 1846 treaty establishing the Oregon boundary had made the border in Puget Sound "the channel which separates the continent from Vancouver's Island." In fact, however, there were two channels with several islands, including San Juan, between them. Naturally enough, each nation claimed a different channel, and soon American settlers were holding San Juan at gun point against agents of the Hudson's Bay Company. Buchanan unhesitatingly ordered Captain George E. Pickett to resist expulsion, and quickly sent a naval force and an army under General Scott to hold possession while a joint occupation agreement was being negotiated.[11] Ultimately, in the post–Civil War arbitration with Britain, the German kaiser, acting as referee, awarded San Juan to the United States.

A sidelight on improved relations with Britain was the American tour of nineteen-year-old Edward, Prince of Wales, in the fall of 1860. As all Washington quivered with excitement, Buchanan held a grand state dinner for his youthful guest, but, as usual, he firmly denied Harriet's plea that he permit dancing. Later in the evening the president found that he would have to sleep on a sofa because all the White House beds had been taken by his guests. Next day at a party on the revenue-cutter *Harriet Lane*, the prince did in fact dance with several young ladies. Later in New York a dance floor caved in during a grand ball for the prince, who reportedly escaped his guardians and spent the night in one of the city's most luxurious brothels. His mother, Queen Victoria, described the visit to America as an "important link to cement two nations of kindred origin and character."[12]

Still farther to the North, Buchanan looked hopefully at Alaska. During the Crimean War between Russia and Britain, the Russians had approached the Pierce administration with an offer to sell Alaska. Pierce, however, had been too busy to be concerned with such a frozen wasteland. In late 1857 the Russian minister discussed the matter with Buchanan, who for a time toyed with the idea of buying it as a colony for the Mormons. When the Russian foreign minister asked if the Mormons would go as conquerors or colonists, Buchanan replied that he didn't care as long as he got rid of them. Two years later Senator Gwin of California, representing Buchanan, proposed $5 million as a starting point for negotiations. The Russians rejected the proposal as too low for consideration. Buchanan replied that the treasury was low and the Congress was hostile. He could not offer more.[13] Actually, while Congress had refused to appropriate $30,000,000 for Cuba, this did not necessarily mean that $7,200,000, the price paid for Alaska later, would have been impossible for that area, but Buchanan never put it to the test.

Meanwhile, William Walker had been overthrown in Nicaragua by a coalition of neighboring Central American leaders organized in part by Cornelius Vanderbilt, who did not appreciate Walker's dealings on trans-Isthmian railroad matters. The United

States jailed Walker in New Orleans, but released him on $2,000 bail. Walker promptly eluded federal officers, whose efforts were probably less than dedicated, and sailed for Nicaragua with another fully equipped army. Buchanan publicly denounced Walker's activities as "robbery and murder." Southerners generally, however, strongly supported Walker and complained bitterly when Commodore Paulding chased Walker to Nicaragua, captured his ship, and brought him back to Washington. The Department of State, directed by the president, ruled that it had no jurisdiction or legal charge against him. Buchanan reprimanded Paulding personally for exceeding his authority in leading an armed force into the territory of a friendly nation. He also based his complaint against Walker partially on the grounds that such invasions would hinder rather than expedite the inevitable expansion of the United States into the area. Newspapers and politicians immediately divided on the issue, with Paulding a hero in the North and a villain in the South. Walker himself went to Mobile and claimed in a public speech that Buchanan had secretly encouraged him to take Nicaragua but had changed his mind in the face of public opinion.[14] John C. Fremont had once said much the same thing to explain his presence in California when Buchanan was secretary of state. Clearly, Buchanan had not wanted Paulding to capture Walker, and had released him as soon as possible. Two years later Walker was captured and shot while attempting once again to establish a new Southern empire.

Nicaraguan and Costa Rican leaders issued the Rivas Manifesto, which accused Buchanan of directing the filibuster attacks. In effect they announced they were under the protection of France, Britain, and Sardinia against the "barbarians of the United States." Buchanan answered that the United States would resist any such European intervention or protection, and threatened to collect reparations for the insulting Rivas Manifesto. The president apparently believed strongly that if the United States did not intervene in Central America to maintain prosperity and security for the transit routes, the European nations would do so. In each annual message he asked Congress for troops to quell lawless violence and protect American travelers in Central America. Congress, with Northern Democrats and Republicans alike opposed to any southward expansion, refused to authorize the use of troops, and the president was thereby restricted to diplomacy. He negotiated a treaty in which New Granada (Colombia) acknowledged responsibility for claims arising out of the Panama riot on April 15, 1856, and he persuaded

Costa Rica to refer claims against itself to a board of commissioners. He also bullied Nicaragua into granting transit rights and even got Mexico to grant the right of American military occupation in cases of disorder. His aims, however, were thwarted by the hostile Congress elected in 1858, and no treaty could be confirmed.[15]

No insult, real or implied, against the United States escaped Buchanan's attention. In 1853 Paraguay, a landlocked hermit nation hundreds of miles from the nearest port, had refused to ratify a treaty of friendship, commerce, and navigation with the United States. The dictatorship of Carlos Antonio Lopez also appropriated the property of certain Americans living in Paraguay, and in February, 1855, his soldiers fired on an American ship engaged in surveying the Parana River. The helmsman was killed. Almost three years later in his annual message of December, 1857, Buchanan informed Congress he would ask for redress peacefully but would have a better chance for success if Congress authorized him to use force if necessary. In June, 1858, Congress responded favorably and voted funds for the expenses of a commissioner if Buchanan wished to appoint one. Buchanan did so wish, and in December, 1858, a commissioner, accompanied by Commodore Shubrick in command of nineteen warships carrying two hundred guns and 2,500 sailors and marines, landed at Montevideo, Uruguay. With the main force in readiness on the Parana River, Commissioner Bowlin and Commodore Shubrick with two ships sailed a thousand miles up the jungle-lined rivers to Asunción, Paraguay. President Lopez understood the message. He paid the family of the dead sailor $10,000, apologized, and concluded a treaty of navigation and commerce. No significant trade developed with Paraguay and the expedition probably cost several hundred thousand dollars, but American honor was vindicated.[16]

Buchanan's most significant diplomatic achievement may have been the successes of William B. Reed, his minister to China. Chinese violations of the coercive treaties imposed by Britain after the First Opium War had led to another conflict in which the British and French again defeated and humiliated the Chinese. Britain and France tried to get the United States involved in the war on the grounds that all three nations had common objectives. Buchanan agreed that this was so, but wisely saw no reason why the United States should fight for something that could be attained peacefully. He instructed Reed to maintain a strict neutrality but to cooperate with the British and French diplomatically to get for the United States the same commercial concessions they were fighting for. Reed followed this policy with tact and ability, and in the Treaty of Tientsin, signed in June, 1858, and two later supplemental conventions, the United States did gain peacefully all the advantages won by Britain and France in the war. The Chinese government also paid the full amount claimed by American citizens for injuries by China, but any break in friendly relations between the two countries was avoided.[17]

With even less effort Buchanan profited from the Perry expedition sent by President Pierce to Japan. A colorful Japanese delegation bearing exotic gifts arrived to sign the first treaty between the United States and Japan. If they were not quite as earthshaking a sensation as Perry's big black ships had been in Japan, they nonetheless attracted a vast amount of attention and inspired a diverting round of dinners and receptions.

Aside from sending nineteen ships to intimidate little Paraguay, Buchanan's most aggressive policies and greatest failures involved Mexico and Cuba. Mexico was again suffering through a series of palace revolutions, and American citizens again were claiming more than $10,000,000 in damages. The natural right of United States citizens to pursue their enterprises both profitable and charitable in Mexico may be questioned, and the occasional mistreatment, expulsion, confiscation of property, and even murder practiced by various Mexican leaders and citizens when they found the Yankees in their way can be understood if not condoned. The Mexican War and the annexation of more than a third of Mexico's territory (excluding Texas; almost half if Texas is included) was after all a very recent memory. In 1857 Mexico approved another in a long series of democratic constitutions and elected a new president and Congress. Within a month President Comonfort was replaced by a military rebellion under General Zuloaga, who also ignored the constitutional successor, General Juarez, the chief justice of Mexico. Zuloaga, however, was soon replaced by General Miramon. Juarez, meanwhile, established his own government at Vera Cruz. The resulting civil war caused the deaths of several Americans, and convinced James Buchanan that stability must be restored under American auspices.

Buchanan was particularly concerned about the ambitions of Louis Napoleon and the French, and ultimately his warnings proved correct. At the time, however, the French, like the British for Calhoun and Polk earlier, may have been only an excuse rather than a reason for his policies. In his December, 1858, annual message, the president described the Mexican situation as critical and recommended that the United States assume a temporary protectorate over the northern parts of Chihuahua and Sonora and establish military posts to enforce it. The Senate Committee on Foreign Relations reported favorably, but the Senate killed the idea by thirty-one to twenty-five. Three months later, in March, 1859, Buchanan sent Robert McLane to Mexico with authority to recognize Juarez at his own discretion, and on April 7 McLane pronounced the government of Juarez to be the only existing government of the republic. Unhappily, however, the government of General Miramon remained in full command of the capital, but this was a challenge rather than a calamity. In Buchanan's own words, "it had now become the imperative duty of Congress to act without further delay, and to enforce redress from the government of Miramon for the wrongs it had committed in violation of the faith of treaties against citizens of the United States. . . . The territory . . . around the capital was not accessible to our forces without passing through the States under the jurisdiction of the constitutional government. . . . No doubt was therefore entertained that it would cheerfully grant us the right of passage."[18]

The president, therefore, in his annual message of December, 1859, asked Congress for authority to invade Mexico and obtain "indemnity for the past and security for the future." The United States, he argued, must establish a military colony to stabilize the region and promote annexation because otherwise some other nation would do so first. Fortunately for Mexico, the Congress was too preoccupied with John Brown's raid and the slavery question to give this request any serious attention.

Early in 1860 McLane and the Juarez government signed a treaty in which Mexico for $4,000,000 agreed to give the United States transit rights from the Gulf of Mexico to the Pacific and the right to police the route, with each government required to send troops on request to the aid of the other if internal disorder should threaten any violation of the pact. The intent was clearly stated by McLane: "Let us take the constitutional government firmly by the hand, and we will in a twelve-month drive out of Mexico every anti-America element and pave the way for the acquisition of Cuba. Indeed, if Spain should execute the threats she is now making . . . against Vera Cruz, American privateers will soon make their anchorage under the Moro." The McLane-Ocampo Treaty got wide publicity, with the North generally opposed to it and Southerners giving it half-hearted support. The Senate rejected it in May.[19]

Buchanan's Mexican policies were rejected because neither the North nor the South had any taste for new territory in that direction. As Frederick Merk has pointed out, Mexico had abolished slavery and its millions of Indians and Mestizoes were both citizens and voters, however they might be abused by their various governments. Many Northerners objected for moral and political reasons to the possibility of new slave territory, few Southerners saw any hope for implanting slavery there, and great numbers of people both North and South objected to the incorporation of new citizens with such dubious origins. Thus the "All Mexico" movement, which had been a significantly noisy part of the Manifest Destiny sentiment in the 1840s, was completely dead by 1858.[20]

For the Southerners and for the president, however, Cuba was a different matter. It was already a slave state in which slavery had long been under attack. Part of the Ostend Manifesto argument had been based on the alleged need to save slavery in Cuba; and for Southerners, therefore, the annexation of Cuba seemed a practical ambition and, like Texas, a symbolic test of Northern good will. Since Spain, like everyone else, was threatening to intervene in Mexico, both the excuse and the means for taking the Pearl of the Antilles seemed apparent. Most American claims against Spain stemmed from injuries against Americans in Cuba, and the island was also the center of the foreign slave trade. Even more important was the long-standing fear of slave revolt, race war, and the destruction of slavery.

On January 1, 1859, the president's close friend Senator Slidell of Louisiana introduced a bill to provide $30,000,000 for negotiations with Spain for Cuba. A long, angry debate followed, and the newspapers North and South reassumed the positions taken on the Ostend Manifesto in 1854. Southerners were almost unanimous for the bill. Republicans, however, denounced it as a scheme to fill the Democratic campaign chest, and Northerners of both parties translated Buchanan's passionate "We must have Cuba" into "We must have slavery." Kentucky Senator John J. Crittenden, who had lost a favorite nephew in the earlier Cuban filibuster attempts of Narcisco Lopez, charged that Buchanan's entire Latin American program was merely a sideshow to divert people's attention from the more important economic and sectional issues. The bill failed and took the homestead bill down with it. In his annual December messages of 1859 and 1860, Buchanan again pleaded for his favorite project, but a nation concerned with John Brown and Southern threats in 1859 and with the election of Lincoln and secession in 1860 did not listen.[21]

If the administration of James Buchanan had not been afflicted with the slavery quarrel and the overwhelming tragedy of secession, the allegedly timid president might well be remembered as the most aggressive would-be imperialist in American history. If he really meant everything he said and really wanted everything he requested from Congress, he was prepared to annex everything from the Rio Grande to Colombia at the risk of war if necessary. And even though threatening weaker Latin neighbors may not have required vast courage, Great Britain was another matter. If the British had chosen to stand their ground in Central America and defend their right to search suspected slave ships, Buchanan might have had to choose between war and a humiliating retreat.

Buchanan left no written evidence in letters or memoirs to suggest that his aggressive posturing toward Latin America and Spain was anything but sincere or that he had any initial assurance that the British would back down in the face of his bold threats. Contemporaries like Crittenden and others suspected that he was trying to restore national unity by acquiring a common enemy or enemies. William Henry Seward, after all, would suggest this tactic to Lincoln just before the battle of Fort Sumter. If this were true, however, Buchanan was strangely blind to the harshly divisive impact of both the War of 1812 and the Mexican War. Indeed, the emotions and issues created by the Mexican War had made the sectional quarrel dangerous for the first time and were still not fully resolved. Still, he had consistently misjudged the Northern reaction to matters like Dred Scott and Kansas, and he may well have hoped that a significant expansion of the national domain would generate a sense of Northern pride stronger than objections to the extension of slavery. The Mexican War conquests had not done this, but Buchanan after all was not a careful student of Northern public opinion. Regardless of motivation, Buchanan almost certainly expected to be taken seriously and was prepared to execute every policy he could get Congress to approve. Whether or not he welcomed the refusal of Congress to give him a free rein, the United States was fortunate that the constitutional powers of Congress in such matters did exist.

The foreign policies enunciated by James Buchanan also strengthen further the picture of a president looking at the world through Southern eyes. Hinton Rowan Helper, Frank Blair, and others had selected Central America as a possible haven for

American slaves being freed by a process of gradual emancipation. Clearly, the Southern members of Congress and cabinet officers who supported Buchanan's ambitions in this area did not share this vision any more than they welcomed the possibility of emancipation in Cuba. William Walker was proslave, and in dealing with him Buchanan stayed barely within the boundaries of propriety. The concept of Cuba as a rich, new slave state for the American South had been clearly stated in the Ostend Manifesto, and was obviously what Buchanan still had in mind. His assumption that Cuba was worth infinitely more than Alaska was probably shared by Northerners and Southerners alike, but his zeal for the one and indifference to the other is at least worth noting. Just what Buchanan expected the status of slavery in Northern Mexico to be is hard to determine. The "All of Mexico" adherents of earlier days however, had assumed it would be slave territory, and what little support Buchanan got for a new Mexican adventure came from the South. His threat against British naval efforts to stop suspected slavers flying the American flag commanded widespread support and was based upon sound international law, but the net result was added protection for the African slave trade.

A final speculation poses the question of what the United States might have done about Mexico and Central America if the slavery quarrel had not existed. Astute British leaders talked as through they both expected and approved an American annexation of much of the area. Would the North if untroubled by fears of slavery extension have been swept along by the concept of Manifest Destiny and united with the South in a dynamic march southward directed by the all-conquering James Buchanan? With British objections minimized, no other nation could have prevented it. Might the self-righteous Northern spirit momentarily represented by free-soilism, and the aggressive Southern spirit indicated by a willingness to die for the right to extend slavery to inhospitable western climes have blossomed together into a crusade for the salvation of Mexico and Central America through annexation to the United States? The racial, political, philosophical, and moral arguments against forcibly annexing citizens darker in hue and unversed in Anglo-Saxon democracy were all trumpeted in 1898, but they did not prevent the annexation of the Philippines. Did slavery, or merely the Northern objections to slavery, keep the United States from committing an immense folly, acquiring an unmanageable empire, or perhaps meeting an enormous challenge with ultimate success? Would the successful incorporation of several million new

Mestizo and Indian citizens have made the peaceful end of Negro slavery easier to achieve? Or, as the anti-imperialists of 1898 feared, would the inability to assimilate the new population on terms of equality have corrupted fatally the values of democracy so eloquently preached by the Declaration of Independence? Would the Civil War have been avoided or perhaps multiplied in its scope and intensity?

9

★★★★★

"WHOM THE GODS WOULD DESTROY"

Stephen A. Douglas won reelection to the Senate in 1858, but most Northern Democrats were less fortunate. Those who had been closest to the president were especially vulnerable, with J. Glancy Jones, administrative whip from Pennsylvania, heading the list of those defeated. Throughout the North the Republicans were swept into governorships, the Senate, and the House. Southern secessionists were pleased, Unionists were appalled, and the president was temporarily reduced to a state of near hysteria. He gave a post-election dinner party, where, he wrote Harriet, they "had a merry time of it, laughing among other things over our crushing defeat. It is so great that it is almost absurd."

The 1858 election produced two far-reaching speeches in addition to Lincoln's. In Illinois, Stephen A. Douglas gave the Southern radicals their new weapon against him by formalizing his Freeport Doctrine. In New York, William Henry Seward, with no significant excuse at all, produced the threat of an "Irrepressible Conflict." forever."[1]

Seward, one of a long line of brilliant New York politicians, had built a powerful Whig party in his state by a judicious combination of democratic, libertarian rhetoric with the traditional Whig economic policies. He and his alter ego, publisher Thurlow Weed, had more than held their own against the Jacksonian Democracy headed by Martin Van Buren and successors like William Marcy. Seward was prone to radical statements geared to short-term purposes, but was in fact essentially conservative when words were reduced to deeds. In 1850 he had spoken of a "higher law," the law of God which took precedence over a Constitution that protected slavery, but only two years earlier he had journeyed to Virginia to persuade Zachary Taylor to become the Whig presidential candidate. Taylor's ownership of more than a hundred slaves had not interfered with Seward's dedication to the equally high principle that politicians should win elections. His efforts to recruit Taylor, incidentally, also had the full support and cooperation of Representative Abraham Lincoln of Illinois. Seward, like Douglas, was a realist and something of a cynic, and also like Douglas he occasionally had difficulty realizing that most other people were not equally realistic. The conclusion is almost inescapable that Seward made statements entirely for political effect, did not take his own words seriously, and was genuinely dismayed to find that other politicians who should have known better took him entirely at his word and acted accordingly. In many cases, also, Southern politicians used his words for their own purposes even though they knew his true character and principles were no threat to the South.

During the campaign, Southern radicals were advocating the seizure of Central America, Cuba, and parts of Mexico, and predicting secession if a Republican should ever be elected president, while Northern Democrats were, in modern terms, trying to cool it. Like Douglas, they denied any wish to spread slavery westward, insisted that no such action was possible anyhow, minimized their differences with Republicans on the issue, and accused the Republicans of needlessly threatening the Union. Invited to speak for a congressional candidate in Rochester, the home of Frederick Douglass, Seward went all-out to show the deep and abiding differences between Republicans and Northern Democrats. He was trying to recruit abolitionists and Know-Nothings into the Republican party and make a dynamic appeal to the emotions of a local New York electorate. His preoccupation with immediate purposes apparently left him blind to the broader implication of his words. The party struggle, he proclaimed, was a collision between free and slave systems of labor. It was "an irrepressible conflict between opposing and enduring forces," and it meant that the United States must "sooner or later, become either entirely a slaveholding nation, or entirely a free-labor nation." A revolution, said Seward, had already begun: "Twenty Senators and a hundred Representatives proclaim boldly today in Congress sentiments and opinions and principles of Freedom which hardly so many men in even this Free State dared to utter in their own homes twenty years ago." The

Democrats, he charged, were the tools of slavery. Republicans, supported by the people, were ready "to confound and overthrow, by one decisive blow, the betrayers of the Constitution and Freedom

Many Northern newspapers protested Seward's speech and, suddenly aware of what he had said, Seward tried to change direction. Four days later at Rome, New York, he blamed Southern radicalism on incitement by Northern Democrats. The damage, however, had been done. The speech cost Seward his party's presidential nomination in 1860 and gave Southern radicals a new rallying cry. For Southern editors and politicians the "Irrepressible Conflict" was the simple, understandable phrase that summarized all the principles of the Republican party. In the words of James Hammond, who was no small phrasemaker himself, "The South is to be Africanized and the elections of 1860 are to decide the question . . . it is to be emancipation or disunion after 1860, unless Seward is repudiated." The oversimplification was in fact absurd, but few if any believed it more strongly than James Buchanan.[2]

To Southerners the overwhelming Republican landslide seemed a popular endorsement of Seward's ideas. The election probably was a firm rejection of James Buchanan's principles, whether economic, social, or political, but this was a far cry from approval of an irrepressible conflict over slavery. Analyzing election returns is still an important American sport; but while the techniques and tools have improved enormously during the past century, the reasons why people vote as they do remain difficult to prove. Certainly Northern city-dwellers just emerging from a painful economic depression had little sympathy for a president whose aid had been confined largely to old-fashioned sermons based on the values of an agricultural society. At such times voters usually identify their troubles with the president, and his party suffers accordingly. True, the Republicans had won support by opposing the Dred Scott decision and fighting to save Kansas from being forced to accept an unwanted proslave constitution. Again, however, the most confirmed Northern racist could hate abolitionists and oppose any tampering with Southern slavery, but with equal enthusiasm support the Republican position on Dred Scott and Kansas. For most Northerners the Southerners and the abolitionists were the radicals, while those struggling merely to keep slavery out of the West were part of a conservative American tradition at least as old as the Northwest Ordinance of 1787. In short, the Republican victories in the Northern elections of 1858 did not indicate any serious threat to slavery in the South. The man who had spoken of an "Irrepressible Conflict" was on the winning side, however, and Southern radicals could be as selective as they wished in describing the Republican party to their constituents.

In retrospect the basic need of the Democratic party was obvious. It could not win the presidency or control the Congress in 1860 without carrying some Northern states, and this would require the breaking of its image as a Southern-dominated party. It would not have to be an anti–Southern-dominated party, but it could not win as the proponent of extreme Southern ambitions. Its Northern leaders could go as far as popular sovereignty, Douglas style, with reasonable hopes for victory, but anything more for slavery could only mean further disaster.

Numerous important Southern leaders had long insisted that a Republican presidential victory in 1860 would leave them no alternative to secession, and the president knew them well enough to take such threats seriously. If saving the Union was really Buchanan's major ambition, he should have set his sights immediately on the task of achieving a united party and the strongest possible candidate for 1860.

In practical terms this meant a reconciliation between Stephen A. Douglas and his Southern critics. It might be impossible, but it was worth an effort. Douglas himself spoke of stepping aside if a suitable alternative could be found, and he publicly praised Vice-President Breckinridge of Kentucky as a possible alternative. As the party's only important winner in 1858 and its most popular Northern leader nationally, Douglas would have to be mollified if not nominated.

Cobb, Thompson, and Floyd in the cabinet and men like Jefferson Davis in the Congress, however, knew that Douglas considered them traitors, real or potential, and that if elected president he would use the power of the White House to weaken them in their own sections. They also knew the Little Giant as a fierce and dynamic competitor who would dedicate himself to the suppression of disunion with both his great persuasive talents and the use of force if necessary. For Southerners, ranging from men like Cobb, who was still essentially a moderate, to the most extreme radicals, the suppression of Douglas was more important than rebuilding the strength of the Democratic party.

The one man with the power to bring the warring Democrats back into reasonable harmony was the president, but unfortunately James Buchanan was still identified emotionally and psychologically with those who wished no reunion except on terms dictated by Southern extremism. Only the South had supported the Democratic party in the 1858 election, and the Southerners therefore deserved to be favored accordingly. The Douglas Democrats, on the other hand, had tried to minimize their differences with the hated Republicans and, with the exception of their leader, had suffered accordingly. To Buchanan the election of 1858 meant that the Northern people had opted for the antislavery side of Seward's irrepressible conflict, and he was determined to use the presidency to protect the South in any way he could. If the Freeport Doctrine of Stephen A. Douglas could not be accepted by his Southern friends, it would be equally intolerable to James Buchanan.

If Southern fears were fueled by a strong touch of paranoia, so were the attitudes of James Buchanan. The absurdity of his position on the Lecompton Constitution remained beyond his grasp, and his continuing sense of betrayal by Douglas was equaled only by his feelings of unfair rejection by the Northern voters. More and more, the Southerners appeared to be his only true friends, and his inability to question the logic of their fears deepened accordingly. Frustrated at every turn by an opposition Congress, he sought personal relief through immersion in administrative affairs. When cabinet members became ill or took time off, he assumed their duties. At the Department of State he busied himself with grandiose but impossible dreams of territorial expansion. With his family and cabinet he grew more and more irritable. He quarreled with Harriet over his ban against dancing and card-playing at the White House, and he became so nosey about her personal affairs that he frequently opened her letters "by mistake." She and a lady friend in Philadelphia guarded their correspondence from his curiosity by sending their letters in the locked brassbound kettle in which Buchanan received his butter from Philadelphia. The president also became more and more possessive with his cabinet and their wives, who continued to act like a happy family in his presence while ridiculing him in private. Kate Thompson reacted to his sanctimoniousness by dubbing him "Old Gurley," after the Senate chaplain. To friends and enemies alike "Old Buck" had become "Old Venison."

In June, 1859, he took a tour through Virginia and North Carolina, which revived his spirits and renewed his affections for the South. "He had a good time in N. Carolina," wrote Kate Thompson, "for Mr. T. says he kissed hundreds of pretty girls which *made his mouth water!*" He also became interested in a Southern widow named Bass, and in July he took her and her three children to

Bedford Springs, Pennsylvania, for a vacation. Some abolitionists promptly ran away with the lady's Negro servant girl, which upset Buchanan more than it did the owner, who remarked only that she hoped others would take good care of the girl.[3]

Obviously not all the president's close friends were Southerners, but even this fact was demonstrated to the public in an unfavorable fashion. Daniel Sickles, destined to lose a leg for the Union but still to outlive all the other generals, had been Buchanan's chief aide in London. In 1853 Sickles had married a seventeen-year-old Italian girl named Teresa Bagioli, but had left her at home in favor of a mistress when he served abroad with Buchanan. This neglect probably continued, and by 1859 Teresa was having an almost open affair with Philip Barton Key, a handsome son of the author of the National Anthem. One Sunday afternoon Sickles shot the unarmed Key to death in the street. It was a brutal, premeditated murder, whatever the provocation, but the president offered moral support by visiting Sickles in jail. With future cabinet-member Edwin M. Stanton as his attorney, Sickles was acquitted and carried from the courtroom on the shoulders of jubilant friends. The approval of violence was obviously not a Southern monopoly, but some thought Buchanan's involvement quite unseemly. Perhaps the religious president was merely trying to follow the divine suggestion that the blessed should visit those in prison, but his enemies probably noted that the accompanying biblical passages did not seem to include slaves or hungry Northern workers who had suffered during the depression.

As Congress prepared to meet for the first time in luxurious but still uncooled quarters provided by an expansion of the Capitol, the Southern radicals planned their strategy. Jefferson Davis, as well as other Southerners, had already agreed publicly with Douglas that the protection of the Dred Scott decision would be meaningless without local laws, but now they would go a step further. They would demand something that most of them knew could not be granted and would be worthless even if conceded. They would insist that Northern Democrats join them in a move to enact a federal slave-code for all territories. In the name of states rights and local power they had long argued that the federal government had no power to bar slavery from a territory. Now they would insist that the same federal government had both the power and the duty to impose slavery on territories even if the inhabitants already there objected to it. The two propositions were hardly consistent, but incongruity has only rarely disturbed the minds of American politicians. If the Southern radicals and their less extreme fellow-travelers could impose this platform on their fellow Southern leaders, there would be no reconciliation with the hated Douglas and no reunification of the Democratic party on common ground.

In retrospect the irrationality of the Southern rejection of Douglas is glaring. Over and over he had defended the Southerners' right to enjoy or endure slavery as long as they wanted it. He had proposed and supported the right of Southerners to take slavery to any territory unless this right should be denied by a refusal of the majority of the settlers acting through a territorial government. Like Buchanan he had long advocated expansion to the South and the annexation of Cuba, and he clearly did not object to adding Cuba as another slave state. And above all, with the Northern and Southern Democrats firmly united behind his candidacy or the candidacy of a compromise leader acceptable to him, the Democrats had an excellent chance to turn back the feared Republicans and win the presidency on the platform he had advocated. Writing in 1881, the former slave and abolitionist Frederick Douglass viewed his ancient enemies with considerable realism: "Happily for the cause of human freedom, and for the final unity of the American nation, the South was mad, and would listen to no concessions. . . . Had the South accepted our concessions and remained in the Union, the slavepower would in all probability have continued to rule; the North would have become utterly demoralized; the hands on the dialplate of American civilization would have been reversed, and the slave would have been dragging his hateful chains today wherever the American flag floats to the breeze."[4]

Certain that the president would support their every move, the Southerners began the session by deposing Douglas from his favorite post as chairman of the Committee on Territories. Douglas and his wife were still visiting in Cuba after a conciliatory tour of the South, and this parliamentary move succeeded only because he was absent. This meant in effect that Douglas would have to make the race for president to prevent the domination of the party by Southern extremism, and Northern Democrats everywhere recognized the fact. As the Republicans celebrated this further show of Democratic schism, the Little Giant journeyed leisurely back to Washington amid enthusiastic receptions throughout the Northeast. The social lines were again quickly drawn, with Harriet Lane and Adele Douglas competing as leading hostesses and with the leaders of each Democratic faction scrupulously avoiding the parties of the other.

Congress and the newspapers immediately began the usual bitter debates over Southern refusal to convict the commanders of captured slave ships, Northern violations of the fugitive slave laws, the distribution of Helper's *The Impending Crisis*, and the great economic questions of homesteads, tariffs, internal improvements, and the Pacific railroad. Underlying every issue, however, was the internal quarrel of the Democrats. Rumors abounded that various Southerners wanted only an excuse to kill Douglas. Slidell, an accomplished marksman, denounced Douglas violently in *The Union*. Douglas in turn hired a well-known Kentucky sharpshooter for a bodyguard. When Buchanan sent the Senate a list of Illinois appointees, Douglas denounced most of them, including the son of Senator Graham N. Fitch of Indiana. Fitch, a Douglas enemy anyhow, took the remarks as a family insult and challenged his colleague to a duel. Douglas made clear his willingness to fight, but after seven notes had passed, Fitch withdrew the challenge.[5]

On February 23, the debate began over the abstract (since no specific territories were involved) questions of popular sovereignty and a federal slave code for the territories. Davis, his fellow Mississippian Brown, and other Southerners announced that if the next Democratic convention should adopt popular sovereignty they would bolt. Douglas and his friends replied that they would do the same if a territorial slave-code plank should prevail. Each side insisted that the other's policy could not carry its section. At one point the angry insults and name-calling were interrupted by an announcement that the Kansas legislature had just passed a law declaring that slavery would cease immediately in Kansas.

With every major issue a stand-off, the session ended on March 4 with an all-night battle over the basic appropriations without which even the federal salaries could not have been paid. Postmaster General Aaron Brown conducted a desperate battle from his sickbed to get an appropriation to cover a large postal deficit, but the bill was lost. Brown died four days later.

Despite the administration's failures and the fruitless debates over slavery in the territories, the fire-eaters had not yet gained a Southern majority, and the Republicans were openly worried because their victory in Kansas had killed their major issue. The move to discredit Douglas in the South was getting weaker, and many Southerners saw no reason to fight over a slave code for distant territories where few if any slaveholders really wished to immigrate. The Leagues of United Southerners launched so hopefully by the radicals Yancey and Ruffin were on the brink of collapse. Unionist presses and leaders were still speaking loudly and being heard. Jefferson Davis expressed a conviction that the Union would survive, and received a hail of radical protests for such apostasy. Ruffin complained bitterly about the lack of radical spirit. James H. Hammond, of King Cotton and mudsills, was certain that the South could and should continue to rule from within the Union. A new burst of high prices for cotton, land, and slaves, coupled with good crops, meant rising prosperity and a corresponding contentment and lack of excitement. Southern Unionists showed surprising strength in the elections of October, 1859.[6]

On October 17, 1859, however, Southern radicalism received an unexpected windfall, when the long and checkered career of John Brown finally reached its climax.[7] For most of his adult life Brown had been a singleminded opponent of slavery, and his attitudes toward American society generally had been thoroughly embittered by a long string of career and business failures. He had been engaged, usually unsuccessfully, in at least twenty-one lawsuits, and on at least two occasions he had been guilty of outright dishonesty. Bleeding Kansas had suddenly provided him the opportunity to rebuild his shattered fortunes while striking a blow for righteousness against slavery. At the height of the Kansas troubles, he and some followers had slaughtered and mutilated five proslave men, none of whom actually owned any slaves. In 1857 he toured New England as a featured lecturer on the troubles in Kansas and raised considerable money and arms for the great work.

Up to this point the radical abolitionists had been occupied chiefly with efforts to raise money for arms and people to send to Kansas, and with a handful of spectacular fugitive slave cases. Ten Northern states had passed laws against the Fugitive Slave Act, and the Wisconsin Supreme Court had declared it to be unconstitutional. In fact, when the United States Supreme Court overruled that of Wisconsin, the Wisconsin Republicans launched a nullification movement based on language quite similar to that of John C. Calhoun and South Carolina in 1832.[8]

To a few who were ready to go further, John Brown suddenly presented a new opportunity. The tall, bearded, wild-eyed hero of Kansas would commit with grim satisfaction the violence that men of less courage, or perhaps more sense, might advocate in theory but shrink from in practice.

As early as 1847 Brown had told Frederick Douglass that he

could create a military base in Virginia and wreck slavery. During his New England tour of 1857 he met Hugh Forbes, an idealist who had served with Garibaldi, and Forbes agreed to train Brown's recruits for $100 a month. In May, 1858, he met with refugee slaves and others in Chatham, Canada, and outlined a program for establishing a new state in Virginia for escaped slaves. His proposed constitution for this new entity justified the killing of slaveholders, the liberation of slaves, the confiscation of property, and the ravaging of enemy lands. The Secret Six, a group of abolitionists from New England and New York, approved the plan and financed it heavily. Forbes, meanwhile, decided Brown was insane, and warned senators Henry Wilson, Charles Sumner, Seward, and others that Brown should be disarmed. At this point, five of the Secret Six had second thoughts and ordered the invasion postponed. Only the Reverend Thomas Wentworth Higginson, later to be an able commander of Negro troops in the Civil War, angrily supported Brown. Boston manufacturer George L. Stearns, chairman of the Massachussets State Kansas Committee, and one of the Secret Six, warned Brown not to use the arms collected for Kansas for any other purpose, but finally gave him two hundred rifles on condition that Brown at least go to Kansas for a few months.

Back in Kansas, Brown helped a Jayhawker band attack Fort Scott, rescue a free-state prisoner, kill a storekeeper, and steal some $7,000 worth of goods. In December, 1858, he led a raid into Missouri. His men killed a slaveholder, looted the house, stole the livestock, and withdrew with eleven slaves. In spectacular fashion Brown personally led the slaves through Kansas, Iowa, Illinois, and Michigan to freedom in Canada. President Buchanan put a $250 price on his head, but Southerners duly noted that no one made any serious effort to stop him.

In early July, 1859, Brown and twenty-one men, including his six sons and a son-in-law, rented a Maryland farm near Harpers Ferry, Virginia, and on October 16 the expedition marched. Their goal had been clearly stated in speeches, conversations, and letters. They would capture the national armory and arsenal at Harpers Ferry, issue a clarion call for the slaves in the surrounding area to join them, and arm the slaves with guns from the arsenal as well as with some 950 iron-pointed spears brought along for the purpose. From this powerful military base, his ever-increasing slave army would spread rebellion, freedom, death, and destruction.

If several thousand slaves had met Brown's expectations, it might have been difficult to dislodge him because Harpers Ferry sits in a pass through mountains and steep hills. Brown, however, did not comprehend the degree of acceptance of slavery by some slaves, the atmosphere of invincible control imposed by the institution on most, and the deadening influence of the system on almost everyone. With virtually no direct communication with the slave population, Brown expected thousands who had been denied the experience of decision-making to decide suddenly without warning or previous reflection to risk life and limb and join him with a taste for bloodshed equal to his own. It was too much to hope.

The mission failed almost before it began. The invaders cut the telegraph wires; seized the federal property; killed a free Negro, in whose honor the Daughters of the Confederacy later erected a plaque; and collected a handful of hostages, including two masters and ten rather confused slaves. Farmers, villagers, and militia companies quickly mobilized against the dreaded slave insurrection and put the liberators under siege in a small building. Buchanan promptly sent federal troops under Colonel Robert E. Lee and Lieutenant J. E. B. Stuart, who stormed the door and ended the fighting. Ten of Brown's men, including two sons and Dangerfield Newby, a freedman hoping to rescue his wife and children, were dead. Seven were captured and hanged later. Five escaped. On the other side, one free black, two slaves, a marine, and three white citizens, including the town's mayor, were dead, and ten were wounded.

The first reaction from both North and South was incredulous anger. Republican leaders quickly denied any connection with Brown, and five of the Secret Six ran for cover. Two fled to Canada, two to England, and one to the temporary safety of an insane asylum with a physical and nervous collapse. Only Higginson remained on call and helped provide Brown with a legal defense. Higginson, however, believed, correctly, that Brown's acquittal would not "do half as much good as his being executed."[9] Brown's attorney and friends pleaded his insanity, but the defendant rested his own case on the righteousness of his goals and a denial that he had ever intended to foment violence. Letters poured in from his former places of residence testifying that insanity had been rife in his mother's family and that he was demented on the subject of slavery.

Those inspired, both past and present, by Brown's martyrdom have questioned the insanity reports because they were for the purpose of saving his life; but regardless of their validity or the actual state of Brown's own mental balance, Governor Henry Wise of

Virginia could justifiably have given them every possible weight. Denying Brown martyrdom by locking him in an insane asylum would have greatly dulled his impact in both North and South, and Wise, however erratic he had always been, was not yet considered a secessionist. Seeing an opportunity to enhance his own status as a defender of the South, however, Wise in every possible way exaggerated the scope of Brown's exploit and insisted upon an immediate six-day trial, which was noteworthy for its sensational aspects. Brown was sentenced to hang for conspiring with slaves to rebel, for murder, and for treason against the state of Virginia. The latter charge was a legal impossibility, but he was assuredly guilty of the first two. The possibility of a commutation on grounds of insanity remained, and Wise did order the superintendent of the state insane asylum to examine Brown. Before this could be done, however, the governor changed his mind and sent the prisoner to the martyrdom he seemed to crave.

On December 2, before an audience that included the future Stonewall Jackson with a corps of Virginia Military Institute cadets and two visitors named John Wilkes Booth and Edmund Ruffin, Brown met his fate with heroic composure. His conduct at the trial and during the brief interval that followed was that of an eloquent saint who had willingly sacrificed his fortunes, his family, and his life for suffering humanity as exemplified by the Southern slaves. At least one contemporary predicted accurately that getting Brown down from the gallows would be much more difficult than it had been to put him there. Small wonder that even Northerners who had been shocked by the initial reports were profoundly moved by his martyrdom and death, and that he has been a hero for vast numbers of Americans ever since. The traditional notion that men do not lie when facing death gave a false validity to his claims that he had meant no violence, had not meant to start a race war, and had in fact intended only an expanded version of his earlier schemes for helping slaves escape northward. This dulled greatly the initial horrified reaction in much of the North. Brown spoke brilliantly and eloquently, but he did in fact lie. An incontrovertible mass of spoken and written testimony by himself and others before the exploit and the choice of an arsenal town for a base prove his intentions beyond a doubt, and he did not take along 950 heavy iron-pointed spears just for the exercise involved in carrying them.

Brown clearly did not expect or wish to fail, and those who financed him probably hoped that their cause would benefit regardless of the result, as it did. By all available evidence, however, the fact that he succeeded only by failing so miserably was an unplanned accident unforeseen by anyone. If several hundred or thousand slaves had enlisted and he could have launched the movement as planned, it probably would have set the cause of emancipation back at least a century. The already strongly race-conscious North would have rallied to the support of their white Southern brethren, a federal army would have crushed the insurgents, and abolitionists and slaves alike would have undergone a new wave of harsh repression. Mass Northern good-will would have been demonstrated so strongly that no secessionist could have made the Southern people doubt it. Nonslaveholding Southern whites would have had a clear opportunity to see that most of the Northern objections to the expansion of slavery were based upon racial prejudice, and the Brown raid would probably have helped them understand and sympathize with these objections.

The historian, however, cannot dally over what might have happened. Brown's failure, his denials of violent intent, his injudicious trial, and his noble composure and lucid rhetoric in the face of death kept his bloodthirsty effort from developing any meaningful sympathy for the South among Northerners. The South, on the other hand, reacted as violently as if the pitiful little exploit had been a frightful success. Edmund Ruffin gathered up the spears for demonstrations during countless new radical speeches. Here was the proof, trumpeted Southern politicians, editors, and preachers, that the Southern radicals had always been right and that Northerners really did mean to invade the South with guns and spears, arm the slaves, and start a second San Domingo to elevate the blacks and enslave the whites. Democratic presses both North and South blamed it all on Seward and the Republicans, even though Seward, Lincoln, Greeley, and most other leading Republicans were appalled by the raid and said so vehemently and publicly. Rumors circulated that Seward knew of the plot in advance, and the New Yorker must have wished he had taken the warnings of Forbes more seriously. A new wave of oppression against slaves, free blacks, and Northern visitors and immigrants like book agents, peddlers, and schoolteachers swept the South, and reports of people being arrested, tarred and feathered, and whipped filled the press. By early 1860 Southern postmasters were stopping Republican newspapers, and *Harper's Weekly,* usually friendly to the South, was banned because its editor was privately against slavery. Books, papers, and magazines considered unfriendly were suppressed and burned.

On the subject of John Brown, Southern moderates remained silent, as their editors and politicians ignored the Northern opposition to Brown and focused on the handful of noted opinion-makers who quickly took up Brown's cause. Before a large crowd in Boston, Ralph Waldo Emerson called Brown "The Saint, whose fate yet hangs in suspense, but whose martyrdom, if it shall be perfected, will make the gallows as glorious as the Cross." "Some eighteen hundred years ago," added Henry Thoreau, "Christ was crucified; this morning, perchance, Captain Brown was hung. These are the two ends of a chain which is not without its links. He is not Old Brown any longer; he is an angel of light." "Saint John the Just," said Louisa May Alcott. Almost alone among the abolitionists, John Greenleaf Whittier had at least momentary doubts. "I have just been looking at one of the *pickes* sent here by a friend in Baltimore," said Whittier. "It is not a Christian weapon; it looks too much like murder." Whittier later atoned for this hesitation with a poetic eulogy, which reads like an effort to convince himself.[10]

Theodore Parker, the great Unitarian clergyman, solved Whittier's problem, at least for himself: "A man held against his will as a slave has a natural right to kill every one who seeks to prevent his enjoyment of liberty. The freeman has a natural right to help the slaves recover their liberty, and in that enterprise to do for them all which they have a right to do for themselves."[11]

A great many Northern whites might have considered Parker's theology valid if faced with their own enslavement, but no significant number shared it in relation to Southern blacks. Southern whites, however, had but few ways of knowing this. Whatever small influence Helper's *Impending Crisis* might have had on poorer non-slaveholding whites was wiped out immediately. In case of emancipation, warned Albert Gallatin Brown, the rich would leave the country, but the poor would be left to face the marauding, plundering, and stealing former slaves. The blacks would demand perfect social equality, which the nonslaveholder would reject. "Then will commence a war of races such as has marked the history of San Domingo."[12] White nonslaveholders everywhere were filled with dread and turned more and more for leadership to those who promised protection from the Northern abolitionists.

In his memoirs later, James Buchanan treated John Brown in terms almost identical to the Southern reaction of 1859, and his annual message of December, 1859, made no contribution to peace.

The raid was important, he said, only because it excited fears throughout the South, which he did not share. He prefaced this realistic analysis, however, with the needless and untrue warning that Harpers Ferry symbolized "an incurable disease in the public mind, which may . . . terminate . . . in an open war by the North to abolish slavery in the South." The South needed reassurance and the opportunity was clear. The Dred Scott case, he insisted, had established the right of every citizen to take slave property into the territories and have it protected there by the federal Constitution, and this right should be enforced.[13] He did not add that such protection would require the passage of federal laws that no Northern Democrat could possibly vote for.

The congressional session lasting into March, 1860, was totally fruitless. The House spent two months electing a Speaker. Charges and countercharges with regard to John Brown and Republican support for Helper's *Impending Crisis* flew back and forth like poisoned arrows. Reuben Davis of Mississippi suggested that Seward should be hanged. Most members carried guns on the floor, and a loss of control by one angry person might have started a bloody melee. Henry Wise had responded to John Brown by putting Virginia on a military footing, and rumors abounded that he was planning to seize Washington by force. Governor Gist of South Carolina offered armed support if needed: "Write me or telegraph me," he assured the South Carolina delegation, "and I will have a regiment in or near Washington in the shortest possible time."[14] A compromise Speaker was finally chosen, but he then gave all the important subordinate posts to radical Republicans, and the tensions remained. A violent exchange between Owen Lovejoy and Roger Pryor of Virginia had members with their fingers on the triggers until quiet was restored. Pryor challenged Potter of Wisconsin to a duel, and Potter selected bowie knives elbow to elbow as the weapons. Too barbarous, said Pryor, and no fight occurred. Attorney General Jeremiah Black refused to answer a duel challenge from Robert J. Walker, still angry over his treatment in Kansas.

In the Senate, James Mason of Virginia demanded a committee investigation to determine who was responsible for Brown's raid and the extent of the subversion intended. The committee was finally voted after two weeks of angry debate covering the Fugitive Slave Law, the right to extend slavery, the recent struggles in Kansas, and the righteousness or evil of slavery itself. Jefferson Davis called the raid an act of civil war, charged Seward with prior knowledge, and called the New Yorker a traitor fit for the gallows. Henry Wilson replied that Brown had won the sympathy of many and that he had become a symbol of freedom rather than madness.

With Mason as chairman the committee finally exonerated the Republican party, but its hearings created many suspicions and frustrations, which added to the Southern conviction that a frightening conspiracy had existed.[15] The correspondence discovered in Brown's farmhouse headquarters clearly implicated Samuel Gridley Howe, George L. Stearns, Gerrit Smith, Thomas Wentworth Higginson, Theodore Parker, and Franklin Sanborn, a young Massachusetts schoolteacher. Proving that these higher-ups who had financed the affair were aware of Brown's specific plans, however, was very difficult. Dozens of letters both signed and anonymous offered the names of people who allegedly could reveal the facts about secret conspirators in high places, secret money solicited for attacks on innocent people, and secret meetings where dark deeds were plotted. The confused committee hardly knew where to begin, but the Democratic members usually chose to believe the worst and did their best to confirm it.

The suspects themselves were uncooperative. Howe had fled to Canada immediately after Brown's capture, but was persuaded by friends to return and face the committee. While agreeing to testify, Howe charged that the investigation was an inquisition, that its purpose exceeded the proper scope of any legislative inquiry authorized by the Constitution, that it threatened the personal liberties of witnesses, and that any such investigations should be handled by the courts. Despite sharp cross-examination by Jefferson Davis and Mason, who in fact forced him to lie, Howe insisted that he and his friends had only tried to protect free-state settlers in Kansas and that Brown had betrayed their trust by going to Virginia. Actually, on March 4, Brown had informed the Secret Six that he planned to invade the South. He had supplied no specific date or place, but they had agreed to far more than his continued activities in Kansas. George L. Stearns, whose long black beard protected his chest from chronic bronchitis, echoed Howe. He had supported Brown with only a general knowledge of the old man's beliefs, and had been shocked by the violence in Virginia.

Others refused to testify at all. On February 15 the Senate got a warrant and deputized a Boston constable to arrest Sanborn and bring him to Washington. As the constable and three aides were leading Sanborn to a carriage, his sister ran screaming down the street, and a neighborhood mob quickly gathered. The angry crowd mutilated the carriage with hoes and chased the frightened arresting

party away without the prisoner. Next day the chief justice of the
Massachusetts Supreme Court ruled that Sanborn's arrest had been
illegal. To Mason and Davis, as well as Southerners everywhere,
this was another lawless insult to both the United States Senate and
the South.

James Redpath and John Brown, Jr., also eluded the committee.
Redpath, the abolitionist reporter who had once portrayed Brown's
murders in Kansas as a Southern outrage, announced that urgent
business required his prolonged absence from home. In fact, the
absence was necessary because United States marshals were chasing
him around the country. He wrote a formal refusal to testify on the
grounds that the investigation was unconstitutional, that his knowledge of Brown was his own private property, and that "Negro-
catchers" had no right to interrogate him. John Brown, Jr., who had
been the money-raising and supply-purchasing agent for the raid,
refused to subject himself to the "author of the fugitive slave law."
Brown took refuge in a newspaper office in Ashtabula, Ohio, where
so many neighbors took turns guarding him that the United States
marshal had to report that an arrest would require additional help.
The help was unavailable, and Brown never testified.

The arrest of another reluctant witness, Thaddeus Hyatt, a
prosperous New York inventor and manufacturer, generated another
long constitutional debate. John Hale of New Hampshire, an abolitionist whose daughter would later be secretly betrothed to John
Wilkes Booth, insisted that the assumed power of the Senate to
compel witnesses to testify was a dangerous violation of the Constitution. Ascertaining anyone's responsibility for violating the law
was "strictly a judicial power," said Hale. "What has it to do with
the necessity of passing laws, whether this or that individual has
been guilty of a certain specified crime?" When Hyatt was jailed,
Hale charged further that the committee was violating the Fourth
Amendment, which protected the "right of the people to be secure
in their persons, houses, papers, and effects, against unreasonable
searches and seizures." Hyatt, after all, had not been indicted or
even charged with a crime. Most of the Senate, however, Republicans and Democrats alike, agreed that the Senate did have the
power to investigate according to its charge and that witnesses must
testify or face punishment for contempt.

Hyatt spent thirteen happy weeks in jail but never testified. He
decorated his prison quarters lavishly, wrote public letters about his
travail, and enjoyed visits from many of the North's social and po-

litical elite. He even had new blank checks printed with his new address, "Washington Jail," at the top.

William H. Seward was the final witness, and the committee listened to his vows of innocence without argument. The majority report of the three Democrats accepted the contention that Brown's financial backers had not known of the Harpers Ferry plan, but denounced the contributing of money to a nefarious cause bound to produce violence and atrocities. The two Republican members denied that abolitionist opinions and fund-raising activities threatened the nation's tranquillity, and complained of the atmosphere of suspicion and the intensive personal examination of the witnesses. The Republicans were of course entirely mistaken. The broadcasting of abolitionist opinions was in fact a major threat to sectional peace because of their impact upon Southern pride and feelings, and the apparent absence of any real practical threat to slavery itself was entirely irrelevant. Most of the Republican senators took the Senate floor to repudiate Brown, but the Southerners would not be mollified. Brown's mad effort, they charged, was the logical result of Republican teachings, and a few words of censure could not compensate for the honor and homage being paid Brown throughout the North.

Between sectional quarrels the House found time to enact the usual homestead and internal improvements programs, and as usual each was stopped either in the Senate or by the president. Even more important, the Southern radicals, encouraged by the president and his cabinet, again insisted upon another full-scale debate over a federal slave code for the territories. Seward, however, suddenly aware that his forthcoming presidential chances had not been enhanced by his growing reputation for radicalism, began making conciliatory speeches denouncing John Brown and insisting that the sectional differences were entirely economic. He denied that the Republican party was sectional and invited the Southerners to join it, but there were no takers.

Clearly, everyone was looking ahead to the presidential election, and in the House the Republicans dealt the administration the first blow. Chaired by "Honest John" Covode, a big Pennsylvania German who had threatened to break heads with a spittoon during the Keitt-Grow brawl in 1858, a committee began investigating pressures used by Buchanan in behalf of the Lecompton Constitution and the English Amendment. The committee took eight hundred pages of testimony and issued a thirty-page majority report, all of which made the administration look both weak and corrupt. Government printing contracts had been used to fund political activities as well as enrich certain editors like Cornelius Wendell, financial manager of the Washington *Union*. Secretary of War Floyd had stupidly bought property for the government for high prices and sold it at serious losses. Without help from Covode, Postmaster General Joseph Holt found that the postmaster of New York had stolen $160,000 before fleeing to Europe. And finally, much testimony, whether true or not, indicated that financial and patronage threats and rewards had been involved in the lobbying for the Lecompton Constitution. Buchanan, who considered himself a paragon of virtue in all financial matters, was hurt and defiant. He challenged the committee to recommend his impeachment, and when no such action followed announced that he had "passed triumphantly through this ordeal. My vindication is complete."[16] In the public mind, however, the vindication of James Buchanan and his party was something less than complete. Time was running short, but the president would at least get one more opportunity to work for a united party, an acceptable presidential candidate, and a national victory, which alone could stave off a Republicn triumph and Southern secession.

10

★★★★★

TO RULE OR RUIN

The American founding fathers had never intended that the president of the United States should be chosen by the mass electorate, and they would have been appalled by the system of selection that had evolved by 1860. They had not even envisioned political parties, but long before 1860 no candidate had a chance without the backing of such an organization. The parties did have one great virtue. They usually spread across the lines of sectionalism and self-interest to maintain a semblance of unity and nationalism among otherwise disparate and competing groups and individuals. They could also, however, polarize the same conflicts they were designed to mute, and the great tests usually came when they were required to select presidential candidates. The task was difficult at best, and the convention process that had developed through the years carried an extra handicap. Any incumbent president, however disqualified for reelection he might be by age, incompetence, or unpopularity, was nonetheless empowered by his control of jobs and favors to play a major role in choosing his party's candidate for the succession.

In 1848 the weary and ailing James K. Polk had had no taste for further involvement, and in 1856 the incompetent and discredited Franklin Pierce had tried unsuccessfully to win a renomination for himself. In 1860 James Buchanan was neither unwilling nor incompetent, although he had from the beginning abandoned any desire for reelection. The forthcoming election would be his last opportunity to realize the goal of his inaugural—the promotion of sectional peace. He knew that determined Southerners were pledged to secession if the Republicans should win the presidency. He should have also known that only party unity behind Douglas or a candidate acceptable to Douglas could prevent the dreaded Republican victory. Clearly, no Democratic candidate pledged to congressional protection for slavery in the territories could win any Northern state. More than enough Northerners had said so in Congress, in their newspapers, and in personal communications, and Buchanan had only to look at the statewide elections of 1858 and 1859 if he needed further proof.

How much of Buchanan's conduct in 1860 stemmed from his personal hatred of Douglas is impossible to measure. The mutual detestation of the two men is understandable, but neither should have allowed it to control his actions. If any personal reconciliation was possible, the first overture should have come from Douglas. Recognizing as he did the momentous issues involved, the Little Giant might well have made one final plea for a truce in favor of a combined effort to save the Union. It would have required an enormous sacrifice of pride, and the president might well have responded with an insulting refusal. The effort, however, would have enhanced the Illinois senator's future reputation as a statesman and peacemaker.

Historians have made much of the control over Buchanan wielded by the so-called cabinet Directory, headed by Cobb and Thompson. Cobb's famous remark on one occasion that the president was "opposing the administration" is often cited as the supreme illustration. It must be reiterated, however, that if the president followed their views most of the time, he did so from conviction rather than weakness. He really did believe that Kansas should have been accepted as a slave state. He was entirely willing to give the South a slave code for the remaining territories. He did consider Douglas a traitor to the party and a force for disunion because the senator was unwilling to placate the South at the cost of losing the Northern electorate. Sharing many of the South's attitudes toward both slavery and Negroes, he insisted upon believing that Northern objections to legal rights for slavery in the territories were limited to a minority of misguided fanatics and that such madness was bound to pass. The decision to throw the power of the White House squarely against Douglas or a Douglas candidate pledged to popular sovereignty and to work for a Southern extremist platform and a pro-Southern candidate was made by Buchanan himself. His eyes were wide open, even though he was wearing blinkers imposed by his unshakable predilections.

The administration's effort was managed by essentially the same men who had accomplished Buchanan's own nomination in 1856. John Slidell of Louisiana, tall, heavy, and floridly handsome with a red face and snow white hair, was a master of every political art, trick, and pressure. Jesse Bright and Graham Fitch of Indiana were men of equal principle and only slightly less ability. Two years later Bright would be expelled from the Senate as a traitor because of his Confederate sympathies. Fitch had been illegally elected in the first place through a blatant fraud in the Indiana state legislature. Elsewhere, men like ex-Senator Daniel Dickinson in New York, Senator and former Governor William Bigler of Pennsylvania, and Senator James Bayard of Delaware were ready to help carry the load. Bayard would later become a conservative Unionist and even join the Republicans until after the death of Lincoln, but in 1860 he was an agent of James Buchanan's. In Massachusetts the administration would count on the tall and suave Caleb Cushing and the future General Benjamin F. Butler, fat, flamboyant, and always looking out for himself. Ultimately, Howell Cobb himself would act for the president at the final convention.

Presidential primaries of the modern type would have revealed the great support for Douglas among Northern Democrats, and might have surprised observers also with his strength among ordinary Southerners. Presidential delegates, however, were and in many cases still are selected in caucuses and local conventions usually dominated by those who make or aspire to make their livelihood through politics. Federal judges and attorneys, postmasters, mail carriers, land agents, Indian agents, clerks, federal marshals, favored editors, members of Congress, and a horde of aspirants for such positions were all subject to favors and promises emanating from the White House. A new census scheduled for 1860 would mean the appointment of hundreds of new marshals. Publishers and editors greedy and hungry for government advertising and printing contracts were often extremely influential in the days before national wire services and television and radio networks. Later federal laws would theoretically exempt all federal employees from such temptations and pressures, but it would not eliminate the obligations and activities of unappointed and unelected aspirants or of the spouses, relatives, and friends of anxious incumbents. The impact of such considerations on election day has been grossly exaggerated, but their significance in the selection of candidates remains formidable.

In New York, Pennsylvania, and Massachusetts, the Democrats were already badly split over various local issues and candidates. Each faction was looking out for its own advantage. All could see the advantages of a party united behind Douglas, but many were also ready to make deals with the administration or with the South for greater strength within the party. The Republicans and Know-Nothings had already captured most of New England, and throughout that region most Democrats available for delegate status were already beholden to the administration for whatever jobs or influence they held. While Douglas had some strong leaders in the Northeast and even in the South, only in parts of the Northwest could he be certain of complete loyalty.

Most election-day voters do not participate in the pulling and hauling that provides the candidates from whom they must choose their leaders, but they are often quite aware of it. When the president, however unpopular he may be, and his supporters make continuing attacks on a potential candidate, dim feelings of doubt about the candidate are bound to penetrate the subconsciousness of the electorate. The all-out attacks on Douglas by the administration through the federal office holders and their friends and relatives, using editorials, news items, rumors, and gossip, did not prevent Douglas from winning a majority of the delegates, but they probably damaged him severely in the minds of those who would make the final decision in November, 1860. Simultaneously, Douglas, as a Democrat, could not escape being identified publicly with the very people attacking him from within the party. He himself gave aid and comfort to the Covode investigation, which was certain to damage any Democrat nominated.

The fear of losing power already held is probably a stronger force than ambition for power not yet gained. The Buchanan men both North and South feared that a Douglas victory would mean an end of their control of the party and the elevation of their worst enemies. Douglas might have tried to allay such fears, particularly in the areas where his enemies clearly outnumbered his friends, but the Little Giant was cast in the image of Andrew Jackson at a time when the wiles of a Martin Van Buren were needed. For Douglas, enemies were to be met head-on and crushed—not softened or placated. The election of a Republican would be even more catastrophic for the professional Democrats, but the so-called Buchaneers apparently refused to face up to this possibility. They were going to Charleston to choose the next president, and it was not to be Stephen A. Douglas. Perhaps because of the same psychological principles that cause the faithful to hate heretics more than infidels, the Buchanan Democrats were prepared to see a Republican elected rather than submit to a victory by Douglas.

The presidential convention system has usually served America at least tolerably well, but at Charleston, South Carolina, in 1860, all of its potential frailties were united in one hideous example. Indeed, the very selection by the Democrats of Charleston as a reward to the South for good behavior in 1856 ranks with the same party's designation of Chicago in 1968 as the two most inane such decisions in American political history. A possible Southern secession from the party was universally recognized as the greatest single threat, but the convention was nonetheless held in the one city most likely to produce this result.

As the weary inland delegates stepped off the crowded, uncomfortable trains, and those from the seaboard disembarked from ships, Judge Andrew Magrath of the Federal District Court set the tone of Southern power with a highly publicized decision. Captain Corrie of the *Wanderer* had been caught red-handed in a cruel and flagrant violation of the federal laws against the foreign slave trade, and Attorney General Black had ordered South Carolina to surrender him to Georgia for trial. Judge Magrath, however, calmly defied the order with a long treatise against the law itself.

Charleston in late April was beautiful and pleasant for Southerners and those administration Northerners accepted in Southern society. Warm air, delightful trees and flowers, striking architecture and a picturesque harbor, bustling commercial activity, and many lovely Southern belles in town for the social season all appeared to strengthen the Southern claims of a superior society. Northerners uncommitted to a Southern position, however, saw a different side. Most delegations brought their own enormous supplies of whiskey. New York brought along its own collection of "friendly females" to combat loneliness in an alien land, and the brass bands, dancers, magicians, and other entertaining performers, as well as the faro tables, did give the city a certain excitement at first. However, the stifling, overcrowded quarters and unrefrigerated food were badly overpriced, the gamblers won the money, and the pickpockets had a field day. Hangovers and discomfort did not make the insulting questions, arguments, and epithets in the streets easier to take, and the irritating arrogance of the Southern delegates supported by cheering galleries strained the tolerance of the Northerners very quickly. Convention speeches were often interrupted by heckling, and most sessions operated near the border of chaos. Delegations caucused and recaucused, always under enormous pressure from the radicals and the galleries if they were Southern and from the Buchanan administration if they were Northern.[1]

On April 23 some 2,500 delegates and visitors crowded into the hall. The Douglas men counted 507 federal office holders there only for the purpose of defeating Douglas, and their estimate may have been accurate. Almost every motion produced a controversy, but the major events can be quickly traced. Because California and Oregon lined up with the slave states, the important committees, with a member from each state, each had a Southern majority of one. The Douglas men, however, had a majority of the total convention on most issues despite the administration's promises and threats. Administration efforts to replace the regular delegations from New York and Illinois with men of its own choosing and to impose a unit voting rule on all delegates failed. The administration and the ultra-Southerners won an important victory, however, when the Committee on Permanent Organization made Caleb Cushing permanent chairman. Cushing was an able parliamentarian thoroughly imbued with Southern sympathies and always ready to serve the Buchanan administration.

The Douglas men made their greatest error by accepting an administration motion that the platform should be completed before the candidate was nominated. The administration and Southerners were determined to write a platform upon which Douglas could not run. The Douglas men, however, knew that they had the convention votes to write the platform, regardless of the decisions in committee. If the nominations had come first, Douglas or a compromise candidate might have won without an immediate bolt by the Southerners, who would probably have remained for the writing of the platform. A sizable number of Southerners compelled to follow their delegations in rebellion later would in fact have voted for Douglas earlier. Also, a Southern bolt over the choice of a candidate or after submission to this choice would probably have damaged Douglas far less than the events that actually transpired. And finally, as long as the platform battle remained unfought there always remained the possibility of a compromise candidate acceptable both to Douglas and the Southern moderates present. The plan of the Southern ultras to wreck the convention before the nomination of a candidate depended upon a decision that the Douglasites might have prevented.

As Roy F. Nichols has pointed out, however, the Douglas men feared a Southern bolt less than they should have because they thought it might strengthen his ultimate Northern vote in the general election. Political prognostication in an emotion-filled atmosphere by weary and uncomfortable people is a dangerous business. Yancey, Rhett, and the Southern fire-eaters wanted a party rift that would elect a Republican and produce a Southern secession. The Buchanan administration and probably most of the Southern delegates, however, thought a divided party and an extra candidate would at worst throw the election into the House of Representatives. With the eternal optimism that is the politician's trademark, they dreamed further that the badly divided House would fail to pick a majority candidate for president, and the Southern-dominated Senate could then elect a pro-Southern vice-president who would become president.

After two-and-a-half long days and nights the Committee on Resolutions by the predictable seventeen to sixteen vote recommended a platform. Fifteen of the sixteen filed a minority report, and Benjamin F. Butler announced his own solo effort. "It is the duty of the Federal Government," announced the majority, "to protect, when necessary, the rights of person and property on the high seas, in the Territories or wherever else its Constitutional authority extends."[2]

The minority countered with a reaffirmation of popular sovereignty and the view that "all questions in regard to the rights of property in States or Territories arising under the Constitution of the United States, are judicial in their character; and that the Democratic party is pledged to abide by and faithfully carry out such determination of these questions as has been made or may be made by the Supreme Court of the United States."[3] Butler called for the 1856 platform on popular sovereignty with no reference to the courts. The Douglas men had gone as far as they could go in reaffirming the Dred Scott decision, and even lost a few Northwestern delegates by so doing.

Chairman W. W. Avery of the North Carolina delegation led off the debate for the majority report with soaring arguments. Mexico, Cuba, and Central America, he announced, were certain to join the United States, and popular sovereignty would exclude slaveholders from these regions. Northern Democrats must stand by their slaveholding comrades and be committed to slavery in these areas.

107

Henry B. Payne of Ohio answered with a call for reason. Quoting Hunter, Toombs, Calhoun, Mason, and other eminent Southerners past and present in favor of nonintervention, Payne begged the Southerners to accept what Calhoun and the others had always advocated. The Northern Democrats would abide by the Dred Scott decision, Payne pledged, but could not abandon the principle of nonintervention "without personal dishonor." If the majority report should be adopted, the South could not "expect one Northern electoral vote, or one sympathizing member of Congress from the free States."[4]

Butler followed with an irrelevant attack on Payne, and the convention recessed, but a driving rain kept most of the delegates in the hall. At 4 P.M., in a damp, chilly atmosphere, with many of the delegates and observers having missed lunch, the debates resumed and continued into the night. Representative Barksdale of Mississippi, who had lost his wig in the House free-for-all in 1858 and would later die at Gettysburg, delivered a bitter diatribe. Ex-Governor King of Missouri answered him with another plea for moderation, and then the South's high moment arrived. The great Alabama orator William Lowndes Yancey took the floor.

Yancey, who had been preaching disunion since 1848, insisted that the Southerners were the true Unionists and the Northerners were to blame for the sectional controversy. Reciting his catalogue of Southern wrongs and Northern transgressions, Yancey finally came to the key point. Not one Northern state that opposed the slave code was safely Democratic, he charged, because the Northern Democrats had accepted the Republican abolitionist heresy that slavery was wrong. The Northern Democrats had defended slavery on the basis of state laws, but not on the assumption that slavery was right according to the laws of God and nature, and this made the Northern Democrats as bad as the Republicans. Black Republicans, Free-Soilers, and popular-sovereignty advocates all shared the common sentiment that slavery was wrong. "It is a logical argument," concluded Yancey, "that your admission that slavery is wrong has been the cause of all this discord."[5]

Yancey had stated clearly the major Southern complaint since the early 1840s. Most Northerners were willing to tolerate slavery, but they were not ready to admit that it was according to the laws of either God or nature. Northern Democrats could make the face-saving gesture of allowing territorial settlers to decide for themselves on slavery because they were certain the settlers would choose free societies. Lacerated Southern sensibilities, however, required moral approval in the form of guaranteed rights for slavery in the territories regardless of the prevailing popular sentiment. To Abraham Lincoln popular sovereignty was a denial that slavery was wrong. To William L. Yancey popular sovereignty was a refusal to affirm that slavery was right. If the Republicans were the infidels on the subject, the Douglas Democrats were the heretics, and as such were the more hateful of the two. Southern self-esteem required a platform and a candidate willing to go further than the often-quoted statement of Douglas that he did not care whether slavery was voted up or down. Whether or not slavery could actually exist in an unfriendly territory was irrelevant. Yancey and his followers were correct. Most of the Northerners present really did consider slavery wrong, and their very presence in Charleston was both a reproach and an affront.

Ohio Senator George Pugh's angry and frustrated reply had the better logic and good sense, but it won few Southern hearts. Pugh read Yancey's own resolutions extolling nonintervention to the Alabama legislature four years earlier. Now, he charged, after years of losing elections at home by defending the South, Northern Democrats must publicly avow the righteousness of slavery to save the party. The Democratic party was not to be "dragged at the chariot wheel of 300,000 slave masters," and its leaders would not "put their hands on their mouths and their mouths in the dust." "Gentlemen of the South," he shouted, "You mistake us—you mistake us—we will not do it!"[6]

A long, frantic weekend separated Pugh's outburst from the final platform vote. George Sanders, Buchanan's New York port collector, wired the president an eloquent reminder that Douglas had supported him once he reached a majority at the 1856 convention, and begged for the same treatment for Douglas. Buchanan, Sanders warned, could not "afford to be the last President of the United States." The president was unmoved by the message, but was probably irritated by the $26.80 bill for the collect telegram. From Washington came a stream of wires from Southern representatives and senators urging their delegations to bolt if their demands on territorial slavery were not met, and always in the background was the knowledge of the Southerners that the president and his cabinet were on their side.

On Monday, April 30, 1860, the national Democratic party forged by Martin Van Buren and Andrew Jackson ran aground. Amid wild confusion, the Douglas minority report for popular sovereignty carried. The 1856 principle calling simply for popular sovereignty passed, with the border states and Virginia giving it sixty votes; but the section tying the party to the Supreme Court's decisions both past and future was defeated, with seven Southern states refusing to vote. Planks advocating protection for naturalized citizens, support for a Pacific railroad, efforts to buy Cuba, and the condemnation of Northern personal-liberty laws quickly passed. Senator Stuart of Michigan, a Douglas leader, harshly attacked the latter plank and thereby helped set the stage for what followed.

In rapid succession, beginning with Alabama, the delegation chairmen from seven Southern states, including Delaware, announced in dramatic tones amid wild cheering that they could no longer remain. Marching out, they retired to another building and formed their own convention. Defying their leaders and the galleries took great courage, but several delegates from Louisiana, South Carolina, Arkansas, and Georgia remained. One Alabama delegate followed his instructions under protest and offered to bet large amounts of money that Douglas could carry Alabama by 20,000 votes.

In the evening the bolters led a wild parade and demonstration through the streets. Yancey assured an excited crowd that "Perhaps even now, the pen of the historian is nibbed to write the story of a new Revolution," and the response was three roaring cheers for a new Southern republic.[7] Next day the group met under the chairmanship of Delaware Senator Bayard and passed the majority report on slavery that the convention had rejected. Ultimately they agreed to a new convention at Richmond and adjourned. The administration leaders may have hoped for an invitation to return to the regular convention, but none came.

When the original convention began its nominations, Cushing ruled that the remaining members of delegations that had bolted could not vote. Thus a group of angry Southern Unionists who had bravely stood up to their own leaders and the galleries were expelled by the parliamentary ruling of an administration spokesman. The number included a Georgian reputed to be the largest single slaveholder in the South.

With Virginia, North Carolina, Kentucky, and Tennessee remaining to vote against Douglas, Cushing ruled further that two-thirds of the total convention as originally constituted would be necessary for a nomination. This meant five-sixths of those present, and directly reversed numerous earlier precedents. No candidate could even come close. On the twenty-third ballot Douglas had 152½ votes, only sixteen away from two-thirds of those present, but it was his high-water mark. After fifty-seven ballots the convention adjourned with a motion to reconvene in June at Baltimore.

Between the Charleston and Baltimore conventions Davis and Douglas renewed the struggle in the Senate. Davis offered his slave-code resolutions. Douglas replied that the Charleston convention had taken a stand and the administration had no right to impose further party tests. Ill and exhausted, Douglas again warned that congressional intervention either to restrict or impose slavery would cause a truly irrepressible conflict, and that congressional action on the side of slavery would destroy the Northern Democrats. Davis himself had often admitted that soil, climate, political economy, and the wishes of the people would determine the question in each territory; so, why destroy the party over an abstraction?

Unable to cope with Douglas's logic on the principles involved, Davis answered that platforms were unimportant. The vital objective was to get a trustworthy candidate. Douglas replied that the seceders at Charleston had left because of the platform. If the platform was insignificant, why wreck the party because of it? The arguments by Davis did indeed illustrate the abstract nature of the quarrel. Once in power, parties only rarely pay much attention to their platforms anyhow. Any serious implementation of the principle over which the Southerners had bolted would require congressional action. There was no way that the House of Representatives, with its permanent Northern majority, could ever be persuaded to enact a slave code for the territories, and the Southern demand for a party statement and a candidate favoring such action was totally worthless except as a cry for approval by some and an excuse for secession by others.

When the Democratic convention reconvened in Baltimore in June, the Charleston seceders, supported by the president, demanded readmission and a chance to repeat their Charleston performance. Moderate delegates, however, many of them for Douglas, from Louisiana, Alabama, Arkansas, and Georgia rose to contest the seats of the bolters. Cushing, again the chairman, would have seated the original delegations, but the Douglas men forced a referral to the committee on credentials. They would accept no delegates unpledged to support the platform and the candidate to be chosen.

After long and bitter wrangling the committee recommended that the Unionists from Alabama, Louisiana, and Arkansas be seated and that Georgia's vote be divided equally between both delegations. During the arguments, Douglas authorized his floor leader to

111

withdraw his name in favor of Alexander H. Stephens if it would keep the peace, but his followers refused. The Southerners would accept no candidate on a platform of nonintervention; so, substituting a lesser candidate for Douglas offered no advantage and would only destroy the Northern Democratic party. Voting state by state, the convention defeated a motion to readmit all bolters. A majority agreed to seat the original Texans and Mississippians, but substituted the Union delegations from Louisiana and Alabama.

At this point, most of the Southerners, this time including those from border states, walked out, followed by the delegations from Oregon and California, and a large bloc from the Northeast, all led by President Buchanan's agents. Chairman Caleb Cushing himself was among the last to go, amid cries of approval from the Douglas adherents. The fiery Unionist slaveholder and duelist from Louisiana, Pierre Soulé, helped send them on their way with a blistering oration blaming it all on Slidell and Yancey and the Southerners' lust for power. Again W. B. Gaulden, the Georgian noted for the number of his slaves, chose to remain.

With the dissenters gone, the convention quickly nominated Douglas on the first ballot. The senator wanted Alexander H. Stephens for a running mate, but the decision was left to the Southerners who had remained loyal. Alabama put forward its own Senator Benjamin Fitzpatrick, who was promptly nominated despite the Douglas preference for Stephens. Fitzpatrick, though a Unionist, bowed to social pressures and his wife's apprehension, and decided not to undergo the hostility at home his candidacy would evoke. His refusal was another serious embarrassment for Douglas, but former Georgia Governor Herschel J. Johnson quickly agreed to be a substitute. As a final effort to regain the South, the convention agreed "That it is in accordance with the interpretation of the Cincinnati Platform that during the existence of the Territorial Governments the measure of restriction, whatever it may be, imposed by the Federal Constitution on the power of the Territorial Legislatures over the subject of domestic relations as the same has been or shall hereafter be finally determined by the Supreme Court of the United States, should be respected by all good citizens and enforced with promptness and fidelity by every branch of the Federal Government."[8] Stripped of its verbosity the plank was a reaffirmation of the Dred Scott decision and an endorsement of any future decision denying the power of any territorial legislature over slavery. The statement that other branches of the federal government should be committed to enforce it came close to the plank demanded by the Southerners, but the effort was a waste of time and pride.

The new seceders, 105 in all, met in Baltimore with Cushing again as chairman and adopted the majority report that had been defeated in Charleston: it was "The duty of the Federal Government in all its departments to protect, when necessary, the rights of persons and property in the Territories, and wherever else its constitutional authority extends."[9] Their candidate was Vice-President John J. Breckinridge of Kentucky, who first had to assure the administration Northerners that he did not accept the doctrine that the South must secede if the Republicans should win. Joseph Lane of Oregon was nominated for vice-president.

Two Democrats were now in the field. Breckinridge could not win without forty-two Northern votes. Douglas could not win without at least sixty-six Southern votes. All that remained undecided was the impact of the campaign, the extent of the Republican victory, and the Southern reaction to it.

Undaunted, however, the Southerners held their convention in Richmond and ratified the actions taken at Baltimore. Buchanan and former president Franklin Pierce endorsed Breckinridge and thereby approved his platform, and the White House soon became the unofficial campaign headquarters for Breckinridge. The president had vigorously opposed party unity behind a moderate candidate and platform, and had willingly promoted a candidate and platform with no chance to accomplish anything except drive a multitude of Northern voters into the arms of the Republicans. With his help the Southern radicals had had their way, and the analysis of the convention by the future Confederate vice-president, Alexander H. Stephens, contained much truth. "The seceders," wrote Stephens, "intended from the beginning 'to rule or ruin' and when they find they cannot rule they will then ruin. . . . Envy, hate, jealousy, spite—these make war in Heaven, which makes devils of angels and the same passions will make devils of men. The Secession movement was instigated by nothing but bad passions. Patriotism, in my opinion, has no more to do with it than love of God had with the other revolt."[10]

11

★★★★★

THE UNCERTAIN VERDICT

The true extremists were only a minority in both the Republican and Breckinridge camps, but the forces of moderation were further splintered by another development. A sizeable group of former Whigs and Know-Nothings in both the North and South could stomach neither Democrats nor Republicans. Their essential agreement with the Douglas Democrats on slavery could not overcome their memories of past battles with the Democrats. Their Republican orientation on economic matters was weaker than their dislike for the Republican position on slavery and their dread of the Southern reaction if Lincoln should win. Some had supported the Know-Nothings in 1856, not because of bigotry toward immigrants but in the vain hope that an emphasis on patriotism and the creation of foreign and religious enemies, however imaginary, might weaken the quarrel over slavery. In 1858 and 1859 in the border slave states they had steadfastly opposed the radicals.

On May 9, 1860, led by men like John J. Crittenden of Kentucky, John Bell of Tennessee, Edward Everett and Amos Lawrence of Massachusetts, William C. Rives of Virginia, John P. Kennedy of Maryland, and Washington Hunt of New York, they met in Baltimore to form the Constitutional Union party and nominate candidates on a brief platform that spoke only for sectional peace.[1] Southerners present wished to nominate Sam Houston. Crittenden, who might have been their strongest man, refused to be considered because of his age. On the second ballot they nominated Bell, a former Speaker of the House who had been one of the Whig party's three candidates against Van Buren in 1836, secretary of war under Harrison, and a long-time senator. Though a large slaveholder, Bell had courageously supported the immediate admission of a free California in 1850, opposed the Kansas-Nebraska bill, and voted against Lecompton in defiance of instructions from the Tennessee legislature. Everett was nominated for vice-president. It was a respectable if somewhat colorless ticket with no chance to accomplish anything except draw votes otherwise most likely to go to Douglas. Indeed, the nominations occurred before the final Democratic split at Baltimore, and may have encouraged the administration to withdraw its forces there on the issue of readmitting the seceders. Bell was expected to score heavily in the border states and thereby increase the likelihood of throwing the final decisions to the House and Senate. The administration had hoped for this from the beginning. American third parties usually do weaken the major party closest to their own persuasion.

Few politicians have ever equaled the genius of Abraham Lincoln for saying exactly the right thing at the best time for his own success. In 1859 and 1860, while denying any presidential ambitions, he managed to travel 4,000 miles and make twenty-three well-reported speeches in ten states. Slowly but steadily he expanded his reputation as the eloquent advocate of a brand of moral righteousness that seemed to require no real effort or sacrifice from those who shared it. His essential message rarely changed: slavery was wrong; it must be contained within its present domain, but must not be disturbed where it already existed; once slavery was legally contained, the North would stop agitating against it and the South would stop pushing for its expansion; he hoped that peace would reign then, but regardless, Republicans and right-thinking Americans everywhere must stand firm against Southern extremism.

Lincoln's greatest opportunity came on March 5, 1860, when a trip East to visit his son at Phillips Exeter Academy was the ostensible excuse for accepting an invitation to speak in New York City. Before 1,500 avid listeners in the Cooper Institute hall, he delivered a masterpiece. To answer the charge of radicalism he named the founding fathers who had voted for slave restrictions in the Northwest Ordinance and the Missouri Compromise and showed that twenty-one of the thirty-nine framers of the Constitution had assumed the right of the federal government to contain slavery, while the remainder had never been known to question it. He expressed great sympathy for Southerners, denied any Republican threat to slavery where it existed, emphatically repudiated John Brown, and insisted that Republicans never had and never would urge slaves to revolt.

After urging his audience and Republicans everywhere to seek peace by yielding to the South whenever duty permitted it, Lincoln analyzed the Southern demands with searching realism. The Southerners, he said, would not be satisfied if given slave rights in the territories. No one was even discussing any specific territories. They would not be pacified if Republicans had nothing to do with invasions and insurrections. The Republicans had never been involved in invasions or insurrections, but were nonetheless being denounced for it. What would satisfy the South? "Simply this: We must not only let them alone, but we must, somehow, convince them that we do let them alone. . . . In all our platforms and speeches we have constantly protested our purpose to let them alone; but this has had no tendency to convince them. Alike unavailing to convince them, is the fact that they have never detected a man of us in any attempt to disturb them." What would convince the South? "This, and this only: cease to call slavery *wrong*, and join them in calling it *right*. And this must be done . . . in *acts* as well as in *words*. Silence will not be tolerated—we must place ourselves avowedly with them." All declarations against slavery "whether made in politics, in presses, in pulpits, or in private" must be suppressed. "We must arrest and return their fugitive slaves with greedy pleasure. . . . The whole atmosphere must be disinfected from all taint of opposition to slavery, before they will cease to believe that all their troubles proceed from us. . . . We do let them alone—have never disturbed them—so that, after all, it is what we say, which dissatisfies them. They will continue to accuse us of doing, until we cease saying." Believing slavery morally right, continued Lincoln, the Southerners were demanding "a full national recognition of it, as a legal right, and a social blessing," and Northerners could withhold this only on the conviction that slavery was wrong. "All they ask, we could readily grant, if we thought slavery right; all we ask, they could as readily grant, if they thought it wrong. Their thinking it right, and our thinking it wrong, is the precise fact upon which depends the whole controversy."[2]

Having minimized the actual issues and reduced the quarrel, probably correctly, to the Southern demand for moral approval, Lincoln then revived the threat of actual slave expansion and closed with an appeal to righteousness and courage that left his listeners shouting and cheering for several minutes. Slavery should be left alone, he concluded, but must not be allowed "to spread into the

National Territories, and to overrun us here in these Free States." Republicans should not be "groping for some middle ground between the right and the wrong," or accept a "policy of 'don't care' on a question about which all true men do care—such as Union appeals beseeching true Union men to yield to Disunionists, reversing the divine rule, and calling, not the sinners, but the righteous to repentance. . . . LET US HAVE FAITH THAT RIGHT MAKES MIGHT, AND IN THAT FAITH, LET US, TO THE END, DARE TO DO OUR DUTY AS WE UNDERSTAND IT."[3]

The words of Lincoln were the direct inverse of Yancey's views at Charleston. Yancey demanded moral approval for slavery. Lincoln reiterated his conviction that the institution was morally wrong. Yancey would accept no policy that did not imply the righteousness of slavery. Lincoln would tolerate no policy that did not suggest the opposite. Neither was talking about any specific event, situation, or actual territorial contest that was remotely likely to occur.

The widespread attention given his New York speech quickly brought new invitations and a general repetition of the same sentiments in other New England cities. At Hartford he added an essentially conservative statement that delighted his audience but added further to the Southern radicals' ammunition against him: "If I find a venomous snake lying on the open prairie, I seize the first stick and kill him at once. But if that snake is in bed with my children, I must be more cautious—I shall, in striking the snake, also strike the children, or arouse the reptile to bite the children. Slavery is the venomous snake in bed with the children. But if the question is whether to kill it on the prairie or *put it in bed with other children,* I think we'd *kill* it!" At New Haven he added to the snake analogy a promise never to bother a snake in bed with a neighbor's children if he had bound himself "by a solemn compact not to meddle with his children under any circumstances."[4] He would not, however, send snakes to join children in a newly made-up bed, and the nation should not allow snakes to be mixed with the children in the new territories. Thus, Lincoln again pledged himself to leave Southern slavery alone while simultaneously describing the institution as a snake fit only for death. The latter was much easier for Southerners to remember.

Also at both Hartford and New Haven, Lincoln made a much publicized appeal for the votes of laboring men. A shoemakers' strike was in progress in Massachusetts, and without taking sides on the specific issue, he extolled the system where a man could strike as compared to slavery, and blamed the strike on the South's unjustified withdrawal of its trade. He also warned that if laborers surrendered their conviction and called slavery right, "instead of *white* laborers who *can* strike, you'll soon have *black* laborers who *can't* strike."[5] This appeal to the workingmen's fear of black competition had worked well for him in Illinois in 1858. It was far-fetched and inconsistent, but it was shrewd politics. Along with his stand for higher tariffs, which labor was beginning to support as a path to higher wages, it helps explain why Northern workingmen who had rarely voted Whig would soon give him their overwhelming support.

Candidates were nominated by convention delegates rather than voters, however, and the Republicans took their turn at this game while Davis and Douglas were still rehashing the Charleston debacle in the Senate. Unlike the sullen and desperate Democrats at Charleston, the Republicans poured into Chicago on a wave of triumphant euphoria. With the Democrats apparently intent on party suicide, they could lose only through some outlandish error, which everyone was determined to avoid. If Chicago in May lacked some of Charleston's unique charm, few of the happy and excited delegates noticed it. The windy city by now boasted some 110,000 vigorous inhabitants, and the estimated 40,000 visitors, brass bands, flags and bunting, and parades only added to its already ebullient atmosphere.

A building picturesquely named the Wigwam had been erected to hold 10,000 delegates and observers, and far more than that many noisy local Republicans were ready to fill it up and shout for Abraham Lincoln if they got the chance. The opportunity soon arose. While the thirteen carloads of New Yorkers and numerous other Seward adherents from points east paraded through the streets, the Lincoln men, many armed with bogus tickets, grabbed the seats in the Wigwam galleries. Chicago, incidentally, had been selected for the convention at the suggestion of a Lincoln friend who argued that it would be neutral territory because Illinois had no candidate.

The Republicans harmoniously approved a magnificent economic platform that promised something to almost everyone except slaveholders wishing to take their minions to western territories. A protective tariff, a homestead act, extensive appropriations for river and harbor improvements, liberal naturalization laws for immigrants, and a railroad to the Pacific would be the national rewards for electing a Republican president. For the original antislavery crusaders the platform repudiated the Dred Scott decision, denounced James Buchanan for the Lecompton Constitution, and called popular sovereignty a deception and fraud. For the conservative majority it classified John Brown's raid as "among the greatest of crimes," reaffirmed the right of the states to control their own domestic institutions, and said nothing about the Fugitive Slave Act. The president, said the platform, should ask Congress for legislation to protect the new territories from slavery, but only if he should judge such action necessary.

The platform apparently made everyone happy except the grizzled and ancient Ohio abolitionist Joshua Giddings, who delivered an impassioned complaint because the preamble from the Declaration of Independence had been omitted. After Giddings staged his own one-man walkout, however, George William Curtis and Frank Blair, Jr., persuaded the convention to obey his wish. The immortal words of Jefferson were added, and amid thunderous cheers the tearful old man was led back to his seat.

The nomination of Lincoln was surprisingly easy. Seward, the front runner, had talked too much and too often and was clearly a risky candidate. Most voters would not be anxious to engage in an irrepressible conflict to defend a higher law. The party's leading editor, Horace Greeley, furthermore, had quarreled with Seward and Thurlow Weed, and was filling the air and his *New York Tribune* with warnings that Seward could not win. Seward's close personal connections with Weed, who was always under suspicion for shady dealings, were also damaging. All of this meant that the convention was receptive when the other candidates decided quickly to unite on a single opponent. The Blairs suggested Edward Bates of Missouri, but he had gained the enmity of recent immigrants by supporting Fillmore and the Know-Nothings in 1856. Cameron of Pennsylvania was weak outside his own state, and Chase had powerful enemies even within his own state of Ohio. The logical answer to Seward was Lincoln, whose formula on slavery satisfied consciences without stirring up fears. The *New York Tribune* and the *Chicago Tribune* were already for him, and his name evoked deafening cheers from the galleries every time it was mentioned. Lincoln's managers helped his cause further by ignoring his instructions and promising cabinet posts to Indiana and Pennsylvania. On the first ballot Seward led with 173½ votes, 60 less than a majority. Lincoln had 102, more than twice that of anyone else. On the second ballot, Pennsylvania switched to give Lincoln 181. On the third ballot the Rail-splitter had 231½, at which point 4 more Ohio delegates shifted and the nomination was completed.[6]

The Republicans had chosen a candidate pledged to honor every Southern interest except the empty right of protection for slavery in the territories. More important, however, Lincoln had steadfastly and often expressed the opinion that slavery was morally wrong, and for this the ultra-sensitive Southerners could never forgive him or accept him as their president.

The convention system had served the Republicans well by selecting the candidate most likely to win—a man who was destined to be widely considered the nation's greatest president. Ironically, however, the Chicago convention probably also helped perpetrate a deception in that the delegates thought they had selected the more conservative of the leading candidates. Despite his inflammatory rhetoric, William Henry Seward, if elected, would not have allowed the Southerners to precipitate a war over the federal forts. As secretary of state he would later try to persuade Lincoln to keep the peace by abandoning the forts, and he would engage in actual ruses to thwart his chief's contrary decision. In seeking to reject a tiger the delegates had in fact rejected a lamb, but this was the fault of Seward himself rather than the convention system. Lambs should not roar if they expect to maintain their identity.

As so often happens, the 1860 election offered American voters a bewildering variety of often unrelated reasons for the choices they made. In the North the Republicans had money, organization, unity, compelling issues, no serious handicaps, and the most marketable candidate since Andrew Jackson. Newspaper articles, editorials, and a rash of campaign biographies both long and short showed the people a man who was truly one of their own. Born in poverty, reared in frontier circumstances, and self-educated, he had joined an Indian war, farmed, labored, kept store, and achieved great success as a lawyer and politician through hard work and intuitive ability. Every symbol of the legendary American success story was present; and, just as sophisticated jibes had only strengthened Jackson's popularity, similar attempts to picture Lincoln as a backwoods barbarian backfired with equal intensity. Simultaneously, the Republicans distributed 100,000 copies of the Covode Committee report damning Buchanan and the Democrats for corruption, hit hard on the economic issues among people who had not forgotten the recent depression and Buchanan's votes, and in general were successful in creating an image of themselves as the advance guard of a bright new day.

The Democratic Senate had already cooperated by again stopping every effort to revise the tariff, and Buchanan made another great contribution to the Republicans with his final veto of their homestead bill. Douglas had fully supported the homestead and Pacific railroad bills and his faction of Democrats had both in their platform, but Democrats generally were firmly identified as the enemy of these projects. Ironically, what passed for big business in the East generally supported Douglas with both money and influence, such as it was. His campaign chairman was the great German-born banker August Belmont, who after an apprenticeship with the Rothschilds had established himself as one of America's wealthiest capitalists, and William B. Astor reputedly contributed $100,000. Businessmen feared Lincoln's election because they knew the economic problems that would follow a Southern secession, and Treasury Secretary Cobb at the crucial moment warned that the South would repudiate $200,000,000 in debts owed to Northern businessmen.

Democratic mayor Fernando Wood of New York and others denounced the Republicans as socialists determined to divide everyone's wealth as well as destroy slave property. These charges caused a stock-market collapse in late October, but the strategy partially backfired. Several Democratic businessmen switched to Lincoln in fear of the chaos that might occur if the election had to be settled in Congress.

"The people . . . are satisfied with you as you are," wrote William Cullen Bryant to Lincoln, "and they want you to do nothing at present but allow yourself to be elected." His friends wished him "to make no speeches, write no letters as a candidate, enter into no pledges, make no promises, nor even give any of those kind words which men are apt to interpret into promises."[7] Lincoln followed this advice religiously. In several interviews he convinced various individual Southerners that he was pledged to their constitutional rights, but he steadfastly resisted all pleas for public statements. Privately he argued that his previous speeches and the platform of the Republican party were available for all to read, and no more words were necessary.

Either Lincoln did not really dread the threat of Southern secession or he did not take it seriously. Otherwise, he might well have given some desperately needed aid to the Southern Unionists by delivering a few well-placed speeches stressing his willingness to tolerate slavery in its present habitat. He was first and foremost, however, an aspiring candidate. No reassurances to the South could gain him any votes from that quarter, but they might cost him some votes in the Northeast, where some disappointment over the failure of Seward still lingered. Also, Lincoln was an old-line Whig. The only two Whig presidential victories during the party's lifetime had been won by candidates who had remained virtually silent throughout the campaign.

Lincoln's silence, however, helped the Southern radicals conduct a thoroughly distorted campaign against both him and his party. The earlier statements of Seward, who by now was speaking everywhere for conciliation, were grist for those working night and day to frighten the South into secession. Lincoln's own "ultimate extinction" statement was taken out of context to imply more immediate extinction than ultimate. Most helpful to the Southern radicals, however, were the statements of radical Republicans who upstaged the silent Lincoln and the Republican moderate majority. Perhaps most damaging was another oration by Charles Sumner on June 4, 1860, called "The Barbarism of Slavery." Among other eloquent phrases, the Massachusetts senator predicted that a Republican triumph would cause the Slave Power to die like a poisoned rat in its hole and urged the free communities to become a belt of fire around the South within which slavery must die.[8]

The Bell campaign, supposedly designed to seek unity and peace, also helped the Southern fire-eaters by concentrating its attack on Lincoln and the Republicans and thereby lending credence to the fears being spread by the disunionists. A widely circulated Constitutional Union pamphlet quoted the rhetorical excesses of the Republican radicals, argued that the Republican party's real goal was abolition, and warned that only the defeat of Lincoln could prevent secession.[9] The realistic warning contributed much to its own fulfillment.

The abolitionists nominated Gerrit Smith and attacked Lincoln as a "slave hound," but the South paid this no attention. With Sumner still exercising his unique talent for enraging Southerners, and Lincoln saying nothing in contradiction, the campaign in the South was one long brainwashing preparation for secession. Politicians and editors at every level filled the air with warnings of Northern conspiracies, new John Brown invasions, slave rebellions, burning homes, and murdered women and children. Expressing an ever-growing sentiment, Lawrence Keitt of South Carolina would never "permit a party stained with treason, hideous with insurrection, and dripping with blood, to occupy the government."[10] In Dalton, Georgia, thirty-six blacks were arrested and charged with a plot to burn the town and kill all the people. In Talladega, Alabama, two whites and eight blacks were arrested, and one white man was hanged. A wave of rumors that the wells were being poisoned swept through Texas, and a moderate opponent of slavery was hanged. One unfortunate vendor of Breckinridge campaign badges was chased down the street and almost hanged because a Lincoln button was found in his bag. The threat of mob violence hung heavy over local conservatives and Unionists who might be tempted to speak out for common sense.[11]

Throughout the summer and fall, the Southern governors were corresponding on ways and means for accomplishing secession after the election. Knowing this, James Buchanan might have supported the contention of Douglas that a Lincoln victory would not justify secession, and he could have combined his support for Breckinridge with severe warnings that secession would be resisted. The president, however, still had the same old problem. He sympathized with the Southerners, although he probably hoped their threats would lead to nothing more serious than a Northern surrender to the demands of the Breckinridge platform. He considered this an eminently reasonable solution, and if threats of disunion could help bring it about, he would not be one to complain. The administration newspaper, the *Constitution*, subject to Buchanan's orders on pain of immediate dismissal as the recipient of the executive patronage, cooperated zealously with the disunionists. Lincoln's election, wrote editor William M. Browne, would put antislavery office holders in every community to spread antislavery ideas among the whites and foment rebellion among the slaves. The post office, meanwhile, would spread the writings of Helper and Garrison everywhere, while the federal marshals would support the trouble-makers against those trying to maintain peace.

John J. Breckinridge was a strange candidate for the Southern radicals. He had taken no stand on Lecompton, he had written a letter of support to Douglas in 1858, and when nominated he had denied that a Lincoln victory would justify secession. He would later be a Confederate general, however, and would command troops fighting as close to Washington as Silver Spring, Maryland. He carried on a moderate campaign with almost no threats or name-calling, but his protestations of loyalty to the Union were more than offset by the circumstances of his nomination and the expressed sentiments of many of his Southern supporters. As Douglas pointed out, while not all of Breckinridge's supporters were secessionists, every secessionist was openly in his camp. Breckinridge was also supported by Cass, Pierce, and Buchanan—the last three titular heads of the Democratic party—and eight of the ten Democratic senators from the North, as well as four-fifths of the Democratic representatives. This, however, only indicated that the Buchanan administration still carried weight with the congressional Democrats. Breckinridge never had the slightest chance to carry a single Northern state.

Obviously, only a withdrawal of the three anti-Republican candidates in favor of one compromise nominee could make possible the defeat of Lincoln. If this could not be achieved, only a Douglas victory in at least some Northwestern states and the same for Bell on the border could throw the election to the House of Representatives, where Lincoln presumably could not win a majority. The men in the White House may have thought of these possibilities, but their primary object was the defeat of Douglas. Some of them were even foolish enough to think Breckinridge might win—Southerners were all too accustomed to having their own way.

In later years Jefferson Davis, who apparently had pushed the disunion threat in the hope of concessions rather than actual secession, described his own efforts to avert the crisis. He proposed to Bell, Breckinridge, and Douglas that all should withdraw in favor of a compromise candidate like Horatio Seymour of New York. Bell and Breckinridge agreed, but Douglas adamantly refused. He had already denounced the idea of throwing the election into Congress and warned that he would throw the election to Lincoln first. He now informed Davis that if he withdrew, the Northern Democrats would prefer Lincoln to any substitute Democrat acceptable to the Southern ultras, and the party's candidates for lesser offices would suffer accordingly. He could not desert them. On the other hand, he reminded Davis, if Breckinridge would drop out, he, Douglas, would have a chance to win and save the party. Whether or not the Davis suggestion offered the Democrats or the nation any real hope for peace, the Mississippian was the wrong person to suggest it to Douglas. Davis had been a harpoon in the back of Douglas for years, and was as responsible as any other single person for turning the South against him.

Douglas, convinced that Lincoln's election was inevitable, chose to use his candidacy for an all-out attack on the secessionists. He believed charges that the Southern radicals were planning a coup if Lincoln won or if no candidate received a majority. Reportedly, if they could carry Virginia and Maryland for Breckinridge, they would declare him president, use their control of the cabinet to seize the federal departments, and call upon the Southern states to recognize the new government. Thus, Washington would become the capital of a new slaveholding nation. Knowing the people allegedly involved, Douglas never doubted that such plans existed.

Driven by this fear, Douglas boldly invaded Maryland, Virginia, and North Carolina to denounce disunion and the radicals. At Norfolk he assured an excited crowd that if the Southern states seceded on the election of Lincoln before any overt act against their constitutional rights, it would be the president's duty to enforce the laws regardless of the cost. In Raleigh, North Carolina, he announced that he "would hang every man higher than Haman who would attempt to resist by force the execution of any provision of the Constitution which our fathers made and bequeathed to us. . . . You can not sever this Union unless you cut the heartstrings that bind father to son, daughter to mother and brother to sister in all our new States and Territories."[12]

When Maine went heavily Republican in the congressional election, the Buchanan Democrats realized they were cutting their own throats and renewed efforts to fuse their electors with those of Douglas. In New York, Douglas answered that if Breckinridge favored "enforcing the laws against disunionists, seceders, Abolitionists and all other classes of men, in the event the election does not result to suit him," he would combine their electors, but otherwise he would not: "I wish to God we had an Old Hickory now alive in order that he might hang Northern and Southern traitors on the same gallows."[13] Ultimately, a fusion of electors in New York and Rhode Island and a partial fusion in New Jersey and Pennsylvania were achieved, primarily because frightened millionaires like Astor, Alexander Stuart, George Law, William H. Aspinwall, and William F. Havenmeyer made fusion the condition for further financial support. The strategy may have helped Douglas win half the electoral vote of New Jersey, but otherwise it was a total failure.

In the final days of the campaign, Douglas made one last effort to rouse Union support in the South. At St. Louis, Nashville, Chattanooga, Atlanta, Montgomery, Selma, and Mobile he delivered his usual fearless message: Lincoln's election would not harm the South or justify secession. The laws must be obeyed, and Lincoln should and would use force to put down disunion if it should be attempted. In Atlanta he was introduced by supporter Alexander H. Stephens. In Montgomery rotten eggs and tomatoes were thrown at him. On the boat between Montgomery and Selma a deck collapsed, causing painful injuries to both him and Mrs. Douglas. On election eve he assured a great crowd in Mobile that they would be far safer in the Union. Wherever he went, the crowds were large and enthusiastic, and Governor Letcher of Virginia endorsed him. Without the mass media of a later day, however, his impact was limited to those who saw him, and most Southerners knew him primarily from the unfair picture drawn by his enemies. Weary, lonely, discouraged, but undaunted, he awaited the final verdict in Mobile.

If, however, Cobb, Thompson, Floyd, and the Southern radicals in Congress had actually hoped to seize the capital with border-state support, Douglas had sidetracked them. Bell carried Virginia, Kentucky, and Tennessee; Douglas himself took Missouri; and Breckinridge won Maryland by only 700 votes, hardly a border-state mandate for upsetting constitutional processes.

The total vote apparently indicated that most Americans were still conservative and that most Southerners still hoped to remain in the Union. Lincoln received 1,866,452 votes, Douglas 1,376,957, Breckinridge 849,781, and Bell 588,879. With less than 40 percent of the popular vote, Lincoln had won a resounding electoral majority, and he would have been elected even if all the votes of his three opponents had gone to one candidate. In addition to all the Northern states he had received 17,000 votes in Missouri, 3,800 in Delaware, 2,300 in Maryland, 1,900 in Virginia, and 1,300 in Kentucky. Oregon and California Democrats had helped the administration significantly in the breakup of their party; Lincoln carried both states. While Breckinridge carried eleven of the fifteen slave states, including South Carolina where the people were not permitted to vote, he won a majority in only seven of them. Thus, the majority in eight of the fifteen actually voted for Bell or Douglas. The combined vote of the slave states was 570,000 for Breckinridge and 705,000 for Bell and Douglas. Even in the states that seceded almost immediately, Bell and Douglas won 48 percent of the votes. A Democratic party united behind Douglas or some other popular-sovereignty candidate at Charleston might have beaten Lincoln, who clearly profited against both Democratic candidates by the foolish conduct of their party at both Charleston and Baltimore and by the warfare of their partisans against each other.

Equally important, the Republicans did not win either house of Congress. They actually lost nine seats in the House while gaining five in the Senate, but they still held only thirty-one of the sixty-six Senate seats until the Southerners walked out. As Douglas pointed out in New Orleans, if the Southerners would but stay in their seats the new president, tied hand and foot by his opposition, should be "an object of pity and commiseration rather than of fear and apprehension by a brave and chivalrous people," and in four short years another election would quickly remedy any real grievances. He might have added, but did not, that the Supreme Court was still under firm Southern control. Whatever the long-range prospects for continued Southern domination of the national government, the Southerners were clearly in no danger from either Abraham Lincoln or the Republican party in 1861. Unless, of course, they abandoned their seats in Congress and tried to destroy a national Union that Abraham Lincoln and most Northerners would be determined to preserve even at the cost of war.

12

★★★★★

SECESSION

As Stephen A. Douglas had pointed out, Lincoln was no radical on the slavery question, he had carried neither house of Congress for his party, and the Supreme Court had not changed in personnel or views since the Dred Scott decision. Lincoln had won only 39.9 percent of the popular vote. If his victory meant that the long-range future of slavery might be dim, it did not indicate any immediate danger in 1860. The price of slaves remained high, although a bad drought and resulting poor crops had brought serious economic hardships in late 1860. Southern statesmen, furthermore, had often demonstrated their awareness of a Northern Jim Crow system for free blacks, which would be unequalled in severity by the Southern states themselves until the 1890s. Free-soilism depended as much upon racist opposition to blacks being admitted to western territories as it did upon moral objections to slavery, and Southern leaders in their more rational moments knew it.

The states of the lower South, however, had announced their ultimata before and during the campaign, and there could be no turning back. In South Carolina, Keitt, Ruffin, and Rhett delivered impassioned speeches as the legislature waited to cast the state's electoral vote. By November 13 Lincoln's election was clear and the legislature immediately voted for a state convention. In the elections for delegates in late November and early December the radicals overwhelmed the Unionists. On December 20 the convention passed a secession ordinance by 169 to 0.

Like the men of 1776, the South Carolina seceders felt a duty to justify their action before the bar of public opinion. The ordinance reviewed extensively the history of the American Revolution, stressed the obvious parallels, and provided an extensive argument for the constitutional right of secession. Even more significant, perhaps, were the specific indictments against the North that presumably made secession necessary. The Northern states, they charged, had "assumed the right of deciding upon the propriety of our domestic institutions, and . . . denied the rights of property established in fifteen of the States and recognized by the Constitution." They had "denounced as sinful the institution of Slavery" and "permitted the open establishment among them of societies, whose avowed object is to disturb the peace of . . . the citizens of other States." They had "encouraged and assisted thousands of our slaves to leave their homes, and those who remain, have been incited by emissaries, books, and pictures, to servile insurrection." And finally, the convention concluded, the Northern states had elected a president who had declared that "that 'Government cannot endure permanent half-slave, half free,' and that the public mind must rest in the belief that Slavery is in the course of ultimate extinction." The new party had announced that the South should "be excluded from the common territory, that the Judicial Tribunal should be made sectional, and that a war must be waged against Slavery until it shall cease throughout the United States." All hope for remedy was in vain because the North had "invested a great political error with the sanctions of a more erroneous religious belief."[1]

The Carolinians conveniently ignored the Republican party platform's pledge to the "maintenance inviolate of the rights of the States, and especially the right of each State to order and control its own domestic institutions according to its own judgment exclusively." The platform did not even require the president to seek legislation against slavery in a territory unless he should consider such action necessary in a specific case. More important, any such restriction would have to be passed by Congress, and neither the existing nor the newly elected Congress was any more likely to pass such a prohibition than it was to enact a territorial slave code—unless, of course, the Southern members should leave their seats. Charles Sumner might have suggested an all-out effort against slavery, but both the Republican party and Abraham Lincoln were clearly on record against any such crusade.

Mississippi, which followed South Carolina very shortly, went even further into its specific reasons for secession, while most of the other seceding states contented themselves with a few well-chosen generalities. Six of the fifteen clauses in the Mississippi secession ordinance were related in one way or another to Northern efforts to entice slaves to escape and help them avoid recapture, although Mississippi was probably the least vulnerable state in the Union to this menace. The problem, furthermore, could hardly be alleviated by a separation that would relieve the Northern states of all federal obligation to help return the fugitives. Replacing the Canadian border with the Ohio River and the Mason and Dixon line as the point of absolute freedom would not make the recapture of runaways easier. Despite the highly publicized cases in which Northerners had defied the Fugitive Slave Laws, such action was still the exception rather than the rule.

Two of the Mississippi complaints dealt with states rights, the recognition of slavery by the Constitution, and the unconstitutionality of "all efforts to impair its value or lessen its duration by Congress, or any of the free states." Certainly no Congress had ever made the slightest threat against slavery where it already existed, and no Northern state legislature, with the possible exception of Massachusetts during the Mexican War, had ever suggested that abolition might be a possibility even in the distant future. The newly elected Congress would clearly be no exception.

The Mississippi ordinance charged further that through "voluntary associations, individual agencies, and state legislation" the Northerners were interfering with slavery, demanding that slavery be excluded from new territories, and opposing the admission of any more slave states. This effort to "force Congress to a condemnation of that species of property" was designed to gain the necessary two-thirds of both houses and three-fourths of the states for enactment of a constitutional amendment to abolish slavery. No one pointed out that such an amendment would require forty-five free states to offset the fifteen existing slave states. Counting the soon-to-be admitted free state of Kansas, this would require the admission of twenty-seven more free states. Since the trend toward large western states had already been established by Texas, California, Oregon, and Kansas, the creation of twenty-seven more states was clearly an impossibility. Also, the supposition that existing Northern states with laws discriminating cruelly against free blacks and barring their further entry would ever support such an amendment was very doubtful.

Also, argued Mississippi, the North had "sought to create discord" by incendiary publications, had "encouraged a hostile invasion of a Southern state to excite insurrection, murder, and rapine," and were continuing "an unfriendly agitation of their domestic institutions." The North had "elected a majority of electors for President and Vice-President on the ground that there exists an irreconcilable conflict between the two sections of the Confederacy in reference to their respective systems of labor and in pursuance of their hostility to us and our institutions, thus declaring to the civilized world that the powers of this government are to be used for the dishonor and overthrow of the southern section of this great Confederacy."[2]

Clearly, the Southern leaders were straining hard to find valid, practical reasons for secession, and those who have since considered it a rational decision have often been compelled to cite reasons that the seceders understood and enunciated but dimly if at all. Perhaps, as Eugene Genovese has argued, the Southern masters did feel they must secede to avoid an internal crisis, but if any kind of nonslaveholding white revolt was threatening in 1861 it was remarkably well hidden.[3] Whatever fears among the gentry had been stirred up by Helper's *Impending Crisis* should have been thoroughly alleviated by the reaction of whites everywhere to the John Brown raid and the mass hysteria evidenced during the 1860 election campaign. True, as both the radicals and the Constitutional Unionists had warned throughout the campaign, Lincoln would now have the power to appoint postmasters and other local federal office holders. These individuals, however, would be entirely subject to local public opinion and the prospect of serious physical danger if they violated local mores and customs. Both the president and his platform were pledged against interference with the Southern states, and the postmaster general and other job-dispensing cabinet members would require a two-thirds confirmation by a Senate in which the Republicans were a minority—unless the South seceded. The new office holders would likely be Southern Whigs and Unionists of the type who followed men like Alexander H. Stephens, but they would hardly be the vanguard of a class revolution. Ralph E. Morrow has brilliantly argued and documented the thesis that the proslavery argument was primarily for home consumption, but he also found that the waverers whose attachment to slavery had to be buttressed were primarily upper-class members of slaveholding families.[4] True, at various times several planters warned that a threat to slavery was a threat to their own political control. The argument that Lincoln's victory actually posed a serious internal threat to planter domination, however, was not emphasized in the secession conventions and probably escaped the attention of many planters and most of the yeomen.

It can be argued with equal logic that the racial prejudices and fears of the nonslaveholding whites were a major instrument of political power for the planters. Presumably, secession and the establishment of a new Southern nation woud alleviate rather than intensify the threat of Northern abolition and thereby would render slavery more rather than less secure. Relieved of this threat, the less affluent Southern whites might well have felt more rather than less free to demand greater political and economic influence for themselves. Surely the abilities needed to acquire and manage plantations and slaves rather than the plantations and slaves themselves explained the planters' domination of Southern society; and, whatever their fears, the abolition of slavery did not bring an end to their control. Indeed, it can be argued that the planter class ultimately accepted abolition with greater equanimity and grace than did the small slaveholders and those who had never owned any slaves at all.

The desperate feeling of the seceders that slavery must expand or die is vital to the Genovese thesis, and this has been amplified in a provocative recent study by William Barney.[5] In Barney's view, both North and South knew that if slavery could not expand, the Southerners would run out of land for plantation agriculture and space for the dispersal of the black population to avoid socially dangerous concentrations of slaves. Undoubtedly, some Republicans hoped this was true and many Southerners believed it, but just how secession would relieve this crushing inevitability was not discussed seriously in any convention. Lincoln expected the process to take at least a century. Although New Mexico had passed a slave code, in large part to seek favor with Buchanan's cabinet, no one really expected either it or California to secede, and neither could be taken from the Union without a war. Cuba, the Pearl of the Antilles, still loomed invitingly only ninety miles from Florida, but its free black population was quite large, its slave code was far more relaxed than that of the Southern states, and it was well on its way toward emancipation. The Cubans themselves would have fought alongside the Spanish to resist any Southern invasion, and any such exploit would have required the all-out support of the nonslaveholding Southern whites. Even if the South could have taken it, the island was not really a prime prospect for a great new influx of slaves. Mexico and Central America could be cited in bombastic speeches as future parts of a Southern empire, but few thoughtful slaveholders really contemplated fighting the wars necessary to gain the privilege of annexing the large Indian and Mestizo populations of either area. The effective conquest and permanent control of alien peoples are difficult enough when the local culture and institutions are left undisturbed. If local hostility to slavery could keep slaveholders out of territories within the existing national boundaries, how could Southerners hope to plant a new brand of slavery among the black, Indian, and Mestizo peoples of Cuba, Central America, and Mexico? The feeling that containment would destroy slavery may have added to the South's bitterness against the North, but it was hardly a realistic motive for secession. As James Buchanan himself later pointed out, secession denied the slave states the support of the total nation against a world unfriendly to slavery, and left the institution far more exposed and vulnerable than when it was inside the Union. Genovese and Barney agree that expansion was an impossible dream, and most Southerners in 1860 probably thought so too.

Among the 183 Southern editorials on secession published by Dwight Dumond, the argument that slavery must expand or die is mentioned only once. A Georgia editor cited this abolition viewpoint and briefly challenged the admittedly widespread opinion that slavery could not expand southward. The point was not a major part of the editorial. Robert Barnwell Rhett's *Charleston Mercury* in one editorial also insisted that the South could in fact take Latin American territory from "the worthless mongrel races that now inhabit and curse the land," but described this goal as a magnificent challenge for the sake of mineral wealth rather than a necessity for the survival of slavery. Both editorials predicted that the North would soon take this territory if the South did not, and both were highly defensive in their arguments that the conquests were possible. The Louisville *Daily Courier* predicted that abolition in the border states would cause race war to the South, but it did not propose territorial expansion as a remedy.[6]

Dumond may have selected his editorials from a biased viewpoint—no evidence supports any such contention—but surely a primary motive for secession should appear more often in so large a collection, which fairly seethes with anger and resentment against Northern threats and insults. The allegedly desperate sense of need for more room in which to disperse the growing slave population is contradicted by both the ever-increasing price of slaves and the several years of agitation by various secessionists for the reopening of the foreign slave trade. In fact, several fire-eaters considered the right to import more slaves one of the blessings to be gained through secession.

Rhett's *Mercury* also insisted that the use of African slaves in the gold and silver mines could turn New Mexico and Arizona into slave states, and the possibility that slavery could be applied to mining has also been suggested by a few historians. That black slaves could have worked in mines is obvious. Whether slave mining could have resisted the new technology that rather quickly replaced the forty-niners and Bret Harte's denizens of Roaring Camp is another question. Even if they had so desired, the mine owners were never numerous or powerful enough to have created western slave states in the face of the white opposition such an effort would have generated. Neither gold and silver rushes nor corporation mining, American style, really offered much hope for a plantation-style slave labor system, and the planters knew it. Rhett pointed to the successful use of slaves in Brazilian and Spanish-American mines as proof of its viability, but this was hardly a model for the perpetuation of an institution which in fact had long since been abolished throughout Latin America except in Brazil, Puerto Rico, and Cuba, and was on its way out in Brazil, where only very light reins were still being applied and legal emancipation for individual slaves was very easy.

Black labor would later mine Southern and Kansas coal, but only a small portion of the total black population would be so employed. These facts are quite irrelevant to the question of how long Southern slavery would have endured and whether it could have been expanded. Aside from the lack of realism in Rhett's suggestions, no evidence indicates that many Southerners took them seriously as a solution to the region's overall problems.

In his discussion of the proslavery argument, Morrow touches only lightly on a theme developed much more fully by Charles Sellers: that the defenders of slavery were actually less concerned with convincing the dissenters than with maintaining their own self-assurance. In a skilled psychological analysis, Sellers points out that Southerners glorified the ideals of the Declaration of Independence and the teachings of Christianity, and found the task of harmonizing slavery with this ideology a difficult intellectual and emotional process. In this view, the inner tensions generated by self-doubt produced the bombast and irrational thinking that ultimately led to secession.[7]

The status of other people's consciences may be logically surmised and illustrated by what they say and do, but it can never be fully proven. Wounded feelings and angry responses to constant moral condemnation and personal insults from others, however, can be seen and weighed. From Calhoun in the 1830s through Yancey and the radicals of 1861, virtually every Southern radical spokesman had demanded that the Northern states compel their citizens to stop speaking and agitating against slavery. Southern anger that Northerners would dare call slavery "immoral," "sinful," "barbarous," "cruel," or "un-Christian" runs like a litany through the Southern complaints, almost as though repeating the hated words would help alleviate their sting. For many Southerners, being "held up to ridicule and contempt, to scorn and execration, in every conceivable mode and on every possible occasion" was more than enough reason for separation.[8] And if the terrible weight of world opinion against slavery did make Southerners doubt their own rhetoric, the gap between North and South had to become more unbridgeable. No people are easier to hate than those who make us think less of ourselves.

Moderate Southerners had argued for years that the abolitionists spoke for only a small minority, but in 1860 an overwhelming majority of the Northern people had expressed the final insult by voting for a president who said slavery was evil. Lincoln's eloquent disclaimers of aggressive intent were irrelevant. Proud Southerners could not accept the authority of a president who considered them guilty of committing, supporting, or tolerating a crime against humanity. In many speeches, Lincoln in fact had tried to emphasize both hatred for the sin and sympathy for the sinners, but on the printed page even the sympathy read like condescension. For politicians, editors, ministers, and other opinion-makers of the deep South, Lincoln personified all the accusations of the most extreme abolitionist rhetoric. "Lincoln's triumph," announced *The New Orleans Bee* on December 10, 1860, "is simply the practical manifestation of the popular dogma in the free States that slavery is a crime in the sight of God, to be reprobated by all honest citizens, and to be warred against by the combined moral influence and political power of the Government. The South, in the eyes of the North, is degraded and unworthy, because of the institution of servitude."[9]

Secession, however, offered a way out. An independent Southern nation could become a great, powerful, prosperous, humane empire based on slavery, and thereby prove to the hated Yankees, to the world, and to the Southerners themselves that slavery really was a boon to mankind. Only through secession did the South have a chance to make the self-righteous, hateful, and threatening New England abolitionists and the patronizing, condescending Lincoln-type Republicans eat their words. As Robert Barnwell Rhett, the "Father of Secession," put it, the historian of the year 2000 would write of the Southerners that "extending their empire across this continent to the Pacific, and down through Mexico to the other side of the great gulf, and over the isles of the sea, they established an empire and wrought out a civilization which has never been equalled or surpassed—a civilization teeming with orators, poets, philosophers, statesmen, and historians equal to those of Greece and Rome—and presented to the world the glorious spectacle of a free, prosperous, and illustrious people."[10] In the age of Manifest Destiny, this magnificent challenge and glorious dream was natural enough for an aristocracy steeped in romanticism, and secession was the necessary first step.

The three-fourths or more of the Southern white population who owned no slaves were reasonably immune to guilt and far less sensitive to Northern criticisms, but their support was necessary for any successful separation. Among these people, however, remained the racial and economic fears that had made slavery possible in the first place. Since the first unhappy, frightened, and frightening-looking Africans had come ashore at Jamestown in 1619, the slave-owners had had no difficulty persuading most nonslaveholding whites to accept black slavery as an alternative to racial competition, conflict, and miscegenation. Constant reminders of the Haitian revolt, various slave rebellions both real and imagined, and the recent John Brown exploit had easily negated the impact of *The Impending Crisis* on the small number of less-wealthy whites who might have had a chance to read it. The 1860 presidential campaign, with its hysterical rumors and charges of rebellions, murders, well-poisonings, arson plots, and invasions, had stirred up the fears of the nonslaveholders as much if not more than those of the more sophisticated planters.

The racial fears and prejudices that made secession and the Civil War possible came naturally enough to people whose white skins were a major social premium and who knew the slaves only through the generalities about them expressed by the masters. The same feelings, after all, existed also throughout the North where the blacks could not be logically defined as a threat to anyone. Fear, prejudice, and bigotry are natural human instincts, which under many circumstances do not have to be taught and can be countered only by the most strenuous intellectual and moral efforts. Without racism both slavery and the Civil War would have been impossible in the United States of 1861, and the ensuing frightful death and carnage should forever be cited as the price paid by Americans for allowing it to dominate their reasoning and shape their conduct.

Secession was a snowballing process, as South Carolina immediately sent commissioners to help the radicals in the other states, and each state that seceded added its voice to the pressures on those not yet converted. By February 1, 1861, seven states had withdrawn.

In Mississippi, Louisiana, and Florida, the secessionists completely dominated the conventions, although the votes for delegates were close in a number of Mississippi counties and Louisiana parishes. In Alabama and Georgia, where Douglas had campaigned, the Unionists made a respectable showing. Secession passed in Alabama by 61 to 39 delegates. The total vote in Georgia was 50,000 for secession delegates and 37,000 for the Unionists, although the secessionists won a big majority of actual seats. Noted Georgians like Alexander H. Stephens and Herschel Johnson fought for the Union until the final vote. In Texas, Sam Houston had resisted the disunionists successfully for years until the advent of John Brown. In 1861 the convention voted 166 to 8 for secession. Texas alone among the seceders allowed the people to vote on the ordinance, and almost a third of the votes supported the Union. When it is remembered that throughout most of the nineteenth century the votes were cast in full view of the public, the courage of the 13,020 Texans who stood by Houston and the Union is remarkable. In the elections for convention delegates, a large portion of the electorate in every state declined to vote.

The convention elections revealed several facts that might have been expected. Secession sentiment was strongest wherever the proportion of slaves to the total population was highest and usually wherever the owners held the largest numbers of slaves per capita. It was weakest where the blacks were fewer and where the people tended to be poorer. Except in a few cases, the variations were rather slight, however, and the areas where slaves were held in larger numbers per owners obviously contained a great many nonslaveholding whites. The statistics actually shed little light on the motivations of the seceders, although they do help identify them more specifically.[11]

Ironically, the seceders were also aided by a drought, which helped produce a sudden economic depression. The Unionists in state after state pointed out correctly that the unrest stirred up by the seceders had depressed cotton prices and closed down the cotton markets by drying up the usual flow of Northern capital. Too many

Southerners, however, preferred to blame their hardships on the North and accept the radical argument that secession would solve their problems.

The other eight slaveholding states rejected secession firmly until after Lincoln's call for troops to suppress their neighbors, and four of them ultimately remained neutral or pro-Union. Thus, while large numbers of the people in these states undoubtedly shared the feelings and motivations of the seceders from the beginning, a majority of both leaders and people in North Carolina, Arkansas, Tennessee, and Virginia turned to secession only after a new situation was created. In North Carolina's election of delegates to its secession convention, fifty-two counties chose Unionists while only thirty elected secessionists, and the people by a narrow vote rejected the convention itself. Even the new convention that followed Fort Sumter and Lincoln's call for troops accepted secession by only 66 to 49. In Arkansas, also, secession had no chance until after Fort Sumter. Unionists won the popular vote and dominated the convention until the Union call for troops brought a reversal. The people of Tennessee voted against holding any secession convention at all, and only after Fort Sumter did the legislature pass a secession ordinance, which the people then approved. East Tennessee in effect refused to secede at all, and has continued to elect Republicans to Congress ever since. And finally, Virginia, which had voted for Bell and would provide most of the battlefields, voted overwhelmingly for Unionist delegates. The convention opposed secession, but also agreed that coercion was unacceptable and that Virginia would join her sisters if all peaceful efforts failed. After Fort Sumter, the people of Virginia ratified a secession ordinance by 125,950 to 20,373.

Meanwhile, in Delaware the legislature rejected all invitations to join the Confederacy, and Fort Sumter left hardly a ripple. In Missouri the late Senator Thomas Hart Benton had for ten years kept his enemies busy denying that they were disunionists, and Missourians therefore had never really been exposed to the idea of disunion as a viable alternative. In 1860 Bell and Douglas together received 70.8 percent of the popular vote, and Douglas carried the state. The vote for convention delegates was 110,000 for the Unionists and only 30,000 for the radicals. The convention voted 89 to 1 for a resolution that no reason for separation existed and 73 to 20 against an amendment calling for Missouri to go with the South if the other border states should secede. A sizeable proportion of Missouri ultimately cooperated with the South after Fort Sumter, but the state as a whole remained loyal.

Kentucky, the birthplace of both Lincoln and Jefferson Davis, and the home of the great peacemaking compromisers, Henry Clay and John J. Crittenden, held no convention. Its legislature, 60.1 percent of whom were slaveholders, appealed to the South to stay in the Union. After Fort Sumter, Governor Magoffin flatly rejected Lincoln's call for troops. The legislature supported the governor unanimously, but also voted to remain neutral.

Maryland, a critical border state because of its location north of Washington, never got a chance to vote for secession. Governor Thomas H. Hicks, who had been elected as a Know-Nothing, refused to call the legislature into session until after Fort Sumter. A pitched battle between Massachusetts troops and citizens from Baltimore forced the governor's hand and, incidentally, gave Maryland its bloodthirsty state anthem, which is sung to the loveliest and gentlest of tunes. The governor transferred the legislature's meeting to Frederick, where the lawmakers voted almost unanimously to appropriate $500,000 for the defense of Baltimore against federal troops. Union soldiers, however, simply occupied the state and arrested thirty secessionist legislators. The state provided soldiers for both armies in about equal numbers. Obviously, if there had been a majority sentiment for secession in the months before Fort Sumter, the governor could not have held back the tide.

The history of the states that seceded only after Fort Sumter or did not secede at all raises obvious questions. These states were losing most of the slaves who escaped, were most vulnerable to abolitionist propaganda and agents, were the likely points of invasion for any future John Browns, and presumably had as great a stake as their neighbors in the expansion of slavery. Virginia in particular depended upon the sale of slaves southward to make the institution profitable. Why, then, did they apparently feel at least reasonably secure against the Northern threats being cited so passionately by the states less exposed?

One explanation more apparent than real is the closer economic interdependence the border states supposedly shared with the North. The seceding states in fact were closely tied economically to their alleged enemies. Even though on the average in the years from 1856 to 1860 the cotton states exported about 88 percent of their crop abroad, the 12 percent sold to the Northeastern states was a major factor in their prosperity. In 1860 American mills consumed 422,703,000 pounds of cotton valued at more than $45,000,000.[12]

Also, most of the cotton sent to Europe was hauled first in smaller ships to New York, where Northern agents arranged for its reshipment and marketing in Europe. Southerners complained constantly about the profits thus made by the Yankees, but they never made any serious efforts to replace the service with their own facilities. The role of Northern bankers in financing the planters' operations was equally vital and was never more apparent than during the economic hardships that accompanied the secession process.

The border and upper Southern states differed from the lower South at just the points most vital to secession. They had fewer slaves and therefore fewer fears about the catastrophic social possibilities of emancipation. Emigration to free states and free territories was easier, and nonslaveholders were therefore far less sensitive to arguments that emancipation would produce an exodus of the wealthy and leave them to become white minorities in black societies. The larger the slaveholdings of the border-state planter, the more likely he was to be a secessionist, which possibly indicates a greater susceptibility to both guilt and anger over the moral condemnation symbolized by the election of Lincoln. Also, of course, the border-state citizen, whether slaveholder or not, was more likely to know at firsthand the racial prejudice of his Northern neighbors, to recognize the small minority status of the abolitionists, to have relatives and friends in the Northern states, and to understand the basic community of interests shared by all. Neither the politicians nor the newspaper editors of the upper South had yet been subjected to the social, economic, and physical threats by which the xenophobic societies farther South had crushed any and all who might dare to deny the essential wickedness and dangers posed by the Republican party. Lincoln, after all, had received several thousand votes in the border states, including 2,300 in Maryland, 1,900 in Virginia, 1,300 in Kentucky, and 17,000 in Missouri, while no citizen of South Carolina, Mississippi, or Alabama would have dared stand in front of his neighbors and ask for a Republican ballot. Indeed, none would have been available if he had asked. The initial reaction of the press in the upper South to secession was anger. Knowing that any war to come would likely be fought on their soil, most editors in Virginia, Kentucky, Tennessee, and Missouri protested bitterly that their neighbors had no right to take such actions without consultation with those states most exposed.

Whatever the definitive explanation, if one exists, those slaveholding states most subject to the reasons given by their neighbors for secession refused to secede until after Fort Sumter or did not separate at all. They were, however, much less vulnerable to the more subtle psychological stresses, fears, and resentments afflicting their neighbors to the South, and their proximity to the alleged enemy made him seem far less threatening than the hateful monster visualized by South Carolina.

13

★★★★★

THE PEACEMAKERS

To James Buchanan the eruption of secession during his administration was indeed a cruel stroke. As he reminded everyone who listened, he had been warning since the 1830s that Northern encroachments on the South would finally produce this result. The timing of the action must have seemed terribly unfair. The Southerners knew that he had long been their faithful ally, and their unwillingness to wait for Lincoln was most ungrateful. The baffling new situation confronted him with a terrible conflict of loyalties and attachments, but he would approach it with his usual strong determination, dogged stubbornness, and confused insight.

All of the Southern members of the cabinet stayed in office until events within their respective states or special circumstances forced their withdrawal. All brought every conceivable pressure of friendship and sentiment to bear on the president. Cobb resigned on December 8 after Buchanan had publicly denied the right of secession, but the others remained much longer to wield a pro-Southern influence and keep the Southern leaders informed of Buchanan's feelings and decisions. South Carolina did not actually secede until December 20; ending with Texas on February 1, the other seceders followed suit one at a time throughout January. Their representatives and senators remained in Congress up to and in some cases even beyond the secession of their states. Many of them participated in debates, served on peace-seeking committees, and in general did all they could to block the achievement of any kind of compromise. They also tried with might and main to influence the president with persuasion, requests, and demands. Jefferson Davis was still trying to negotiate with Buchanan for Southern advantages even after he was inaugurated as Confederate president. On January 27, the day after his home state of Louisiana seceded, John Slidell wrote Buchanan a curt note asking if the president had been responsible for relieving Major Beauregard from his post as superintendent of the military academy at West Point. Beauregard, who was Slidell's brother-in-law, would soon command the initial Southern assault on Fort Sumter, but Buchanan was still reluctant to rebuff a friend. There was no alternative, however. As Secretary of War Holt, who had replaced Floyd, put it: "We have heard this crack of the overseer's whip over our heads long enough. This is an outrage—it is one that Senator Slidell has no right to address you."[1]

"With every sentiment of personal friendship and regard," Buchanan wrote Slidell, "I am obliged to say . . . that I have full confidence in the Secretary of War; and his acts, in the line of his duty, are my own acts, for which I am responsible."[2]

Ultimately, the Southerners who were angry at Buchanan's refusal to accept the legality of secession, the Northerners who thought he should have used force against it, and a few associates who were anxious to escape their own records of "softness" toward the South created a most unflattering portrait of the president in crisis. They remembered him as being utterly distraught, tearful, hysterical, and generally almost beyond control of his emotions and actions. However, his cabinet members, both Northern and Southern, remembered him in no such light. He met with them almost daily in long, often agonizing sessions, and while he occasionally vacillated on details and disappointed and angered some of them with specific decisions, most of them later recalled that he had always appeared firm and energetic. His biographers have agreed that the sheer volume of his paperwork, letters, and consultations required enormous energies, which no person in less than full command of himself could have managed. He continued a fairly active social life. He found time to write a charming letter of advice to a young lady about to be married, and was at her wedding reception on December 21 when an alarming commotion turned out to be the jubilant shouts of Lawrence Keitt, who had just learned of South Carolina's formal secession. Keitt, a recent bridegroom himself, would later die in battle for the cause that had inspired his joy. Only the day before, the president had written a friend that he had "never enjoyed better health or a more tranquil spirit than during the past year. All our troubles have not cost me an hour's sleep or a meal's victuals, though I trust I have a just sense of my high responsibility. I weigh well and prayerfully what course I ought to adopt, and adhere to it steadily, leaving the result to Providence."³ The president clearly was not quite as serene as he pretended, but he did have the advantage of a clear conscience and an invincible faith in his own rectitude. He would go to his grave without ever betraying the slightest awareness of any possible mistake that he might have made.

The 1860 election had hardly been tabulated when the secession procedures began in most of the Southern states. Two weeks before the election, Buchanan's attention had already been called to the possibility that the Southern states would soon be seizing federal property. The nation was rapidly becoming unglued, and, as in most national crises, most eyes were turned to the White House for guidance. With the growing threat to the federal forts and other national property in the background, the president had to decide upon an overall policy and approach to secession. Was secession constitutional? Did the federal government have the constitutional power to coerce a seceding state back into the Union? If he decided these questions in favor of the seceders, the problem of the forts and federal property would take care of itself. If he decided either question otherwise, the enforcement of the federal laws, the collection of federal taxes, and the retention of the forts and other property would become problems to haunt his dreams, assuming he always slept as well as he had boasted.

At first both president and cabinet were virtually unanimous in their sympathy for the South. On November 18, Pennsylvania Judge George W. Woodward wrote Attorney General Black a long justification for the expected secession and a bitter diatribe against the Republicans who had caused it all. "As a Northern man I cannot in justice condemn the South for withdrawing," wrote Woodward. "I believe they have been loyal to the Union formed by the Constitution—secession is not disloyalty to that, for that no longer exists. The North has extinguished it." Buchanan, Woodward continued, should dissuade them if possible, but if unsuccessful, should "let them go in peace. I wish Pennsylvania could go with them. They are our brethren. . . . We are the wrong doers. We have driven them off and if we raise an arm to strike the 'stones of Rome will move to mutiny.' "⁴

Black considered the letter admirable and read it to the president and cabinet together, where "It excited universal admiration and approbation for its eloquence and its truth. . . . They wanted to publish it very much." Black, however, believed that it exaggerated the abolition danger, and advised against publication unless Woodward revised this part of the letter.[5]

According to Black, all the cabinet agreed fully with Woodward's letter and the Southerners were ecstatic. They may or may not have also been influenced by the views of Horace Greeley, the Republican party's own best-known editor, whose *New York Tribune* insisted until after Fort Sumter that the Southern states had "a clear moral right" to separate and form their own nation. Buchanan himself later blamed Greeley for thus encouraging the Southern radicals. Soon, however, an overwhelming majority of the Northern press began to evince a more belligerent attitude against secession, and Black and Cass began to have second thoughts as to what Buchanan's actual policies should be.

As Americans everywhere waited for the president's annual message to Congress, Buchanan agonized over what to say. He conferred almost daily with his cabinet and often with various Southern friends like senators Mason, Hunter, Slidell, and Jefferson Davis. As usual he managed to avoid all contact with Republicans, free-soil Democrats, or anyone else willing to discuss the irritations, grievances, and fears being felt by the North. He considered a presidential call for a national convention, but the cabinet persuaded him to recommend this step to Congress. Had he possessed more charisma and a more dramatic style, he might have commanded the spotlight with an eloquent appeal to both sides, but it was probably too late for this under any circumstances. Also, anything he said would be filtered to the people through the editors of intensely partisan local newspapers. Many of these would have supported his appeal. Probably even more would have misrepresented it. He has often been condemned for keeping the Southerners in his cabinet despite their obvious feelings of sectional allegiance. Supposedly, their dismissal would have strengthened the Southern Unionists, but this result is by no means certain. The Southern cabinet members were all highly influential at home, and with them at his side the president could at least try to influence them for the Union. Perhaps more serious was his tolerance for editor William E. Browne, who openly advocated and defended secession in the *Constitution*, a paper subsidized by administration patronage and generally considered to be the president's own organ. Buchanan, with regret, finally broke publicly with the editor's viewpoints, but did not cut off the patronage until the end of January, 1861.

In late November, Yancey and Keitt stated publicly that the

president supported secession, but at the White House Buchanan assured a group of secessionists that this was false. He announced that he would deny and oppose any right of secession, but he did agree that they had suffered greatly at the hands of the North. He promised that he would "appeal to the North for justice to the South," and at least one listener remembered that he added a promise to be "with them" if this justice should be denied.

In cabinet meetings Cass, Black, and Toucey agreed that the president could not acknowledge any right of secession. Cobb, Thompson, and Floyd considered secession a basic right of any state, although Thompson and Floyd for the moment expressed opposition to it. Groping for legal authority or perhaps for a constitutional prohibition against exercising it, the harried Buchanan turned to Black, his official legal officer. Demanding definitive answers rather than general advice, Buchanan asked what powers he had to collect duties and imports where the laws were being resisted, what right he had to defend public property if it should be attacked, and what legal actions he could take to execute laws usually administered through federal courts? And finally, could he use military force against a state where no judges, marshals, or other civilian federal officers existed?

Black's answer solved no problems. The president, he said, had a clear duty and right to collect the duties, defend public property, and execute the laws. The military act of 1795 had authorized the calling of the militia "whenever the laws of the United States shall be opposed . . . by any State, by combinations too powerful to be suppressed by the ordinary course of judicial proceedings." The president would have to decide for himself when such a condition existed. Black added, however, that troops could be used with equal justice against those Northern states that had defied the Fugitive Slave Act. At this point, after all, South Carolina was still merely talking, and had not yet actually defied the federal government.[6]

Despite Black's later reputation as the administration's strong arm against secession, his views were essentially conservative. He warned that the American system had always depended upon law enforcement by the courts only, except in cases of extreme necessity. If the revenues could not be collected by normal peaceful means, Congress would have to legislate any new procedures. The government could preserve itself with force against a "direct and positive aggression upon its property or its officers," but it could not make "an offensive war, to punish the people for the political misdeeds of their State Government." While the Government could enforce the decrees of its courts on individuals, any coercive enforcement against united opposition in a state would be to make war upon them and expel the state.[7] No one in Buchanan's cabinet really wanted to fight a war for the Union, and until much later none of his advisers were even ready to accept war as an alternative to a permanent separation.

To Jacob Thompson, Howell Cobb, and other Southerners, the right to defend federal property or enforce the law upon individuals meant the right of coercion against a seceded state. It also bore directly upon the question of the federal forts. Thompson immediately challenged Black and persuaded Buchanan to review the Constitutional Convention records for light on the subject. After much contemplation and prayer the president agreed with Thompson that the founding fathers had never intended to confer any such powers against individual citizens of a seceded state.

Buchanan's annual message on December 3, 1860, was presented and widely publicized before any state had actually seceded, although most of the federal officials and judges in South Carolina had already resigned. Unfortunately, it was hardly well designed to discourage secession. As always, the president ignored completely the Northern side of the argument. Since the Mexican War, at least, a multitude of Northerners had come to consider the Southern complaints and demands as part of a gigantic Slave-Power conspiracy to spread the blighting institution and gain control of the nation. Northeasterners had long resented the Southern role in blocking tariffs, and Northwesterners blamed the slaveocracy for their failure to get homesteads and internal improvements. Northerners everywhere had long chafed under the domination of Southern and pro-Southern presidents, Southern cabinets, a Southern-dominated Senate, and a Southern-minded Supreme Court. Southern leaders had never comprehended the fact that much of the Northern enmity they resented so bitterly was a normal response to their own words and actions. They had long needed a president who would at least try to make them understand this, but such a challenge, unfortunately, was also beyond the comprehension of James Buchanan.

The South needed reassurances but not a presidential endorsement for the wildest arguments of the Southern radicals. Buchanan, however, blamed the crisis entirely upon the "long continued and intemperate interference of the Northern people with the question of slavery." The danger, he said, did not "proceed solely from the claim on the part of Congress or the territorial legislatures to exclude slavery from the Territories, nor from the efforts of different States to defeat the execution of the fugitive slave law." These could have been endured, but "the incessant and violent agitation of the slavery question" had "produced its malign influence on the slaves, and inspired them with vague notions of freedom. Hence a sense of security no longer exists. . . . Many a matron throughout the South retires at night in dread of what may befall herself and her children before the morning." Self preservation was the first law of nature, and "no political union, however fraught with blessings and benefits" could endure "if the necessary consequence be to render the homes and firesides of nearly half the parties to it habitually and hopelessly insecure. Sooner or later the bonds of such a Union must be severed." Reviewing the last twenty-five years of "inflammatory appeals," Buchanan found the solution obvious: "How easy would it be for the American people to settle the slavery question forever, and to restore peace and harmony to this distracted country! They, and they alone, can do it. All that is necessary to accomplish the object, and all for which the slave States have ever contended, is to be let alone and permitted to manage their domestic institutions in their own way."[8]

Having thus agreed with the truth of the South's announced reasons for secession, Buchanan then argued that the South was in no real danger from either the election or administration of Lincoln, and should wait for some "overt and dangerous act" before resorting to secession. The president, said Buchanan reassuringly, could execute, but not make the laws, and no Congress, except in the case of the Missouri Compromise, had ever passed any laws impairing slave rights. No such law would be possible in either the present or the next Congress, and the South should follow the precept of "Him who spake . . . that 'sufficient unto the day is the evil thereof.' "[9]

Having made this wise appeal, the president could not resist returning to his original theme of Southern wrongs. The Supreme Court, he said, had ruled that a territorial legislature could not bar slavery, but there were those who would give such a legislature the "power to annul the sacred rights of property." Neither Congress nor any state, except in the act of framing or amending its constitution, had any such power, and the contrary doctrine "from its intrinsic unsoundness" could not survive or justify a dissolution of the Union.[10]

True, he continued, many Northern states had openly defied the Fugitive Slave Act, but all courts, both state and national, except that of Wisconsin, which had been reversed by higher authority, had upheld its constitutionality. Surely the incoming president would enforce it, and the South should wait until some overt act proved otherwise. If, however, the state legislatures did not "repeal their unconstitutional and obnoxious enactments" promptly, no human power could save the Union. "In that event, the injured States, after having first used all peaceful and constitutional means to obtain redress, would be justified in revolutionary resistance to the government of the Union."[11]

Unfortunately for Buchanan's hopes, no Northern state was going to repeal its personal-liberty laws, and the Southerners knew it. By declaring the salvation of the Union dependent upon such an action, Buchanan was only strengthening the hand of the secessionists.

After admitting that certain grievances would justify secession, Buchanan then insisted that secession was unconstitutional. The founding fathers had never intended any such right, and the principle had been clearly "refuted by the conclusive arguments of General Jackson" in 1833. The Union "was intended to be perpetual and not to be annulled at the pleasure of any one of the conflicting parties." Also, the "solemn sanction of religion" had been added by requiring the officers of the federal and state governments alike to take an oath to support the constitution.[12]

The president's rather brilliant constitutional analysis was tempered, however, by a paragraph that appeared to justify the right of secession as long as it was called revolution instead of an inherent constitutional right. The "right of resistance on the part of the governed against the oppression of their governments" existed "independently of all constitutions" and was "embodied in strong and express language in our own Declaration of Independence. But the distinction must ever be observed that this is revolution against an established government, and not a voluntary secession from it by virtue of an inherent constitutional right."[13]

Meanwhile, said Buchanan, the president must obey his oath of office, but how and to what extent? The machinery for enforcing federal laws in South Carolina had already disappeared, and only Congress could amend existing laws to restore federal authority in that state. He did not expect anyone to try to expel the United States from its property by force, but if this should happen, the commanding officer had orders "to act strictly on the defensive" and the "responsibility for consequences would rightfully rest upon the heads of the assailants." The federal government, Buchanan insisted, had no power either to recognize secession or to coerce any state to remain in the Union. The Constitution delegated no such power to either the president or Congress. Madison, himself, had said, "The use of force against a State would look more like a declaration of war than an infliction of punishment, and would probably be considered by the party attacked as a dissolution of all previous compacts by which it might be bound."[14]

The president, however, did have a practical recommendation beyond his injunction against the Northern states to stop attacking slavery and to enforce the Fugitive Slave Laws. To ease the resentments and fears of the cotton states and expose them to universal condemnation if they seceded despite adequate Northern concessions, the Congress should call a constitutional convention or ask the states to call one. Such a convention should pass a constitutional amendment that would recognize the right of property in slaves in the states where it existed or might hereafter exist. It should emphasize the duty of the federal government to protect this right in all the territories throughout their territorial existence, reconfirm the right of masters to have escaped slaves returned, and declare all Northern state laws hindering this process to be null and void.

Again poor Buchanan was on the same worn-out track that had elected Abraham Lincoln in the first place. John Breckinridge, running on a platform that only stated the protective duty of the federal government toward territorial slavery in vague terms, had received almost no Northern votes, and had not even won a popular majority in the slaveholding states. Federal protection for slavery in territories whose people were opposed to the institution violated a basic precept of democracy and was the equivalent of a public announcement that slavery was moral and righteous. By voting overwhelmingly for Lincoln and Douglas the North had made clear that no such amendment would ever be considered.

Thus the president defended the Southerners' own excuses for secession, denied them any such right, announced his unwillingness to coerce them, and declared that secession could be prevented only by concessions that every Southerner knew would never be made. The impact of his message on the secession conventions cannot be measured, but it could not have helped the Unionists in either the South or the North. Northerners were infuriated by his indictments and his arguments against coercion. His message was just another evidence that Southerners were ruling the country, and it probably made most Northerners less rather than more receptive to compromise proposals. Southerners, on the other hand, found their radical arguments vindicated, but were angered by his refusal to admit the right of secession.

To his credit, however, Buchanan showed a greater awareness of the bloodshed and mass suffering a civil war would bring than did either Abraham Lincoln or Jefferson Davis. Through his Southern associations and sympathies he understood the depth of Southern anger, pride, fears, determination, and courage. As a Northerner and Union lover he also knew the blood, treasure, and power the North could and would expend for the Union if a military confrontation occurred. When Lincoln and Davis ultimately put their faith in war, each apparently expected only a quick, easy victory, but James Buchanan had no such illusions. He hoped the border states could be kept from seceding and prayed that peace could be maintained until the erring sisters recognized their mistake and rejoined the nation voluntarily. In late December when the New York bankers were reluctant to float a badly needed government loan for fear the money would find its way south, Buchanan protested that even if the cotton states should secede, the remaining states would still have "all the elements of wealth and prosperity." He continued that "this great and enterprising brave nation" was "not to be destroyed by losing the cotton States even if this loss were irreparable, which I do not believe, unless from some unhappy accident."[15]

In Congress, the Union-lovers and peace-seekers began their final desperate efforts. On December 18, two days before South Carolina actually seceded, the Senate established a Committee of Thirteen to deal with the crisis, and vice-president and recent candidate John Breckinridge selected the members.[16] Chairman John J. Crittenden, his Kentucky colleague Larazus Powell, and R. M. T. Hunter represented the border South. Jefferson Davis and Robert Toombs of Georgia spoke for the lower South. The Northern Democrats were Douglas, William Bigler of Pennsylvania, and Henry Rice of Minnesota. The five Republicans were Seward, Jacob Collamer of Vermont, the radical Benjamin F. Wade from Ohio, ex-Democrat and moderate James Doolittle of Wisconsin, and James W. Grimes of Iowa. The committee was the Senate in microcosm. A majority were moderates, but the radicals on both sides would dominate. Unfortunately, the president had almost no influence left with either the committee members or the Senate itself. Seward and Doolittle were the Republican voices of compromise, but all the Republicans as well as the Southern radicals ultimately took their cues from president-elect Lincoln in Springfield, Illinois.

Crittenden was well-suited for the peacemaking mantle of his late friend and Kentucky colleague Henry Clay, but Clay had never faced a committee or a Senate in which only principles and virtually no concrete issues were at stake. Crittenden's reputation for fairness was universal. In the famous Kentucky court struggle of the 1820s, the young Crittenden had served as attorney for one claimant to the court clerkship after signing the bond for his client's opponent, Francis P. Blair, on the basis of personal friendship. Conflict of interest was not even mentioned and Crittenden won his case. He had opposed both the Mexican War and the Kansas-Nebraska Act without losing any significant support in Kentucky. Eventually two of his sons would serve as major generals on opposite sides in the Civil War.

On the same day the Crittenden committee was appointed, Andrew Johnson of Tennessee warned his fellow Southerners bluntly that a civil war would mean the end of slavery, and Crittenden proposed six new amendments for the United States Constitution. He would extend the old Missouri Compromise line of 36°30′ to the Pacific Ocean and prohibit slavery north of the line, while granting federal protection to slavery in all territories south of it. All future states would be admitted with or without slavery, according to their own choice. Congress should be forbidden to abolish slavery in any place of national jurisdiction within a slave state. There should be no abolition in the District of Columbia as long as either Virginia or Maryland had slavery, or without the consent of the people of the District or without compensation. There should be no federal interference with the interstate transportation of slaves. Congress should have the power to reimburse the owners of fugitives rescued by force with money to be collected from the county in which the rescue occurred. And finally, there should never be any future tampering with those parts of the Constitution that shielded and protected slavery.

As a practical matter, the 36°30′ proposal, the pledge regarding slavery in the District, and compensation for escapees were the only concessions that did not already exist. Of these, the first soon dominated the others, the second was not considered important, and the third was clearly impossible. The only remaining territory south of 36°30′ was New Mexico, which after twelve years of popular sovereignty had a slave code and twenty-two slaves, ten of them in transit. As both Crittenden and his opponents understood well, however, the approval for slavery implied in these propositions was the bait being offered the South.

Jefferson Davis, who had already reached the point of no return and was unamenable to any concessions, moved that no proposals should be reported to the Senate unless they were supported by a majority of both the Republican and Democratic members of the Committee. This meant that a nine to four approval could be vetoed by four Southerners and a ten to three vote could be nullified by three Republicans. He and Toombs were clearly not looking for a compromise. Toombs demanded constitutional amendments for the recognition and protection of slavery in all territories, the surrender of all fugitive slaves without habeas corpus or a jury trial, the prohibition of any law pertaining to slavery without the consent of a majority of the slave states, and a final proposition that none of the foregoing or any other constitutional provisions related to slavery except provisions on the African slave trade could be changed without the unanimous consent of all the slave states. To these inflammatory ultimata, Davis added a proposal to put slave property on the same footing with all other property and exempt it from impairment by the local laws of any state or any enactment by a territory or by the United States.

As usual, Douglas tried to appease both sections and offered a plan to keep the status of each existing territory unchanged until its population reached 50,000, at which point it could become a state with its own choice on slavery. Also, however, the United States could make no further territorial acquisitions without the consent of two-thirds of each house of Congress. With regard to fugitive slaves, the domestic slave trade, and slavery in the district, he echoed Crittenden; but he would also deny the vote and office holding to all blacks, and he proposed that land might be acquired at federal expense for colonizing Negroes.

Only the Crittenden plan received serious attention. Hundreds of letters and petitions promised that the states would ratify it. In New York City, 63,000 signed a petition. Another petition had 14,000 women signers. St. Louis sent 100 pages of names wrapped in an American flag. Greeley, among other prominent editors, believed that a large majority of the public favored it, and President James Buchanan thought it the ultimate in reasonableness. Without the support of those states already involved in the exhilarating process of secession and new-nation building, however, no compromise could do more than hold the border states, and barring violence these states were likely to remain loyal anyhow.

The moderate Republicans on the committee waited for word from Seward, who was in touch with Lincoln and was slated to be the next secretary of state. The New Yorker was personally inclined toward conciliation, but his views were somewhat contradictory. He feared that concessions might encourage rather than discourage secession, but he also knew that too much firmness would generate an equally dangerous sense of exasperation in the South. He resolved the problem by doing what was almost necessary for him in any case. He simply followed the wishes of the president-elect. Soon his friend Thurlow Weed was en route to Springfield for definitive instructions.

Like everyone else, Lincoln was somewhat confused and was being bombarded by conflicting advice.[17] The Northeastern big business community feared both the loss of some $150,000,000 in long-term notes owed by Southerners and a decline of the business connections that had been profitable for so many years. Men like Belmont, Barlow, Astor, and Vanderbilt were busy with their own empires and were unconcerned with the status of territorial slavery. Republicans and Democrats alike in this group were pressuring both Congress and the president-elect for concessions to the South, and Weed had already publicly advocated the Crittenden proposals. In response, however, the more radical Republicans were showering Lincoln with warnings and pleas to stand firm against the slaveocracy. In his New York *Evening Post* William Cullen Bryant sounded the tocsin against any "plan manufactured in Wall Street." The feelings of the average Northerner were not recorded, but his later response to Fort Sumter indicates that he was neither alarmed about Wall Street's finances nor looking southward with any great sympathy.

Lincoln's first public announcement came on November 20 in a speech by Illinois Senator Lyman Trumbull to a "Grand Republican Jubilee." Lincoln informed the press that his own views would be in the address. In the two paragraphs he wrote for Trumbull, the president-elect again promised that with the Republicans in power all states would have "perfect liberty to choose, and employ, their own means of protecting property, and preserving peace and order within their respective limits." In fact, he continued, the disunionists were "in hot haste to get out of the Union, precisely because they perceive they can not, much longer, maintain apprehension among the Southern people that their homes, and firesides, and lives, are to be endangered by the action of the Federal Government." With his usual shrewdness, Lincoln probably had diagnosed correctly one reason for the haste of the fire-eaters. In a second paragraph, however, which Trumbull wisely omitted, he indicated a woeful misjudgment. He was "glad of this military preparation in the South," which would "enable the people the more easily to suppress any uprisings there, which their misrepresentations of purpose may have encouraged." Trumbull also pledged that Lincoln would be "President of the whole country" and would "protect the constitutional rights of the lower South, where he received no votes, as resolutely as he will defend the North which elected him." Slavery would not be bothered, but if the seceders should assail the constituted authorities of the Union, Americans would have but one sentiment: " 'The Union, it must and shall be preserved,' and woe to the traitors who are marshalled against it."[18]

These sentiments were highly praised throughout the North, but most Southern editorials denounced them as meaningless for not spelling out the specific Southern rights Lincoln was promising to defend. Also, the radical Republican press thought him entirely too gentle. As various historians have pointed out, the South had the problem of the boy who had cried "Wolf!" once too often. Its radical spokesmen had gained concessions so often by threatening secession that most Northerners, including Lincoln, did not take them entirely seriously and were tired of appeasing them.

Some Northern papers, including the influential *Chicago Tribune*, treated the secession threat almost as a joke. They cited the strong vote for Bell as evidence of strong unionism and ignored numerous reports that the Bell followers were rapidly becoming secessionists. Former Congressman Long John Wentworth in the *Chicago Democrat* taunted the Southerners with the prediction that they would "eat dirt" and "back out." Able only to "bully, and brag, and bluster," he charged, they were "wonderful hands at bragging and telling fantastical lies, but when it comes to action, count them out." Lincoln quickly announced that Wentworth spoke only for himself.[19]

The public reaction to the Trumbull speech convinced Lincoln that he should say no more, despite a continuing swell of demands for a more definitive statement. The *Boston Courier* and its followers, he complained, were citing the speech as a betrayal of Republican principles, while the Washington *Constitution* was describing the speech as "an open declaration of war against the South." He ultimately became certain that no compromise would change the South. Either it would secede and would have to be resisted, or the whole matter, as he continued to hope, would prove to be a bluff. He knew that he was no threat to slavery where it existed, and he refused to believe that the South was not equally aware of his sentiments. He was also constantly besieged with letters and visitors urging him to accept no compromise. Representative Gilmer of North Carolina, a member of the House committee that was the counterpart of the Crittenden Committee in the Senate, wrote Lincoln an eloquent plea for a statement to help the Southern Unionists. The president-elect replied that he could not "shift the ground" upon which he had been elected. A new letter would make him "appear as if I repented for the crime of having been elected, and was anxious to apologize and beg forgiveness." He added page references to the Lincoln-Douglas debates where Gilmer could find reassurance that slavery would be safe in his administration.[20]

Despite his public reticence, the position of the president-elect was in fact very clear from personal statements, letters, and the views of the editors and friends in constant touch with him. He would not even consider a right of secession and would not "entertain any proposition for dissolution or dismemberment." Neither he nor his administration would touch slavery where it existed, and he would enforce the Fugitive Slave Laws. But on the question of giving the South a legal right, however useless in practice, to extend slavery he would not compromise. This he considered a moral judgment, which would divide and bring chaos to his party, which would not help the South even if granted, which would not affect the secession process one way or the other, and which he personally could not make.

The abstract moral issue was perhaps revealed most clearly in Lincoln's famous exchange of letters with Alexander H. Stephens. He assured Stephens that the South had no more reason to fear any tampering with slavery than it had in the days of Washington, but he realized that more was involved: "You think slavery is *right* and ought to be extended; while we think it is *wrong* and ought to be restricted. That I suppose is the rub. It certainly is the only substantial difference between us."[21]

Stephens replied that Southerners really did not fear Lincoln's antislavery opinions any more than they had feared those of Washington and Jefferson. Antislavery views, however, had become public policy, and the South would not permit its beliefs to be put "under the ban of public opinion and national condemnation. This . . . is quite enough of itself to arouse a spirit of general indignation, but of revolt on the part of the proscribed."[22]

Various noted historians of both North and South have agreed with James Buchanan that Lincoln put his party's interest ahead of statesmanship in not throwing his weight behind the Crittenden Compromise. Lincoln, however, was probably correct in his belief that it would be a useless gesture, and his reluctance to violate his own conscience as well as sacrifice his party with a concession that would not be accepted anyhow is entirely understandable. Lincoln wrote:

> We have just carried an election on principles fairly stated to the people. Now we are told in advance, the government shall be broken up, unless we surrender to those we have beaten, before we take the offices. . . . if we surrender, it is the end of us, and of the government. They will repeat the experiment upon us *ad libitum.* A year will not pass, till we shall have to take Cuba as a condition upon which they will stay in the Union. They now have the Constitution . . . and acts of Congress of their own framing, with no prospect of their being changed; and they can never have a more shallow pretext for breaking up the government, or exhorting a compromise, than now.[23]

Clearly, Lincoln believed that a confrontation would have to come before any long-range peace could be attained, and that if he backed away under Southern threats the whole process would have to be repeated later by someone else. He also genuinely believed that an acceptance of popular sovereignty might trigger a wave of Southern filibustering throughout the Caribbean and Central America. On at least one occasion he suggested that no compromise would be workable that did not include a constitutional amendment barring any further territorial expansion. After all, Buchanan was still recommending an invasion of Mexico.

To Weed the president-elect gave his instructions for Seward, who acted accordingly. To the Crittenden Committee, Seward proposed an amendment whereby the Constitution could never be altered to permit congressional interference with slavery, a change in the Fugitive Slave Law to give escapees a jury trial, and a congressional resolution recommending the repeal of all state personal-liberty laws. The Southern members considered the propositions downright insulting. Editor William Browne of the administration-supported Washington *Constitution* wrote that Seward had almost made a disunionist out of Crittenden.

Meanwhile, the committee had already voted on Crittenden's chief proposal. Four Republicans following Lincoln opposed the extension of 36°30'. The Southerners had already said they would not support it unless the Republicans did also, and Davis and

Toombs therefore also voted against it. The measure thus lost by a six to six tie. The closeness of this vote sent the Southern radicals into a new flurry of speed to get their states to secede before some acceptable compromise could be offered.

With his committee dead, the desperate Crittenden on January 3 proposed to the Senate that his compromise be submitted to the whole people for a popular vote. On January 16, the motion to consider his resolutions was defeated 25 to 23, with 6 Southern Democrats not voting and 25 Republicans in opposition. The Republican refusal kept the people North and South from expressing their will, but the actions of the six Southerners helped validate Lincoln's view that the seceders would not be influenced by any such compromise anyhow.

In the House, meanwhile, a committee with a member from each state had been established under the chairmanship of Thomas Corwin, who had once suggested that Mexico should welcome American soldiers with "bloody hands and hospitable graves." Corwin was a dedicated chairman, but the Speaker appointed too many radical Republicans, too many secessionist Democrats, and no Douglas Democrats at all. Weeks of haggling and quarreling produced no significant results. John Sherman of Ohio proposed that all remaining territories immediately become states and settle the slavery question in their constitutional conventions. His plea that disunion would mean war did not persuade the committee even to discuss his idea. Charles Francis Adams and Marylander Henry Winter Davis offered to admit New Mexico, including present-day Arizona, as a state with its own choice on slavery. New Mexico was the only territory left in the United States that might in reality actually become a slave state, and it did in fact have a slave code to accommodate the owners of its twelve resident slaves. Lincoln himself, meanwhile, had relented to the point of writing a letter indicating that he would not oppose New Mexico if it chose slavery, as long as everyone understood that no further concessions would be made. The border states supported this idea with enthusiasm, but the states in the process of seceding refused it as a plot to add another free state. The cotton states thus rejected an offer of the only territory left in the United States where slavery might have had a chance for at least a temporary survival. The committee ultimately found itself lacking a majority for either a report or an adjournment. By 16 to 13 the committee finally authorized the chairman to report all the main proposals with his own opinions on them.[24]

Chairman Corwin reported five propositions to the House. A call for repeal of the personal-liberty laws and a faithful execution of the Fugitive Slave Act passed on February 27 by 137 to 53. A constitutional amendment providing that the Constitution should never be altered to abolish or interfere with the domestic institutions of any state passed on the following day by 133 to 65, and cleared the Senate by 24 to 12. The immediate admission of New Mexico was defeated by 115 to 71, although several Republicans supported it. A proposition to give fugitive slaves jury trials in the states from which they had fled, certainly not calculated to help the slaves, also passed the House by 92 to 83. The House, it must be remembered, had both a Northern and a Republican majority, since those elected in November, 1860, would not take office until December, 1861. The constitutional amendment to bar any future move against slavery received 66 Republican and opposition votes in the House and 9 Republican or opposition votes in the Senate. It had been ratified by Ohio and was being considered by several other states when Fort Sumter was finally attacked.[25] It would have been the thirteenth amendment, and with cooperation the South would easily have received it instead of the thirteenth amendment abolishing slavery forever in 1865.

Grasping at straws, the desperate and unhappy President Buchanan could not understand why Congress would not pass the Crittenden proposals, and as usual he believed that the true will of the Northern people was being thwarted by the radical Republicans. In late December he dispatched General Duff Green to Springfield with a plea for Lincoln to come to Washington and join the president in a plea for a national convention or for a popular referendum on the Crittenden proposals. On December 28, Green wrote that Lincoln agreed that the compromise might temporarily quiet the agitation but also believed that if Southerners got territorial rights south of 36°30′ the quarrel would be renewed by an attempted annexation of Mexico. Lincoln, however, also agreed that the decisions "belonged to the people and States in legislatures and conventions," and he would support "their will thus expressed." The president-elect promised Green a letter to this effect on the following morning but quickly changed his mind. He addressed the letter to Green but sent it to Senator Trumbull in Washington with instructions to deliver it only if six of the twelve senators from Georgia, Alabama, Mississippi, Louisiana, Florida, and Texas would sign a statement pledging their states to suspend all secession efforts until the new administration actually committed some act against their

rights. In the letter Lincoln said that despite his personal objection
to any constitutional amendments he would not oppose a popular
vote because the amending power belonged to the people. Again,
he affirmed the right of every state to control its own domestic institutions and denounced the lawless invasion by armed force of any
state or territory "no matter under what pretext, as the gravest of
crimes." Trumbull and others may have decided that the statement
could not be attained from the Southern senators, or, more likely,
they probably feared that Southerners would interpret Lincoln's
denunciation of activities typical of John Brown as a pledge not to
put down secession by force. Although the letter was neither delivered nor published, Buchanan soon learned of its contents and
did assume from it that his successor would not make war against
the seceders.[26]

Unable to get any support from Lincoln, the president on
January 8 sent a special message to Congress. He described in detail the economic disasters that had befallen both the government
and the country as a result of the civil-war threat. He eloquently
reviewed the great blessings the American Union had bestowed
upon its people. He pointed out that a considerable amount of
federal property had already been seized and that Fort Sumter was
under severe pressure. He insisted that only Congress had the
power and responsibility to find a peaceful solution or to authorize
the use of force to protect federal property. The secession, he
argued, had been caused by a misapprehension in the South of the
true feelings of the Northern majority. If the question could "be
transferred from political assemblies to the ballot-box . . . the people themselves would speedily redress the serious grievances which
the South have suffered," but the Congress must quickly find a "distinct and practical proposition for conciliation." Again Buchanan
had analyzed the sentiments of the Northern electorate as if the
election of 1860 had never occurred at all.[27]

The closest thing to the national convention the President
wanted came when the Virginia legislature invited delegations from
all states interested in peace to convene in Washington. Buchanan
gave the effort all the support he could muster, and the movement
apparently did strengthen the Unionists in the border states.

Busily seceding and forming new governments, the seven states
of the lower South, as well as Arkansas, refused to attend. Michigan, Minnesota, and Wisconsin also declined, and California and
Oregon were too far distant to respond on such short notice. Ultimately, on February 4, 131 delegates from twenty-one states gath-

ered in cold, damp Washington. Ex-President John Tyler became chairman, and various critics pointed out the preponderance of older men no longer influential. Delegates like Lot M. Morrill, Salmon P. Chase, George Boutwell, William P. Fessenden, James Grimes, James Harlan, Reverdy Johnson, and David Dudley Field, however, were clearly men of the future as well as the past.

Despite the eloquent appeals of moderates like Tyler, former Senator William C. Rives of Virginia, former General William Butler and James Guthrie of Kentucky, John Morehead and Thomas Ruffin of North Carolina, Reverdy Johnson of Maryland, William S. Dodge of Connecticut, and Curtis Noyes of New York, the deliberations were quickly dominated by noisy extremists on both sides. Most of the Republicans were implacable free-soilers, and Martin Conway of Kansas demanded immediate emancipation. At the other extreme were James Seddon of Virginia and former Commodore Robert Stockton of New Jersey. Stockton, the primary conqueror of California from Mexico, had evolved into a pro-Southern radical. The followers of Seddon and Stockton would accept nothing short of a complete acquiescence to Southern demands that even the Northern moderates could not approve.

On February 7 Tyler led the delegates to the White House for an official call on the president. According to Vermont delegate Levi Chittenden, who later published a record of the convention, the Northern delegates were hoping for evidence that the president was ready to curb the secession and suppress treason. Buchanan, however, was concerned only for concession and compromise. He embraced each delegate and with tears in his eyes begged them to save the country from a bloody fratricidal war. He offered no condemnation or even criticism for disunion, secession, or treason. He clearly considered the South a deeply injured party to whom the North owed apologies and pledges for better conduct in the future.

According to Chittenden, the visit convinced the Northern delegates that the president would not oppose the South in any way and that they must stand firm for the Union. As he had done so often, Buchanan had made the Northerners more rather than less determined to resist what they considered the threat of Southern aggressions. Later on the same day most of the Republican delegates adopted a resolution to delay or prevent any action by the convention not previously approved by a Republican caucus.[28] Henceforth the Republican delegates voted almost as a unit, and the positions were usually determined by the more radical members.

Sixteen days and many bitter arguments later, the delegates

held a reception for President-elect Lincoln. When asked point-blank about his policies toward slavery, Lincoln reassured his listeners that he would preserve, protect, defend, and enforce the Constitution equally in all parts of the country. The moderates of both sections were enormously encouraged for different reasons. Lincoln had made clear his tolerance for slavery where it already existed, while standing firm on the Chicago platform and for the preservation of the Union. The Southern radicals stalked out while he was still speaking. They wanted no concessions that would discourage secession, and they were even more adamant against the implication that disunion would be prevented by coercion if necessary.[29]

The convention had been doomed from the beginning, but radical Senator Zachary Chandler of Michigan was unwilling to take any chances. After wiring the Michigan governor to send delegates, Chandler wrote, "I hope you will send *stiff-backed* men or none. . . . without a little bloodletting, this Union will not, in my estimation, be worth a rush."[30] Soon published, Chandler's letter hurt the peacemaking effort more than any radical delegates who might have been sent. The Peace Convention finally agreed to resolutions similar to the already-rejected Crittenden Compromise. A Senate committee voted them down by twenty-eight to seven. The House would not even consider them.

Thus all attempts at compromise failed. The incumbent president, who prayed daily for their success, was powerless to do anything except add to the irritation of Northern sensibilities already raw from many of his own earlier policies. The president-elect, who did have great influence, would grant no concession that implied a moral approval of slavery, however meaningless the concession might be in terms of practical policy. He believed that a crisis had to be reached and passed. The South had to learn once and for all that a Republican administration would not interfere with slavery in the South, that slavery could be expanded no farther, and that the Union could not be divided. With these questions settled, thought Lincoln, the North and the South could live together in peace and let the future take care of slavery in its present domain. Having triggered the crisis by winning the 1860 election, Lincoln would not shirk his responsibility to see it through. He would preserve the Union regardless of price, and unlike Buchanan he would give the Constitution only a passing nod if it should interfere with his efforts.

Allan Nevins and others have criticized James Buchanan for not ignoring Congress and calling a national convention on his own immediately after the 1860 election. The president's historical reputation as a dynamic peace-seeker might have been thereby enhanced, but the practical results would probably have made no difference. Two top-level congressional committees, the ad hoc Peace Convention called by Virginia, and the Congress as a whole labored long but unsuccessfully to find a basis for agreement. Each of these bodies simply reflected contradictory viewpoints that divided the nation, and there is little evidence that a national convention would have been any different. The delegates to such a convention would have stood by the views of their constituencies— as did the other groups striving for a peaceful settlement. Most of the nation's leaders wanted both Union and peace, but few were willing to compromise any basic principles to prevent either secession or war. A majority of the people in each section felt the same way, and an additional convention for the airing of their views would not have changed their minds. Southerners wanted an open expression of approval for slavery in the form of territorial protection granted by the North, and they insisted further upon a Northern suppression of all antislavery ideas. Despite the widespread racist attitudes toward blacks throughout the North, and in fact partly because of such feelings, most Northerners resented even the implication that they should make any such concessions. Nothing the North could offer would keep the lower South from seceding, and nothing would induce Abraham Lincoln to allow the Union to be divided. Neither James Buchanan nor a national convention could change these facts in 1861.

The president, however, could make his successor's goal far more difficult or he could leave him with a situation uniquely designed to place the burden for commencing hostilities squarely upon the South. If Buchanan gave up Fort Sumter peacefully, Lincoln's problems would be compounded. Numerous editorials, letters, and speeches indicate that any such surrender by Buchanan would have triggered a massive wave of Northern anger. Whether the fury would have equalled that caused later by the actual military attack and whether the animosity, which would have been leveled as much at Buchanan as at the South, would have lasted long enough to sustain Lincoln's ultimate call for all-out military action are different questions. The constant pressures by his Southern friends on Buchanan to abandon the forts peacefully indicate how strongly they wished to present Lincoln with a *fait accompli*. The president-elect was equally aware of the situation. Hearing a rumor that Buchanan had decided to capitulate, Lincoln said that if this were true the president should be hanged. Only strong persuasion by friends and advisers kept the Rail-splitter from announcing publicly that he would retake the forts if they should be abandoned, and he did send General Winfield Scott a message to that effect.

Buchanan's final efforts to achieve compromise through concessions to the South were all made within the context of his almost daily confrontation with the problem of the forts. The issue almost wrecked his cabinet, did drive some of its members out, and cost him, at least temporarily, most of the Southern friendships he had enjoyed for a lifetime. It was the only issue during his administration on which his head triumphed over his heart.

14

★★★★★

THE ORDEAL

In late October, 1860, a week before the national election, the president was astounded by a letter to Secretary of War Floyd from General Winfield Scott, commander in chief of the United States Army. Scott's long, erratic career had included some questionable strategy against the Seminole Indians, competent diplomacy in a crisis with the Canadians over the Maine boundary, controversial but successful leadership in the Mexican War, and a crushing defeat for the presidency in 1852 after years of angling for a nomination. A huge, impressive looking man of six feet, five inches, he was seventy-four in 1860, and had become so enormously fat that mounting his over-burdened horse required the assistance of several aides. He had never been endowed with keen political judgment, and his "Views" of October, 1860, indicated no sudden improvement. Citing Paley's *Moral and Political Philosophy*, in which Buchanan could find no relevance to the matter being discussed, Scott advised that while states had the right to secede, the federal government could "reestablish by force, if necessary, its former continuity of territory" against "an *interior* State or States." Thus, peripheral states had the right to secede, and force could be used by the federal government only against a seceded state that blocked the way to another state that had chosen to remain in the Union. A broken Union, continued Scott, could be reunited only by a horrible civil war, and a lesser evil would be to allow the nation to form itself into as many as four new confederacies. The general even suggested the boundaries and capitals for the four new nations to be thus created.

Having spelled out a highly permissive doctrine, Scott then suggested that "from a knowledge of our Southern population" he feared a seizure of some of the federal forts in the South even before secession. He strongly recommended that nine forts be immediately "garrisoned as to make any attempt to take any one of them by surprise or *coup de main* ridiculous." And finally, after suggesting this dynamic policy, Scott pointed out that only five companies, totalling four hundred men, were available for the task.[1]

As Buchanan well knew, the entire army numbered only sixteen thousand men, and most of these were busy protecting settlers on the vast western frontier. He considered a call for volunteers at this point to be both unconstitutional and unwise, and feared correctly that any transfer of troops from the west to the Southern forts would strengthen rather than retard the secession movement. Also, to scatter four hundred men among nine forts would be a demonstration of weakness rather than strength, and would very likely reassure as well as incite the secession forces. The president's memoirs are the source for analyzing his thoughts in late 1860, but there is little reason to doubt the accuracy of his memory. He also believed that Scott's "Views" were immediately relayed southward by Floyd to give aid and comfort to the radicals. In January, 1861, Scott contributed openly to the secession debate by publishing his treatise. As commander in chief of the armed services, James Buchanan, like most American presidents, was ill informed on military strategy and potential and was heavily dependent upon his professional advisers. In most matters, General Winfield Scott was a frail reed.

Scott, however, had put his finger squarely on the issue where a war for the Union or a peaceful secession would be decided, and Buchanan knew it. Except for those in the west, the federal forts in peacetime were virtually unmanned except for a handful of maintenance personnel. They were usually held on the basis of contract with or a conditional cession from the states in which they were located. Since an independent South Carolina would no longer use the forts to defend the United States, the Carolinians argued from the beginning of secession that their state's original grants were no longer valid. Whatever the legal aspects, a peaceful transfer with compensation could be easily arranged if the North should take Greeley's advice and let the erring sisters depart in peace. To the Southerners, therefore, the forts were a barometer to be anxiously watched as an indicator of Northern intentions. If the Union would give them up or if they could be taken without inciting a war, a peaceful secession would be a reality. If the Union chose to retain them, the forts could become a handy fuse if either or both presidents should decide that war would serve a useful purpose.

The most obvious percussion caps were the three Charleston installations, Fort Moultrie, Castle Pinckney, and the still unfinished Fort Sumter. In their existing state they were no danger to Charleston and of no great value to the United States. In federal hands they were a hated symbol of Yankee power; but if the Carolinians should choose to attack them, they could not be defended without massive naval support from the Union. If the Carolinians would permit a token Union force to remain in the forts indefinitely, no explosion would occur, the border states would remain in the Union, and peaceful efforts to win back the others could continue. A Southern attack, as Buchanan well knew, could bring Northern public opinion immediately up to the point of an all-out war.

On the day after Lincoln's election, Colonel John L. Gardner, in command at Charleston, tried to transfer some ammunition from the city arsenal to Fort Moultrie, but an angry crowd prevented the move. Floyd and Buchanan quickly decided to replace Gardner with Major Robert Anderson, who was of Kentucky birth and Virginia ancestry, and whose wife was a Georgian. Anderson was friendly to slavery and presumably would handle the situation with tact and understanding.

Anderson, however, was first of all a Unionist and a military professional determined to do his job. He was fifty-six, and his long career included genuinely heroic deeds in the Mexican War. He began calling for reinforcements as soon as he reached Charleston, and argued that making the forts invulnerable to attack would be the best way to prevent bloodshed. He wanted at least two companies for Fort Sumter and Castle Pinckney and reinforcements with ordnance stores and technicians for Fort Moultrie. Cass and Black insisted that the troops should be sent, while Cobb, Thompson, and Assistant Secretary of State William H. Trescot, a Charleston native, vehemently protested. Buchanan finally ordered them sent, but Secretary Floyd persuaded him to wait for a conference with General Scott before taking the final action. Scott was ill and delayed coming to Washington, and during the interim the harried president made an agreement. Cobb, Trescot, and Thompson promised for Governor Gist of South Carolina that Charleston would not take the forts. In return Buchanan revoked his order sending the reinforcements.

At no time, however, did Buchanan ever indicate any willingness to abandon the forts.[2] They were federal property and could not be taken legally under either the right of secession, which he opposed, or the right of revolution, which he defended. The same constitutional scruples that denied him the right to coerce the seceding states also denied him the right to bow to Southern demands for the evacuation of Charleston harbor. His feelings may have been related in part to the same regard for the sanctity of property ownership that he was constantly expressing in defense of the slaveowners. His resolve, furthermore, could not have been immune to the force of public opinion. The Northern press, including papers that had long been pro-Southern, and almost all other ascertainable Northern opinion were angrily opposed to any suggestion that the forts would not be held, and Buchanan had always had a strong instinct for personal and political survival. He was concerned for his future place in history, and he would soon be retiring to an estate in Pennsylvania. Secretary of War Floyd later remembered that as early as November 7, 1860, the president had warned that if the South Carolina forts were lost " 'in consequence of our neglect to put them in defensible condition, it were better for you and me both to be thrown into the Potomac with millstones tied about our necks.' "[3]

Fort Pickens, near Pensacola, Florida, posed a problem similar to that of the Charleston forts, but with one major difference. It was located just outside the harbor, and could be reinforced from the sea without danger from shore batteries. At Charleston, however, Castle Pinckney, usually inhabited by a single ordnance sergeant, was on a small island near the city docks. Fort Johnson and Fort Moultrie were on tips of land about three miles apart, which formed the entrance to the harbor. Both were part of the mainland and could easily be put under siege or stormed and taken. Fort Johnson was actually an abandoned barracks and hospital area rather than a fort. Moultrie, with some seventy-five men, was the best equipped of the installations. Fort Sumter, a brick pentagon only fifty feet high on a rock no bigger than the fort itself, was located in the harbor channel almost midway between Forts Moultrie and Johnson. Any ships trying to reinforce Sumter would be highly vulnerable to shore batteries, as was the fort itself. The shore batteries themselves, however, would be equally clear targets for heavily armed warships if the federal government should decide to use them.

The distance between Washington and Charleston, and the lack of instant, direct communications between the forts and Washington added to the uncertainty. Neither the civilian telegraph service nor the mails provided real privacy, and neither the War Department nor Anderson risked many telegrams. Neither was ever completely certain of the other's intentions and plans. Anderson's most startling move caught Washington entirely by surprise, and Buchanan's one effort to send reinforcements was equally unexpected by Anderson.

Until his resignation on December 20, Assistant Secretary of State Trescot actually represented Governor Gist of South Carolina in the White House, and afterwards he continued as an official envoy to whom Buchanan's doors were always open. When Floyd assured Trescot that he would cut off his right arm before he would sign any order strengthening the forts, Trescot promptly relayed this word to Gist. Gist replied through Trescot that all would remain quiet until passage of the secession ordinance if no more troops were sent, but warned that he would use the state's full military power to prevent any reinforcements. Buchanan responded by sending Trescot to South Carolina with a copy of his annual message. He apparently hoped in vain that the message and his forbearance toward Sumter might persuade South Carolina to postpone secession until the inauguration of Lincoln.

Through the early weeks of December, Anderson sent more warnings of danger. State troops were drilling in Charleston and openly boasting that they would take Fort Moultrie. Anderson had ordered repairs on Castle Pinckney, and to protect the workmen there and at Moultrie he requested a hundred muskets with ammunition from the Charleston arsenal. Colonel Huger at the arsenal refused to issue the arms without a direct order from the War Department, and wrote Floyd for instructions. The Huger letter reached Washington on December 6 and quickly became common knowledge. Floyd denied Anderson's request and informed Huger that authority to supply arms to the forts would be temporarily deferred.

At this point Floyd sent Major Don Carlos Buell to Charleston to explain the situation to Anderson. A few days later Anderson and Buell composed a set of orders for Anderson, which Floyd himself signed. Anderson was to avoid any act that might "needlessly tend to provoke aggression." He was to hold the forts, however, and if attacked was to defend himself "to the last extremity." Also, vitally important, Anderson was given an option. Since he lacked the troops to defend more than one of the three forts, "an attack on, or an attempt to take possession of, either of them will be regarded as an act of hostility, and you may then put your command into either of them which you deem most proper. . . . You are also authorized to take similar defensive steps whenever you have tangible evidence of a design to proceed to a hostile act." Buchanan later approved these orders, but modified them to relieve Anderson of any obligation to fight to the death.[4]

December 8 was a hard day for the president. Howell Cobb, the friend and subordinate whom Buchanan loved most, resigned. Cobb knew that his home state of Georgia would probably secede, and though he had been a Unionist throughout the 1850s he was now ready to work for secession. He was completely open and honest, and he and Buchanan parted on the best of terms with profound mutual regret. On the same day the South Carolina congressional delegation headed by Lawrence Keitt and Porcher Miles came to the White House with a proposal. Their state would not bother the Charleston forts pending "an offer . . . through an accredited representative to negotiate for an amicable arrangement of all matters between the State and the Federal Government, provided that no reinforcements shall be sent into these forts, and their relative military status remain as at present."[5] Buchanan asked them to put any communications in writing, and on December 10 the proposition was formally submitted.

Buchanan wrote on the document that he had objected to the word "provided" because it "might be construed into an agreement on my part which I never would make." The president noted further that two of the men called again and repeated that the forts would not be molested until after commissioners appointed by South Carolina should "treat with the Federal Government in relation to the public property. I informed them that what would be done was a question for Congress and not for the Executive." Buchanan wrote that any attack on the forts "would put them completely in the wrong, and making them the authors of the civil war." He did, however, point out that under existing circumstances he had no plan to strengthen the forts.[6] As might have been expected, the Carolinians, after years of considering Buchanan their friend and supporter, left the White House believing that he had promised not to change anything in Charleston harbor.

On December 12 the president's burdens continued to mount. General Scott finally arrived from New York and the aged secretary of state, Lewis Cass, resigned in a letter protesting Buchanan's refusal to send troops to Charleston. The irritated president noted that only two weeks earlier Cass had argued that Buchanan's message to Congress was *"not sufficiently strong against the power of*

Congress to make war upon a State for the purpose of compelling her to remain in the Union; & the denial of this power was made more emphatic & distinct upon his own suggestion." Accepting the resignation, Buchanan stated their differences clearly: "The Secretaries of War and of the Navy, through whom the orders must have issued to reinforce the forts, did not concur in your views . . . . believing as I do that no present necessity exists for resort to force for the protection of the public property, it was impossible for me to have risked a collision of arms in the harbor of Charleston, and thereby defeated the reasonable hopes which I cherish of the final triumph of the Constitution and the Union."[7]

The resignation brought a storm of public criticism against Buchanan and made Cass momentarily the hero of the hour. Northern editors everywhere denounced the president as though he had actually abandoned the forts. This was most unfair, but quite understandable. The president who had instigated and supported the Dred Scott decision, had declared Kansas as much a slave state as Georgia, had alienated the Northern wing of his party, and only recently had echoed the South's most angry complaints could not possibly have escaped suspicion under the circumstances. The Northerners in his cabinet, including Cass and Black, had been equally pro-Southern, and Cass had simply seized an opportunity for a public recantation at the expense of his chief. Two days later, on December 15, Cass sent word through Jacob Thompson that he had changed his mind and would like to rejoin the cabinet. The public damage had been done, however, and the angry Buchanan felt only that he was well rid of an officer whose duties had been largely performed by others anyhow. He would later refuse a request from a magazine for a sketch of Cass.

Buchanan promptly moved Black into the State Department and promoted Assistant Attorney General Edwin M. Stanton to attorney general. Earlier Joseph Holt of Kentucky had replaced Aaron Brown as postmaster general. Black, Stanton, and Holt became the strong antisecession, pro-Union warhawks in the cabinet. All three had supported the Dred Scott decision and advocated the election of Breckinridge in 1860, but all three could also see the wave of the future.

Stanton was a moody, quarrelsome, and often rude individual with various afflictions and peculiarities. He had once lost a brother to suicide, and had roamed the woods in wild grief until he had to be captured. On another occasion he returned home to find that a young lady for whom he felt great affection had died of cholera and

173

had been promptly buried in the course of the day. Unwilling to accept the tragedy, Stanton dug up the body to make certain she was dead. When his first wife died in 1844, he almost went insane. He had her buried in her wedding dress and stayed by the grave for a month. His first-born child, a daughter, died in infancy and was buried for a time, but the tortured father later rescued the little casket from the grave and kept it on his bedroom mantlepiece for several years. He also suffered from constant asthma. Stanton would later prove a personal burden for presidents Lincoln and Johnson, and his conduct immediately prior to Lincoln's assassination was so erratic that some historians have suggested his possible involvement in the murder. No hard evidence has ever been mustered to support such a contention, and no valid motive can be adduced, but the mere fact of the suspicion indicates the impact of Stanton on his associates. Buchanan rarely found his presence congenial.[8]

Holt was an equally bizarre personality. He had emerged from boyhood poverty through the patronage of the eminent Kentucky attorney Robert Wickliffe, who had taken him into his family and trained him in the law. Holt had also married Wickliffe's niece. The Wickliffe family later charged, however, that Holt was primarily responsible for the five months' imprisonment of Robert Wickliffe's two young grandchildren who had refused to take the oath of allegiance to the Union at a Northern boarding school. An older Wickliffe grandson who served in the Confederate Army wrote later that Holt had taught him that "South Carolina was the true school of political faith, that the States were sovereign and the Federal Government subordinate and dissoluble, and that the time would soon come, the sooner the better, when the same battle with the same final result, would be waged between the Cavalier of the South and the hated Puritan of the North." The angry soldier charged that Holt's cruelty to the family of his benefactor and wife was an effort to escape his earlier pro-Southern reputation.[9] Whatever the reasons, Holt was a Southern secessionist until 1859, but experienced such a sharp conversion that his reputation for vindictiveness toward Southerners would continue through reconstruction. Like Stanton he was morose and disagreeable, and his obvious animosity against the South occasionally weakened his influence with the president. In later years, however, he spoke and wrote of James Buchanan with great respect.

Philip Thomas, a Marylander who had replaced Cobb at the Treasury Department, was a moderate Southerner who wielded little influence. He would later resign under a trivial pretext and join the Confederacy.

Some historians have given Black, Holt, and Stanton all the credit for Buchanan's refusal to abandon Fort Sumter, but the president himself indicated no great respect and certainly no affection for either Stanton or Holt. He did usually listen to Black, but the position he followed on Fort Sumter was probably influenced far more by Northern public opinion than by any of his cabinet. Every hint of weakness brought a storm of public abuse. Every show of defiance toward South Carolina brought momentary praise. Fortunately, James Buchanan was not isolated from the public; and, while he often misread its views, the message on Fort Sumter was consistently loud and clear.

On the day he accepted the resignation of Cass, the president conferred with General Scott, from whom he had heard nothing since the celebrated "Views" suggesting both a reinforcement of the forts and a peaceful division of the Union into four new nations. Scott had been in touch with Lincoln through Senator Lyman Trumbull, who was convinced that Buchanan would surrender the forts. Almost as a test, the general urged the president to send three hundred men to Fort Moultrie. Buchanan refused for the same reasons given Cass. He had already sent orders to Anderson. Congress was just beginning to discuss the Crittenden and other compromise proposals, and no state had yet actually seceded. Anderson and his men were still being treated kindly in Charleston, and it was no time to commit a warlike act. Later in the day Scott sent a note reminding the president of Jackson's success in squelching the South Carolina nullification in 1833.

Two years later, in a celebrated feud, the general charged that the president had refused to send reinforcements because he was waiting for a South Carolina commission to negotiate about secession and the disputed property. Scott also wrote that Buchanan had said he would leave it all up to Congress. He would send reinforcements and order Anderson to hold out only if Congress decided against secession. Buchanan and his biographers have denied the Scott version with considerable logic.[10] Buchanan had already given Anderson his orders. He had not agreed to negotiate with the Southerners about anything, and when a commission did arrive, he refused to receive it. On the other hand, a general anxious to erase his own earlier position of "softness" toward secession did have documentary ammunition against his old chief. Buchanan did state clearly on numerous occasions that the Congress and not the executive should decide on the proper response to secession, and his friendly biographers have always argued that he might have done more at Fort Sumter if Congress had granted his requests for more authority and military power. Also, he probably did tell Scott that a South Carolina commission would be sent—a fact that was common knowledge throughout Washington. And finally, Buchanan did hope that such a commission, even though he himself could not accept it, might work out a peaceful settlement with the Congress. Thus, as in the case of the resignation of Cass, Buchanan was innocent but vulnerable.

Public reaction to the Cass affair was quickly heightened a few days later when the Mississippi government directed Secretary of the Interior Jacob Thompson to visit North Carolina and discuss secession. Thompson asked for Buchanan's approval and offered to resign if the president objected. Still fond of both Thompson and the beautiful Kate, Buchanan accepted Thompson's version of why he was going and approved the venture. The president was reading Northern sentiment correctly on the forts, but he was still obtuse on many facets of the crisis. He did believe that Thompson would try to keep North Carolina from seceding, and Thompson did argue in North Carolina that secession should come only after some extreme provocation, which had not yet occurred; but approving the mission was a serious political error. Alongside the secessionist editorials of William Browne in the administration newspaper, Thompson's journey convinced people all through the North that Buchanan was a secessionist. Lincoln was swamped with letters denouncing the president as a traitor, and Greeley in the New York *Tribune* ran a headline calling him insane.

Just before South Carolina formally seceded, Buchanan sent Caleb Cushing to Charleston with a final plea to their Southern friends to wait until the North had time to react to the president's annual message. The gesture was futile. Even as the final speeches were shaking the air, another incident infuriated the people of Charleston. Captain Foster, in charge of construction at Castle Pinckney and Fort Sumter, feared for the safety of his workmen, and requisitioned forty muskets from the federal arsenal. South Carolina gunboats began a twenty-four hour patrol around Sumter, and angry street crowds demanded the surrender of the forts. Governor Pickens agreed. On December 20, the day of secession, a special messenger handed James Buchanan a blunt note from Governor Pickens demanding the immediate delivery of Fort Sumter to South Carolina.

Secretary Floyd cooled the situation by ordering the return of the muskets, but Governor Pickens had gone too far with his letter. Trescot noted Buchanan's indignant reaction and rushed off to find the South Carolina members of Congress. The letter was a clear violation of the earlier pledges by the delegation, and would release the president from any obligation, real or implied, against sending reinforcements. Later in the evening Trescot reported back to Buchanan that the Carolina delegation had wired Pickens a request to withdraw the letter.

Buchanan had already written his answer, which he now did not have to send, but which made his views clear. Only Congress, he wrote, could decide on relations between the federal government and South Carolina, and he had no power to recognize the dissolution of the Union or surrender Fort Sumter to anyone. He did not say so, but he appeared to imply that if Congress should agree to cede the forts he would acquiesce in the decision. He added, however, that an attack would make South Carolina an assailant in a war against the United States: "It will not then be a question of coercing a State to remain in the Union, to which I am utterly opposed . . . but it will be a question of voluntarily precipitating a conflict of arms on her part, without even consulting the only authorities which possess the power to act upon the subject."[11]

Having formally seceded on December 20, South Carolina began to erect shore batteries to threaten the forts and dispatched three commissioners to Washington to negotiate.

December 22 was another terrible day for James Buchanan. A new cabinet scandal suddenly exploded in the War Department. Several months earlier the Covode Committee in Congress had given the Republicans a powerful array of political ammunition based upon the incompetence of Secretary of War John Floyd, but Buchanan apparently had never even considered asking for his resignation. Even earlier Floyd had been writing acceptances for Russell, Majors, and Waddell to cover the government's debts for their services during the Mormon crisis. In effect, Floyd was making the War Department responsible for money not yet appropriated by Congress. Buchanan had long since ordered Floyd to stop doing this, but the secretary had foolishly disobeyed his chief. Far worse, Floyd's relative Godard Bailey, who worked in the office of Interior Secretary Thompson, had been trying to help Floyd by giving Russell negotiable bonds held in trust for the Indians by the Interior Department. No proof ever surfaced to indicate that either Bailey or Floyd profited from the transaction, but Russell managed to swap

Floyd's acceptances for some $870,000 worth of bonds. Secretary Thompson knew nothing of it, and Floyd angrily pleaded ignorance also. When the bonds came on the market, the press pictured a gigantic theft in which the government was being looted by potential rebels. One paper even claimed that Riggs and Company, Buchanan's bankers, had bought six of the bonds for the president himself.

Even after this blow, the soft-hearted Buchanan was reluctant to discharge Floyd and asked Black to suggest that he should resign. Black refused, but Vice-President Breckinridge carried the word. Floyd, however, indignantly refused to resign, and Buchanan decided not to discharge him on Christmas day. The Virginian had also made another serious tactical error, either carelessly as usual or perhaps with intent. On December 20 he had ordered his ordnance chief to send a shipment of heavy guns from the Pittsburgh armory to some unfinished forts in Texas.

As Floyd licked his wounds on Christmas day, Senator Wigfall of Texas took the occasion to suggest that the Southerners should kidnap Buchanan and make Breckinridge president. Floyd indignantly refused, and at least two of Buchanan's biographers have credited the secretary with great virtue for declining to cooperate with such an insane proposal. Just when he reported the threat to his chief is not clear, but Wigfall remained in the Senate until March.

On December 26 the cabinet met with a full agenda. Thompson furiously denounced Floyd and threatened to prosecute everyone, including Floyd, connected with the bond affair. Black too had a complaint. He and Holt had received numerous angry telegrams from Pittsburgh citizens about the impending shipment of cannon to the Texas forts. Buchanan promptly cancelled the order, and Floyd, already beginning to look for a reason to resign more honorable than the threat of prosecution, took the action as a personal insult. The president's chief concern was the expected South Carolina commission. The cabinet finally agreed that he should receive the commissioners, but only as "private gentlemen." Trescot scheduled a procedural meeting for December 27.

On the morning of December 27, however, more dramatic news arrived from South Carolina. Under cover of darkness, Major Anderson had spiked the cannon and destroyed the gun mounts at Fort Moultrie, and had moved his forces into the more defensible Fort Sumter. The South Carolina commissioners promptly cancelled their meeting with the president, while the angry Trescot hurried to Floyd's office and got a promise that the secretary would order Anderson back into Fort Moultrie. Floyd telegraphed Anderson that he could not believe this action had been taken, because no such command had been given. Anderson quickly answered: "The telegram is correct."

As messages began to fly back and forth, the Southern leaders hurried to the White House. Jefferson Davis arrived first to denounce Buchanan and warn that he was now "surrounded by blood and dishonor on all sides."

According to Trescot, the distraught president answered: "I call God to witness, you gentlemen more than anybody *know* that this is not only without but against my orders. It is against my policy."[12] Hunter, Lane, Yulee, and even John Slidell called to condemn, cajole, and threaten. Buchanan must order Anderson back to Moultrie or face a civil war. The president was again confused and tortured by conflicting emotions. He made no commitments, and his visitors left not knowing what he would do. Neither did he.

In the afternoon the cabinet convened and argued far into the night. Black, Holt, and Stanton defended Anderson and insisted that he had only followed the president's orders. Floyd, who had opposed secession until his disgrace from the bond scandal, loudly argued that Anderson had violated the president's earlier pledges and announced that he would resign unless the president immediately withdraw Anderson's command from Fort Sumter. Black angrily produced the latest presidential orders to Anderson, written in Black's own hand and signed by Floyd himself only a week earlier. Waving the orders in Floyd's face, Black warned that "There never was a moment in the history of England when a minister of the Crown could have proposed to surrender a military post which might be defended, *without bringing his head to the block.*" Floyd's rage was almost uncontrollable, but the president had finally run out of patience with both Floyd and his own Southern friends from Congress. The orders, he announced, justified Anderson's move, and he would not order a return to the more vulnerable Fort Moultrie.[13]

Floyd promptly resigned, having substituted a conflict on principle for a discharge based on shameful conduct. His formal letter was filled with compliments and friendship for Buchanan, but for once the president did not answer in kind. During the Civil War, General Scott charged that Floyd had in fact done much to arm the South, but a congressional investigation decided that most of the armaments transferred southward in 1859 had been condemned as "unfit for the public service," that the total numbers had been exaggerated, and that the arms had been transferred by routine decisions involving storage facilities. The artillery ordered from Pittsburgh to Texas in December, 1860, might have been more useful to the South, and this step had been taken after the secession process had begun. Floyd's record for carelessness and maladministration was such, however, that even this effort, stopped by Black and Holt, was probably innocent. Without any of Scott's charges, however, Floyd must still be considered one of the weakest and least competent cabinet officers in American history. That he remained in office almost to the end of Buchanan's term was no credit to the president's administrative ability.

Before the South Carolina commissioners came to the White House on December 28, their government had vindicated Anderson by seizing Fort Moultrie, Castle Pinckney, the United States Post Office, and the Customhouse, but this apparently enhanced rather than diminished the arrogance of the commissioners. Their interview with the president lasted two hours. They announced that they would not negotiate unless all federal troops were removed from Charleston. Buchanan, who had already declared his own objections to any official negotiations, flatly refused their demand, but again referred them to Congress. "You are pressing me too importunately," he complained. ". . . you don't give me time to say my prayers. I always say my prayers when required to act upon any great State affair."[14] The Carolinians withdrew and composed an insulting written answer for the following morning. Solemn pledges, they wrote, had been violated. South Carolina had erred in trusting Buchanan's "honor rather than its own power," and bloodshed was inevitable unless the troops were withdrawn.

With Thomas and Thompson now the only Southerners left in the cabinet, the group met on December 29 to frame a reply to the commissioners. Buchanan had already written his own version, which unfortunately has been lost or destroyed, although parts can be reconstructed from the memories and comments of those who read it. Apparently still hoping for a congressional compromise and support from Lincoln for a national convention, he was ready to send Anderson back to Moultrie in return for another pledge by South Carolina that none of the forts would be molested. He was also willing to recommend that Congress deal wth the commissioners. Black, Stanton, and Holt, however, objected strongly. They wanted a vigorous denial that any previous pledges had been made, and opposed any possible intimation that South Carolina, like a foreign state, could be officially represented by diplomatic officers. They also could not approve a statement in which Buchanan expressed his belief that Congress had no constitutional power to coerce a state to remain in the Union. At one point the ever-blunt Stanton avowed that any president who would "make such an order" as sending Anderson back to Fort Moultrie "would be guilty of treason." After a full day of argument, Buchanan finally announced that he would stand by his own version.[15]

This produced a cabinet crisis. Knowing "by experience that when Mr. Buchanan made up his mind he was immovable," Black spent a sleepless night. The following morning was Sunday; and, perhaps while the president was saying his deferred prayers, Black was informing first Toucey and then Stanton that he would resign. Stanton replied that they would go or stay together. Toucey rushed to the White House with the bad news, and Buchanan immediately sent a messenger for Black. "I know," said Black to Stanton, "the sort of appeal he will make to me in the name of our sacred and long standing friendship. To resist will be the most painful duty of my life." Stanton exhorted his colleague to stand firm.[16]

Black had predicted accurately. The harried president gently accused Black of desertion in his hour of need, and pleaded that in this dark moment he needed all his friends. Black responded with equal emotion: "There is no storm of popular indignation I would not breast by your side, no depth of misfortune into which I would not descend provided you had a course to defend. But your answer to the Commissioners leaves you no cause, it sweeps the ground from under our feet, it places you where no man can stand with you, and where you cannot stand alone."[17]

To Black's surprise, Buchanan did not argue. He admitted "the force and justice" of Black's position, repeated that he was only trying to avoid an open rupture for which the Union was militarily unprepared, and concluded: "I cannot part with you. If you go, Holt and Stanton will leave, and I will be in a sorry attitude before the country . . . . Here, take this paper and modify it to suit yourself; but do it before the sun goes down."[18]

The cabinet crisis was over. Black and Stanton listed their objections, and Buchanan rewrote the letter accordingly. Except for the president's refusal to evacuate Fort Sumter, it was highly conciliatory. Only Congress, he repeated, could decide their relations with the federal government, and he could treat them only as private citizens. However, he had hoped "such a disposition might be made of the whole subject by Congress, who alone possess the power, as to prevent the inauguration of a civil war between the parties in regard to the possession of the Federal forts in the harbor of Charleston," and he deeply regretted that in their opinion, "the events of the last twenty-four hours render this impossible." The statement was almost an admission of hope that Congress might give them what the Constitution and his fear of Northern public opinion forbade him to surrender. Anderson, the president wrote, had acted on his own responsibility and without authority unless he had "tangible evidence of a design to proceed to a hostile act." Anderson, however, was a "brave and honorable officer" and "should not be condemned without a fair hearing." His own first impulse, Buchanan insisted, had been to order Anderson back to Moultrie pending evidence of aggressive intent by South Carolina; but before he could do anything, South Carolina had taken Moultrie, Castle Pinckney, the Post Office, and the Customhouse. Now they were demanding that he withdraw all forces from the city, but he could not do so: "Such an idea was never thought of by me in any possible contingency. No allusion had ever been made to it in any communication between myself and any human being." He had now received word that the arsenal had also been seized, and this left him no alternative but to defend Fort Sumter with every means at his disposal. Still, however, he did not see how this could be "construed into a menace against the city of Charleston."[19]

The commissioners' reply of January 2 to Buchanan's letter was so insulting that after Thompson read it to the cabinet the president had a messenger return it as unacceptable. The Carolinians had not come to negotiate anything with Congress, but wanted only assurances that the president in some way would give them the Charleston forts. He had refused this demand over and over, but their hope that he was only trying to capitulate in the least painful way or that he might change his mind was natural enough in the light of his past relations with the South.

Whatever Buchanan's heart might have suggested he do for or about his Southern friends, his head remained fully aware of the state of Northern public opinion. In fact, without his knowledge, Stanton, Daniel Sickles, and others telegraphed various politicians throughout the North to fire salutes, stage public meetings, organize parades, and send telegrams congratulating the president for standing behind Anderson's move. Anderson had become a national hero, and Buchanan knew it. So did the former Southern sympathizers Black, Holt, and Stanton.

On the same day, Trescot again tried to persuade Buchanan to send Anderson back to Fort Moultrie, but both the president and Navy Secretary Toucey pleaded that hauling down the flag at Sumter was impossible with Northern public opinion in such a fury. At Trescot's insistence, Senator Hunter of Virginia suggested to Buchanan that the South Carolina militia might march out of Fort Moultrie if Anderson would march in again. Emerging from the interview, Hunter warned Trescot: "The case is hopeless. The President has changed his ground and will maintain it to the last extremity. Telegraph your people to sink vessels in the entrance of the harbor immediately. They have no time to lose."[20] James Buchanan would have been less than human if he had not resented the constant badgering and name-calling of Southerners whom he had always served so well. Indeed, his former friends may have contributed much to the increasing zeal of his efforts toward Fort Sumter.

On December 30, General Scott wrote another formal letter asking permission to send 250 troops to Fort Sumter with some extra ordnance supplies. He hoped a sloop of war and a cutter could be ordered for their delivery. Next morning Buchanan gave the orders. The sloop of war *Brooklyn* with troops, stores, and provisions was to sail immediately to Fort Sumter. Later in the evening, the president suggested to the general that it might be proper to delay the *Brooklyn* until the South Carolina commissioners answered his letter of the previous day. The delay would be no more than forty-eight hours, and Scott agreed. The unacceptable reply of the commissioners was delivered on January 2. Meanwhile, General Scott himself suggested that the *Brooklyn* might have trouble maneuvering in the Charleston harbor because of her deep draft. Also, her departure would be quickly known. A fast side-wheel steamer might accomplish the mission with greater secrecy and success. Scott would later charge that Buchanan had sabotaged the effort by sending the relatively unarmed *Star of the West* instead of the *Brooklyn*, but this was just another example of the general's bad memory as applied to 1860–1861.[21]

On January 5, 1861, the *Star of the West*, carrying men and supplies discreetly below decks, sailed from New York. On the same day, however, Anderson notified Secretary Holt that he felt entirely secure and needed no assistance, while another observer reported that the Carolinians had erected among the sand hills at the harbor entrance a heavy battery that could sink any unarmed ship trying to enter. Scott immediately sent the *Star of the West* a countermanding order, which reached New York after she had sailed. The *Brooklyn* then sailed from Norfolk in pursuit of the *Star of the West,* and was ordered to lend aid if the other ship should be damaged. If the *Star of the West* could not land, she was to return to Norfolk and discharge her cargo. The orders were signed by Scott. On January 9 the *Star of the West* arrived off Charleston. The shore batteries opened fire, and the ship beat a hasty retreat. The shore batteries were within range of Anderson's guns, but the major had received no warning that the relief ship was coming, and was quite unprepared to start a battle without either orders or an attack upon his own command.[22] The results of this attempt to reinforce Fort Sumter could not have been lost upon President-elect Abraham Lincoln.

The Unionist cabinet members had managed to keep Secretaries Thompson and Thomas in the dark about the expedition. On the day the ship sailed, Thompson had wired friends in South Carolina and Mississippi that no troops had been sent or would be sent while he was in the cabinet. Embarrassed and angry, Thompson felt betrayed and promptly resigned. There had never been any doubt that he would go with Mississippi into secession, but the angry Kate Thompson blamed everything on the president, whose heart was "as black as the man of War Brooklyn. . . . I wish I was a *Military Dictator.* I would take his head off to the tune of Yankee Doodle!"[23]

For a brief time Buchanan was something of a hero for his rejection of the Southern commissioners, but when the *Star of the West* failed to complete her mission, the newspapers in both North and South attacked him. Northern editors called him a weakling. Secessionists were speechless with anger because the ship was sent at all, while Southern Unionists agreed with the Northerners that the *Brooklyn* should have been allowed to bombard the shore batteries.

A few days later, the last Southern cabinet member, Philip Thomas, also resigned, ostensibly over a minor disagreement with Buchanan over a loan policy. He would later join the Confederacy. Thomas was replaced at the Treasury Department by John A. Dix of New York. Dix had opposed the annexation of Texas in 1844 and had later been denied appointments as secretary of state and minister to France because of his free-soil sentiments. He would later serve competently as a major general and eventually become president of a transcontinental railroad. Dix spent much time at the White House and did much toward restoring the administration's prestige during its final weeks. When he sent an officer to

New Orleans to take over the federal revenue cutters, a Southern captain refused to surrender his ship. Dix had the officer arrested and the ship seized, and issued a general order: "If anyone attempts to haul down the Union flag, shoot him on the spot."[24]

At Charleston, meanwhile, Anderson and Governor Pickens made an unauthorized truce. Anderson quite properly demanded an explanation for the attack on the *Star of the West* and gave the governor a reasonable time in which to disavow the act. Pickens responded by justifying rather than disavowing, and demanded that Anderson deliver the fort in return for a written pledge guaranteeing full reimbursement to the federal government. Anderson refused to comply, but offered to send an officer along with a representative of the governor to Washington for instructions. Neither side would resort to arms until the matter was settled. The administration thus found itself with a new stalemate. Lieutenant J. Norman Hall and J. W. Hayne were in Washington awaiting what could only be a repetition of the president's earlier decision, but until this information could be formally transmitted the truce forbade any further effort to reinforce Anderson. Buchanan as usual insisted that Hayne communicate only in writing.

For three weeks a group of Southern senators headed by Jefferson Davis prolonged the truce by persuading Hayne to delay his communication with the president. Buchanan complained about this both at the time and later, but he may have been as willing to keep the truce going as the Southerners were. Anderson was preparing Fort Sumter for action, while the Carolinians were building up their shore batteries and sinking hulks across the harbor entrance. Jeremiah Black wanted immediate reinforcement, and wrote General Scott a long inquiry about tactics and strategy. Scott responded by publicizing his "Views" of October 29, 1860. On January 18, the date of release, the general's suggestion that secession was permissible under certain circumstances and was preferable to civil war must have encouraged the secessionists. Throughout the rest of January various Southerners continued to hound Buchanan for a promise either to withdraw Anderson or refrain from sending reinforcements. Meanwhile, the other Southern states were seceding one by one, and the Confederacy was being organized at Montgomery, Alabama.

Buchanan kept answering that he was not planning to send reinforcements, but would do so if Anderson should ask for help. In a secret letter probably aimed at protecting his own future reputation, Black complained about the president's gullibility in believing

South Carolina's threats of war. In Black's view, the refusal of the *Brooklyn* to engage the shore batteries at Charleston had made the United States the laughing stock of the world.

The Anderson-Pickens truce finally ended on January 31, when Hayne presented the Pickens letter to Buchanan. On February 6, Secretary of War Holt rejected Pickens's demand as an attempt to buy the fort and a threat to seize it if the United States wouldn't sell it. The United States, wrote the angry secretary, would keep Sumter and reinforce it if Anderson should make the request. Hayne answered with another insulting letter accusing Buchanan of bad faith.

For the remainder of his term Buchanan and his cabinet debated not whether to reinforce Fort Sumter but how to do it. Scott, Toucey, and Holt organized a relief expedition of four small steamers in New York under Commander J. H. Ward, who had orders to be ready to sail instantly. Former navy Captain Gustavus Fox, soon to be assistant secretary of the navy for Lincoln, proposed a convoy of several large ships carrying launches and two shallow-draft harbor tugs. The tugs were to load supplies outside the harbor and, protected by cotton bales, make a run for the fort in darkness. The launches would bring in the troops. Military historians have generally felt that the Fox plan might have worked, but by the time it got a fair hearing the Southerners had bought the two tugs Fox wanted. Presumably, however, other tugs could have been found if Buchanan had decided to make the effort. Scott, Black, and Stanton wanted to send Ward's fleet to Charleston before the harbor defenses could be made stronger, but Anderson reported again that he was safe and advised that any such expedition would suffer heavy casualties and do more harm than good. In his reluctance to send troops to Sumter, Buchanan was supported throughout by his commander on the scene. Up to the day of Lincoln's inauguration, Anderson kept insisting that his position was secure. Unless the major should call for help, Buchanan would resist his advisers and deliver Sumter as a well-deserved problem to Abraham Lincoln.

Congress, meanwhile, continued its private war against the president by refusing him every request for authority to do the things he did not really want to do anyhow. Bills for calling the militia and increasing the president's military power were quickly defeated, and no bill to raise money for defense was even proposed. When he appointed a new collector for the port of Charleston, the Senate refused to confirm his nominee. He was showered with public criticism for not acting on his own, but he replied quite correctly that to do so with Congress in session would be to make war on the representatives of the whole nation. Abraham Lincoln would start with not only a very different approach to the problem, but also with the advantage of having Congress in a state of adjournment.

In January a congressional committee investigated charges that Secretary Floyd had conspired to send huge quantities of arms from the North to the South. The committee found the charges groundless, but various Northern papers continued to stir up suspicions that the president was trying to arm the South.

General Scott's first report to Lincoln and his later wartime charges were in the same vein, but were quite unfair. Buchanan did strengthen Fort Taylor at Key West, Fort Jefferson on Tortugas Island, and Fort Pickens at Pensacola, and all three would remain secure throughout the Civil War. His dispatch of the *Brooklyn* to Fort Pickens brought an angry complaint from John Tyler as chairman of the Peace Convention, but Buchanan replied only that the vessel was on an "errand of mercy and relief . . . in no way connected with South Carolina." By mutual agreement the *Brooklyn* did not land its troops, but stood by in case of need, while the Southerners left the fort unmolested. The troops could be landed anytime the Southerners threatened the fort. Lincoln would later cite the failure to actually land the reinforcements at Pickens as one of his reasons for sending ships to Sumter, but Pickens remained safe. The later charge that Buchanan left it undefended was false.

On February 12 the Confederate Congress assumed control of the problem of the forts. Governor Pickens immediately wired a vehement demand that Fort Sumter be captured while Buchanan was still president. This, he said, would confront Lincoln with the question of a war separated from any hostile act during his own administration. Pickens wanted to know only whether President Jefferson Davis would appoint a general for the exploit or if he should manage it himself. The Confederate government, however, delayed until February 22, when the Congress resolved that forts Sumter and Pickens must be taken by either negotiations or force as early as possible, and authorized Davis to make the necessary military preparations. Finally on March 1 Davis sent General Beauregard to Charleston, but warned Governor Pickens that no attack should be made until victory was absolutely certain.

Why did Davis delay when the evidence indicated that Buchanan's response would probably be less vigorous than Lincoln's?

The Charleston batteries and manpower were being increased daily, but they were already strong enough to reduce the undermanned fort unless it should be heavily reinforced. Perhaps Davis agreed with those who argued that it would be inadvisable to have Lincoln inherit a war for which he would not be responsible. Certainly, the side that fired the first shot would carry a heavy burden of guilt in the eyes of the uncommitted in both the border and Northern states. Perhaps the peacemaking efforts of Seward, who was frantically trying to appease both the Southern and the border states, had convinced him that Lincoln would be more tractable than Buchanan. Perhaps also, however, Davis was reading Lincoln correctly and had himself opted for a conflict broad enough to pull the uncommitted border states into the Confederacy. Buchanan had consistently indicated that he would respond at most to an attack upon Fort Sumter by sending a naval force to defend or retake it. Would a limited struggle over Fort Sumter with no announcement of any federal program to suppress the entire rebellion have aroused the border states and triggered the Civil War? If the North had been able to retain or regain Fort Sumter, would the entire South have commenced an all-out war? If, after a respectable show of resistance, Buchanan had surrendered the fort without a national call to arms, would the Congress have compelled him to make war? Was Lincoln's call for 75,000 militia to put down the rebellion his only possible response to the loss of Fort Sumter? Was it the response Davis and his advisers expected and perhaps hoped for?

The Confederate leaders expected and hoped that the battle would bring Maryland, Kentucky, and Missouri, as well as Virginia, North Carolina, Tennessee, and Arkansas into the Confederacy. If they had guessed correctly on Maryland, Missouri, and Kentucky, an unconquerable Confederacy might have been a reality. They also miscalculated the force of the Northern reaction to the attack and the extent of the Northern willingness and power to make war.

Lincoln in fact showed no more determination than Buchanan to defend Fort Sumter successfully. Buchanan left the new president a much stronger naval force than Lincoln chose to use. After weeks of vacillation, Lincoln finally sent a relief force incapable of doing anything except provoke a successful attack by South Carolina. Davis waited until Lincoln's relief expedition provided an excuse for an attack. Lincoln sent a force too weak to justify the attack. Each could then accuse the other of starting the war. True, Seward diverted the expedition's most powerful ship elsewhere by a ruse, but Lincoln never once expressed any disapproval. Northern spirit for a total war on all the seceded states was easily aroused by South Carolina's victory at Fort Sumter. If a federal fleet had won the battle and kept the fort, Lincoln's efforts to save the Union by military coercion might not have been launched so successfully.

After decades of glorifying strong presidents and damning donothing congresses, numerous historians have suddenly become acutely sensitive to the dangers of presidential power. The Buchanan and Lincoln administrations can provide much fuel for debate on the subject. Buchanan left all decisions with regard to secession and the seceded states to the Congress, and he was probably aware that Congress was unlikely to do anything coercive at all. He asked Congress for added military forces and increased authority, and bowed meekly to its refusal. Lincoln, apparently supported by the Northern public and temporarily unhampered by Congress, took a different course. If continued, the policies of Buchanan and the Congress would have allowed the seven seceded states to establish their own nation, which might or might not have remained permanently separate. Buchanan, however, considered Fort Sumter a question apart from the overall problem of secession. His response to Anderson's sudden mark-up in the price for the fort's survival can only be guessed. No such force was available, and Congress had showed no willingness to create it. In all likelihood, he would have given Davis no excuse for the attack, and neither he nor the Congress would have expanded the battle into an all-out war, although the Confederacy itself might well have done so. In any case the border states would have had far less reason to join their sisters. Lincoln's response to Fort Sumter rather than the battle itself gave the Confederacy four more states and began the war.

By February, 1861, both the administration and the Congress were frightened by rumors that secessionists might seize Washington, make Breckinridge president, and claim the city as the capital of a new Southern nation. A congressional committee appointed to consider legislation for strengthening the president's military authority also investigated the evidence of a conspiracy to take the city. The suspicious Congress had a dilemma. Numerous members feared an attack on the government if the president had no troops, while others suspected the possibility of an attack by such troops if Buchanan was their commander. Blamed on all sides both for having insufficient troops and for having too many, Buchanan mobilized 653 men to keep the peace. The Southerners denounced him fiercely for what Kate Thompson called "such *Tom foolery*."

Remembering the actual kidnapping threat against himself, Buchanan agreed with Black, Holt, and Scott that an attack on the city was possible. "If they *can* take it and *do not* take it," said Black, "they are fools." The congressional committee, however, could find no evidence of such intentions, and this only increased the denunciations of Buchanan for arming the city.[25]

As Buchanan's final days in office slowly passed, confusion and uncertainty dominated the capital. Still busy with his futile efforts to find a compromise, John Tyler persuaded Buchanan to keep the federal soldiers out of the annual Washington's Day parade. Holt had already ordered the men to march, however, and the press had made the announcement. Buchanan ordered Scott to stop their parade, but as the people of Washington waited for the festivities to begin, Daniel Sickles rushed to the War Department with a plea that cancelling the parade would cause more trouble than the participation of the troops. The department and the president finally conceded, and the soldiers had to get back into their dress uniforms and march.

One at a time the final compromise efforts failed, as the president's oldest and dearest Southern friends denounced him as a traitor. The Thompsons were angered by a report that Lincoln's friends Senator and Mrs. Lyman Trumbull were at the White House on good social terms with Buchanan and Harriet, but they did reluctantly attend his farewell dinner. During his last few days, the clerks came to small parties at the White House, and the judges and foreign ministers came to pay their respects. Buchanan's day of deliverance was at hand.

March 4 was cold and windy. Buchanan was signing last-minute bills in the president's room at the Capitol when Holt rushed in with a surprising and ominous message. After weeks of sending reassurances, Anderson had just reported from Fort Sumter that a successful reinforcement of his command would take at least 20,000 men. With a sigh of relief the president ordered his carriage and rode off to pick up Lincoln for the parade and inauguration.

In the carriage Buchanan and Lincoln chatted amiably, and observers noted Buchanan's almost joyful expression. "My dear sir," said the retiree, "if you are as happy in entering the White House as I shall feel on returning to Wheatland, you are a happy man indeed."

"Mr. President," answered Lincoln, "I cannot say that I shall enter it with much pleasure, but I assure you that I shall do what

I can to maintain the high standards set by my illustrious predecessors who have occupied it."[26]

The procession down Pennsylvania Avenue was marked by elements familiar enough in the late twentieth century, but entirely new in 1861. General Scott had concealed sharpshooters with rifles on the rooftops along the route. Platoons of soldiers were stationed every hundred yards. The cavalry guarded the side streets. A guard of honor from the regular army and the marines marched so close to the open carriage that spectators had difficulty seeing the occupants. Two batteries of artillery were posted near the Capitol, and more riflemen manned its windows.

As the carriage neared the Capitol, Buchanan and Lincoln could see a huge crane swinging from the dome. The great bronze statue of Freedom waiting to be hoisted to the top was still lying on the ground nearby. The two men entered the building through a boarded tunnel and the inaugural procession walked to the platform. Buchanan appeared withered and bowed beside the taller Lincoln, and the ancient and shriveled Chief Justice Taney resembled a "galvanized corpse." As Lincoln stood to deliver his address, Stephen A. Douglas rose from a front seat to take his hat and cane.

Buchanan sat impassively listening to Lincoln deliver a highly conciliatory inaugural, which appeared to echo most of his own positions. The new president repeated that he had neither the lawful right nor the inclination to interfere with slavery where it already existed. He would support the proposed thirteenth amendment just passed by Congress, which forbade forever any federal interference with slavery in the states. He would hold, occupy, and possess the federal property, and collect the duties and imposts, but beyond this there would "be no invasion—no using of force against, or among the people anywhere." At the insistence of Seward, to whose arguments Lincoln had reluctantly bowed, the earlier threats to retake federal property were conspicuously absent, as were the other aggressive declarations Trumbull had made in his name. Federal officers would not be sent in to perform federal duties, and the mails would be delivered unless repelled. "In *your* hands, my dissatisfied fellow countrymen, and not in *mine*," said Lincoln, "is the momentous issue of civil war. The government will not assail *you*. You can have no conflict, without being yourselves the aggressors."[27]

The opportunity for Southern aggression, however, was imminent. On the evening of Lincoln's inauguration, Buchanan should have been celebrating his deliverance, but instead he held another cabinet meeting. Before Anderson's startling last-minute dispatch Buchanan had had very little to tell Lincoln that had not been reported in the press, and his brief contact with the new president at the inauguration had provided no time for any serious discussions. The ex-president and his associates did not wish to be misrepresented by future historians, however, and Anderson had suddenly left them highly vulnerable to charges of gross negligence if not worse. At this meeting and again the following morning at the War Department, they held their final discussions of Fort Sumter. Holt read a letter which he had prepared for Lincoln, and everyone agreed with its content and purposes. It summarized all previous dealings on Fort Sumter, quoted extensively from Major Anderson's earlier optimistic reports, and explained the existence of the naval force in readiness at New York. Delivery of this document was the Buchanan administration's final act. The watch had been changed, and the new helmsman could now plot his own course.

15

★★★★★

EPILOGUE

In the preface to his memoir, James Buchanan restated a firm faith in the principles of his administration and an unshakable conviction that he had served without fault. The war, he wrote, had been caused by "the long, active, and persistent hostility of the Northern Abolitionists . . . against Southern slavery, until the final triumph of their cause in the election of President Lincoln; and . . . the corresponding antagonism with which the advocates of slavery resisted these efforts. . . ." He himself had "never failed, upon all suitable occasions, to warn his countrymen of the approaching danger, and to advise them of the proper means to avert it." When, however, the war had become inevitable, the Congress had "persistently refused to pass any measures enabling him or his successor to execute the laws against armed resistance or to defend the country against approaching rebellion."[1]

Buchanan needed his own self-assurances because unlike other former American presidents he was denied the full repose of an honored and respected retirement.[2] En route home, he was cheered by crowds in Baltimore, where Southern sentiment still predominated. Lancaster welcomed him with a thirty-four gun salute and the ringing of church bells, and for a month he enjoyed friendly visitors and getting reacquainted with the delights of his beautiful farm. From Washington, Black, Stanton, and Holt all assured him that Lincoln would abandon Fort Sumter and that his own efforts to find a peaceful solution would be continued. Both Seward and General Scott were in fact doing their best to persuade Lincoln to withdraw Anderson whenever his food supplies should run out. Lincoln, however, decided otherwise, and the Civil War began at dawn in Charleston harbor on April 12, 1861.

The Southern sympathies that the ex-president had exhibited all too often now gave credence to ridiculous Republican charges that he had somehow been responsible for the fall of Fort Sumter and for the war itself. His pleasant trips into town had to stop because of angry rumors that his life would be in danger. Insulting and threatening letters began to arrive daily. Anonymous notes stuck under the back door warned that the house would be set afire. He refused to publicize his troubles by hiring detectives, but volunteers from the local Masonic Lodge supplied volunteer guards for many months. Stores exhibited bank notes picturing a red-eyed Buchanan with a rope around his neck and the word "Judas" written on his forehead. Lincoln's war message of July 4 drew heavily upon a report from General Scott and quite unfairly poured fuel upon the fire that was rapidly destroying what reputation poor Buchanan had left. Lincoln charged that too many rifles and muskets had been sent to the South, that quantities of money had been left exposed in Southern mints, that the navy had been scattered to distant seas, and that his own effort to reinforce Fort Pickens had been foiled by an "armistice of the late administration."

The partisan press joined with an all-out effort to convince readers that Buchanan had conspired to aid secession. The terrible defeat of Northern troops at the first battle of Bull Run and the final realization that the expected short skirmish was going to be a long and bloody war added to the old man's troubles. A Senate resolution to censure and condemn him because "from sympathy with the conspirators and their treasonable project" he had "failed to take necessary and proper measures to prevent it" did not pass, but received wide publicity.[3] According to the Republican newspapers, he could have stopped secession and prevented the war if, like Jackson, he had dared to send troops to Charleston in the beginning. Furthermore, they wrote, he had negotiated truces with the enemy when he should have been using force, overruled General Scott by sending the *Star of the West* instead of the *Brooklyn*, and vetoed Scott's proposal to reinforce Sumter after the *Star of the West* had failed. He had scattered the fleet around the world, and had armed the South.

Both Thurlow Weed and General Scott published articles replete with false tales of events at cabinet meetings and incorrect analyses of who had been responsible for which decisions. Buchanan's ex-cabinet officers could have come to his rescue with true accounts, but five of them had accepted federal positions with Lincoln, the others were frightened by adverse public opinion, and none would speak a public word in his defense.

Congress abolished the franking privilege of ex-presidents to prevent the free mailing of any pamphlet or letter he might write. Abolition papers charged that he was constantly urging foreign governments to recognize the Confederacy, and printed false lists of the villains allegedly gathering at Wheatland for dark conspiracies. On successive days they announced that he was in England selling Confederate bonds, and at Bedford Springs, Pennsylvania, plotting with spies. The Indian bond story was revived, with Buchanan the culprit and the amount raised to six million dollars. The Commissioner of Public Buildings reported that he had to remove Buchanan's portrait from the Capitol rotunda to keep it from being defaced. New York papers accused Buchanan and Harriet of stealing portraits from the White House and keeping the gifts brought to Washington by the Japanese delegation.

At first the attacks made the old ex-president violently ill. He soon recovered, however, and set about preparing his defense. At every possible opportunity he publicly supported Lincoln and the war effort. He opposed the peace plank in the Democratic platform of 1864, and was relieved when the party's candidate, McClellan, also rejected it. He did, however, suggest in November, 1864, that "A frank and manly offer to the Confederates that they might return to the Union just as they were before . . . might possibly be accepted."[4]

Meanwhile, in October, 1862, he demolished the charges of General Scott in an exchange of public letters, and a few weeks later finished the first draft of his memoirs. Titled *Mr. Buchanan's Administration on the Eve of the Rebellion*, the book was published in 1866. The author quite successfully refuted the charges of malfeasance in 1860–1861, and made accusers like General Scott and Horace Greeley look very bad indeed. He established a firm base of innocence for future biographers, and restored his own peace of mind. He was seventy-one years old in 1862, but he was neither sick nor weak in his own defense, any more than he had been sick or weak in office. When the Confederate army invaded Pennsylvania, he rejected all warnings that he should flee, even though the advance guard came within ten miles of Wheatland.

He continued the active management of the financial affairs of numerous relatives, and further enhanced his own personal fortune with shrewd management and accounting. Old friends both Northern and Southern who had fallen upon hard times often wrote. They always received sympathy and sometime generous financial aid as well. A few of his dearest Northern friends who had lost loved ones in battle blamed him personally, and this gave him much pain. After the war, he hoped to be reunited with some of his Southern friends; but when Harriet brought an overture from Howell Cobb, the old man wisely but sadly answered that he did "not wish to see him now or hereafter. . . . I wish him well and hope he may obtain his pardon; but this is all."[5] Buchanan had spent too many long, lonely hours fighting to regain his reputation without risking it again by immediate postwar visits from Confederate leaders. As might have been expected, however, he did not favor emancipation and he considered the federal imposition of Negro suffrage to be a dangerous and unconstitutional blow at states rights for a cause he thought dubious at best.

On June 1, 1868, James Buchanan died at seventy-seven from a severe cold and the infirmities of old age. Over 20,000 people attended his funeral and heard various orators extol his "great private virtue, integrity, charity, kindness, and courtesy." On the day before he died, he assured a friend: "I have always felt and still feel that I discharged every public duty imposed on me conscientiously. I have no regret for any public act of my life, and history will vindicate my memory."[6]

History has indeed cleared Buchanan's name of the unfair charges spawned by the fear, anger, and sufferings of wartime. Also, later historians who have questioned the necessity and value of the Civil War when weighed against its destruction and bloodshed have admired his moderation and praised his efforts for compromise.

There is a strange irony in this, however. The historians who have considered the war a necessary and justifiable price for the destruction of slavery should feel a debt to James Buchanan. Those who think the war could and should have been avoided owe him nothing. His blindness to Northern feelings about slavery extension added much to the war spirit that developed in both sections by 1861. The Dred Scott case, for which he must bear important responsibility, infuriated the North while providing the South with the constitutional arguments and the psychological basis for demanding a slave code in the territories. When Northern Democrats friendly to the South desperately needed proof at home that popular sovereignty would not create new slave states, Buchanan gave them the Lecompton Constitution and his view that Kansas was "as much a slave state as Georgia or South Carolina." When the Republican party was struggling for a national base, Buchanan's Democratic administration gave the voters worn-out bromides and antiquated advice for an economic depression. When Republicans and Northern Democrats passed legislation designed for economic progress, Buchanan contributed vetoes based upon obsolete principles directly attributable to the South. When the Democrats, the only national party left, desperately needed respect and support everywhere, Buchanan could only serve up John Floyd and the army scandals. After important Southern leaders threatened to secede if the Republicans should elect a president, Buchanan used his high office to help divide the Democrats and enable the Republicans to win. Even after secession began, his annual message to Congress echoed the Southern complaints and further alienated Northerners who might otherwise have been prone to accept compromises. Even his aggressive foreign policies, which fortunately were checked by Congress, gave credence to the Republican charges that popular sovereignty or the Crittenden Compromise would produce filibustering expeditions to acquire slave territory in Latin America if none could be found within the continental limits of the United States. With a Southern cabinet and Southern policies Buchanan roused false and unattainable hopes followed by bitter disappointments throughout the South, and simultaneously alienated Northern public opinion to the point where no Northern concessions were possible. His love, admiration, and deep sympathy for Southerners were entirely sincere and inescapable, but they did not make him an adequate president for all the people.

Why, in the 1840s and 1850s, was the United States unable to elect a president with the broad vision and the ability to understand the complaints and the legitimate needs of both sections? Each section desperately needed a clearer and more accurate picture of the aims of the other. Why could the people not find a president capable of providing this? Why Polk, Taylor, Fillmore, Pierce, and Buchanan, instead of a Clay, Webster, Benton, Douglas, or Crittenden? Did the American people get what a majority of them actually wanted? Pierce and Buchanan were elected because most Northern voters were quite ignorant of their pro-Southern views, and because the alternatives were the impossible General Scott in 1852 and the radical Fremont and the Know-Nothing Fillmore in 1856. Could a different selection process have provided the voters with a better set of choices? Or did the public state of mind in 1852 and 1856 make impossible the nomination by any process of candidates genuinely qualified for the responsibilities and challenges of the office? Was Abraham Lincoln an intelligent choice or a happy accident? If Pierce and Buchanan had conformed to their images as projected during the election campaigns, their administrations would have been entirely different. Does this mean that American presidents should be denied the luxury of false image-making; and, if so, how can this be accomplished? Could procedures be established to require that every candidate for a presidential nomination be interviewed publicly not once but several times by a panel of his strongest opponents? This problem has been multiplied many times with the advent of modern public-relations techniques and electronic technology, but it was no less a factor in the building of a national tragedy in the 1850s.

Fortunately, the historian is not required to furnish definitive answers to his own questions. The answers must be sought, however, if the all-powerful American presidency is to be filled regularly by men who can lead and serve with foresight, wisdom, and ability as well as with mere good intentions. No president ever had better intentions than James Buchanan. Few have done more to frustrate their own objectives.

Notes

CHAPTER 1

1. Winthrop D. Jordan, *White Over Black: Development of American Attitudes Toward the Negro* (Chapel Hill: University of North Carolina Press, 1968); Leon F. Litwack, *North of Slavery: The Negro in the Free States* (Chicago: University of Chicago Press, 1961); David B. Davis, *The Problem of Slavery in Western Culture* (Ithaca: Cornell University Press, 1966); and William R. Stanton, *The Leopard's Spots: Scientific Attitudes Toward Race in America, 1815–59* (Chicago: University of Chicago Press, 1960).

2. Eric Foner, "Racial Attitudes of the New York Free Soilers," *New York History* 46 (Oct., 1965): 311–329; "Politics and Prejudice: The Free Soil Party and the Negro, 1849–1852," *Journal of Negro History* 50 (Oct., 1965): 232–256. Also Foner, *Free Soil, Free Labor, Free Men* (New York: Oxford Press, 1970), pp. 261–300.

3. Benton cited by Elbert B. Smith, *Magnificent Missourian* (J. B. Lippincott Co., 1958), p. 313.

4. Thomas H. McKee, *The National Conventions and Platforms of All Political Parties 1789 to 1905* (Baltimore: The Friedenwald Co., 1906), p. 92; pp. 88–94 for entire platform.

5. Buchanan cited by Philip S. Klein, *President James Buchanan* (University Park: Pennsylvania State University Press, 1962), p. 257; see also pp. 254–260; and George T. Curtis, *Life of James Buchanan* (New York: Harper and Brothers, 1883), 2: 169–186.

CHAPTER 2

1. "The Autobiography of Martin Van Buren," *Annual Report of the American Historical Association for the Year 1918* (1922), p. 496.

2. Klein, *Buchanan*, p. 21.

3. Aaron V. Brown to Mrs. James K. Polk, Jan. 14, 1844, *Polk Papers*, Library of Congress.

4. Klein, *Buchanan*, pp. 239–241.

5. John B. Moore (ed.), *The Works of James Buchanan* (New York: Antiquarian Press Reprint, 1960), 11: 377.

6. James Buchanan, *Mr. Buchanan's Administration on the Eve of the Rebellion* (New York: D. Appleton and Co., 1866), pp. 9–20, 57–66.

CHAPTER 3

1. Curtis, *Life*, 2: 185; Klein, *Buchanan*, p. 253.

2. Stephens to Thomas W. Thomas, June 16, 1856, "The Correspondence of Robert Toombs, Alexander H. Stephens, and Howell Cobb, *Annual Report of the American Historial Association,* 1911 (1913), 2: 372.

3. Oliver P. Chitwood, *John Tyler* (New York: Russell & Russell, Inc., 1964), pp. 286–287.

4. Blair to Buchanan, Aug. 31, 1841, Buchanan MS, Historical Society of Pennsylvania.
5. Buchanan cited by Klein, *Buchanan*, p. 284.

6. Ibid., p. 259. Robert Johannsen, *Stephen A. Douglas* (New York: Oxford University Press, 1973), p. 533.
7. Klein, *Buchanan*, pp. 275–285.

CHAPTER 4

1. Missouri Supreme Court cited by Allan Nevins, *The Emergence of Lincoln* (New York: Scribner's Sons, 1950), 1: 85.
2. Ibid., 1: Appendix I, 473–477; Stanley I. Kutler (ed.), *The Dred Scott Decision: Law or Politics?* (Boston: Houghton-Mifflin Co., 1966) provides an excellent summary along with both contemporary and historical opinions attacking and defending the decision.
3. Catron to Buchanan, Feb. 19, 1857, reprinted in footnote by Moore, *Works*, 10: 106.
4. Grier to Buchanan, Feb. 23, 1857, reprinted in footnote by Moore, *Works*, 10: 106–108.

5. Moore, *Works*, 10: 106–107.
6. *Report of the Decision of the Supreme Court of the United States in the Case of Dred Scott versus Sandford* (New York: Da Capo Press, 1970), p. 13; for entire decision as reported by Taney, pp. 5–60.
7. Leon F. Litwack, "The Federal Government and the Free Negro, 1790–1860," *The Journal of Negro History* 43 (Oct., 1958): 261–278. Also reprinted in Crowe, *Civil War and Reconstruction*, pp. 7–17.
8. Thomas H. Benton, *Historical and Legal Examination of the Dred Scott Case* (New York: D. Appleton & Co., 1957).

CHAPTER 5

1. The Kansas story has been thoroughly researched and written by Nevins, *Lincoln*, 1: 133–175, 229–304; Roy F. Nichols, *The Disruption of American Democracy* (New York: Macmillan, 1948), pp. 94–131, 150–175; and Alice Nichols, *Bleeding Kansas* (New York: Oxford Press, 1954). James C. Malin, in *The Nebraska Question* (Ann Arbor: Edwards Brothers, 1953), summarizes his earlier pioneer work on the sources of conflict unrelated to slavery. Paul W. Gates, *50 Million Acres* (Ithaca: Cornell University Press, 1954), stresses the conflicting land claims.
2. *National Intelligencer*, July 16, 1857, cited by Nevins, *Lincoln*, 1: 146. For Walker's role see James P. Shenton, *Robert John Walker* (New York: Columbia University Press, 1961), pp. 147–174. For a glimpse of Walker's

rhetorical talent see *Letter of Mr. Walker of Mississippi Relative to the Annexation of Texas* (Washington: Globe Office, 1844).
3. Maclean cited by Nevins, *Lincoln*, 2: 155.
4. Klein, *Buchanan*, p. 292.
5. Ibid., p. 295.
6. "Toombs, Stephens, Cobb Correspondence," *Annual Report of A.H.A., 1911*, 2: 401–408; Klein, *Buchanan*, pp. 273–277; Nevins, *Lincoln*, 1: 76, 170–172.
7. Bernard Weisberger, "The Newspaper Reporter and the Kansas Imbroglio," *Mississippi Valley Historical Review* 36 (Mar., 1950), 633–656.
8. Conversation cited by Klein, *Buchanan*, p. 301, and various other sources.
9. Moore, *Works*, 10: 150–151.
10. Klein, *Buchanan*, pp. 305–306.
11. Moore, *Works*, 10: 190.
12. Hammond, *Speech on the Admis-*

sion of Kansas, Under the Le-compton _Constitution _(Louis-ville: Lost Cause Press, 1966, on microcards); Nevins, *Lincoln,* 1: 285–286.

13. James T. Dubois and Gertrude S. Mathews, *Galusha A. Grow* (Boston and New York: Hough-ton Mifflin Co., 1917), pp. 166–175; Nevins, *Lincoln,* 1: 288.

CHAPTER 6

1. Roy P. Basler (ed.), *The Col-lected Works of Abraham Lin-coln* (New Brunswick: Rutgers University Press, 1953), 2: 255, 256; 247–283 for entire speech.
2. Ibid., 2: 461–469.
3. Robert W. Johannsen (ed.), *The Lincoln-Douglas Debates of*

1858 (New York: Oxford Uni-versity Press, 1965).
4. Basler, *Works of Lincoln,* 3: 18.
5. Ibid., 3: 16.
6. Ibid., 2: 500–501; repeated at Alton in slightly different words, 3: 315.

CHAPTER 7

1. Moore, *Works,* 10: 129–135.
2. Frederick Law Olmsted, *A Jour-ney in the Seaboard Slave States* (New York: Mason Brothers, 1856); *A Journey Through Texas* (New York: Dix, Edwards & Co., 1857); and *A Journey in the Back Country* (New York: Ma-son Brothers, 1860). All abridged and combined in *The Cotton Kingdom* (New York: Mason Brothers, 1861–1862).
3. Hinton Rowan Helper, *The Im-pending Crisis of the South and How to Meet It* (New York: A. B. Burdick, 1860), pp. 120, 128; see also 1963 edition by Collier Books, New York.
4. Ibid., pp. 155–187.
5. Buchanan, *Mr. Buchanan's Ad-ministration,* pp. 59–62.
6. Samuel M. Wolfe, *Helper's Im-pending Crisis Dissected* (New York: J. T. Lloyd, 1860); George Fitzhugh, *Sociology for the South; or the Failure of Free Society* (Richmond: A. Morris, 1854; New York: B. Franklin, 1965), and *Cannibals All! or Slaves Without Masters* (Rich-mond: A. Morris, 1857; Boston: Belknap Press of Harvard Uni-versity, 1965). I could not locate Gilbert J. Beebe, *Review and Refutation,* and have cited it

from Nevins, *Lincoln,* 1: 214. See also Harvey Wish (ed.), *Antebellum Writings of George Fitzhugh and Hinton Rowan Helper on Slavery* (New York: Capricorn Books, 1960).
7. Pamphlet *Letter on the Interest of Non-Slaveholders in the Per-petuation of American Slavery* (1860), cited by Nevins, *Lin-coln,* 1: 214.
8. Thomas Prentice Kettell, *South-ern Wealth and Northern Profits* (New York: George W. and John A. Wood, 1860; Louisville: Lost Cause Press microcard edi-tion, 1966). Samuel Powell, *Notes on Southern Wealth and Northern Profits,* cited by Nevins, *Lincoln,* 1: 219.
9. Most convincingly stated by Charles and Mary Beard, *The Rise of American Civilization* (New York: Macmillan Co., 1927), 2: 3–13, 19–21, 28–54, also reprinted in Edwin Rozwenc (ed.), *The Causes of the Amer-ican Civil War* (Lexington, Mass.: D. C. Heath and Co., 1972 edition), pp. 68–99. In Rozwenc volume see also Frank Owsley, "The Irrepressible Con-flict," pp. 99–120.
10. Charles G. Sellers, "Who Were the Southern Whigs?," *American*

Historical Review 19 (Jan., 1954), 335-346.

11. Cited by Avery Craven, *Civil War in the Making* (Baton Rouge: Louisiana State University Press, 1959), p. 104.

12. Alfred H. Conrad and John Meyer, "The Economics of Slavery in the Ante-Bellum South," *The Journal of Political Economy* 66 (Apr., 1958), pioneered the technique and approach. The latest is Robert W. Fogel and Stanley L. Engerman, *Time on*

the Cross (Boston: Little, Brown and Co., 1974), 2 vols.

13. Stanley Elkins, *Slavery: A Problem in American Institutional and Intellectual Life* (Chicago: University of Chicago Press, 1959); Fogel and Engerman, *Time on the Cross*; Eugene Genovese, *The Political Economy of Slavery* (New York: Pantheon Books, 1961).

14. J. C. Furnas, *Goodbye to Uncle Tom* (New York: H. Wolfe, 1956).

CHAPTER 8

1. Klein, *Buchanan*, p. 324; Moore, *Works*, 10: 113, 174.

2. The Mormon story is detailed in Robert R. Mullen, *The Latter-Day Saints* (Garden City: Doubleday, 1966), pp. 145-155; Nels Anderson, *Desert Saints* (Chicago: University of Chicago Press, 1942), pp. 112-192; Stanley P. Hirsshon, *The Lion of the Lord* (New York: Alfred A. Knopf, 1969), pp. 137-183. See also Cornelius Conway, *The Utah Expedition . . . by a Wagon Master of the Expedition* (Louisville: Lost Cause Press on microcards, 1960). Various official messages and reports in *House Ex. Doc. 71* (35th cong., 1st sess., 1857-58). Cf. Nevins, *Lincoln*, 1: 314, 320-323; Klein, *Buchanan*, pp. 315-317; Nichols, *Disruption*, pp. 98-102. Buchanan's views in Moore, *Works*, 10: 151-154, 202-206, 242-245.

3. *National Intelligencer*, Sept. 17, 1857, cited by Nevins, *Lincoln*, 1: 320.

4. Young cited by Klein, *Buchanan*, p. 316.

5. Klein, *Buchanan*, pp. 317-321; Moore, *Works*, 10: 296-299.

6. Malmesbury cited by J. Fred Rippy, *Latin America in World Politics* (New York: F. S. Crofts and Co., 1940), p. 107; see also pp. 103-108. Cf. Kenneth Bourne, *Britain and the Balance of Power in North America*

(Berkeley: University of California Press, 1967), pp. 199-205.

7. Klein, *Buchanan*, pp. 318-320; Moore, *Works*, 10: 136-139.

8. Senate Resolution cited by Nelson M. Blake and Oscar T. Barck, Jr., *The United States in Its World Relations* (New York: McGraw Hill Book Co., Inc., 1960), p. 261; Buchanan quotation in Moore, *Works*, 10: 247.

9. *Senate Ex. Doc. 59* (35th cong., 1st sess., 1857-58); *House Ex. Doc. 132* (35th cong., 1st sess., 1857-58).

10. Moore, *Works*, 11: 26-27.

11. Ibid., 10: 293, 336-337, 350-352; 11: 27; Klein, *Buchanan*, p. 325.

12. Klein, *Buchanan*, p. 350.

13. Ibid., pp. 325-326.

14. Ibid., pp. 319-320; Moore, *Works*, 10: 171-175.

15. Moore, *Works*, 10: 258-261, 349-350; 11: 29. Klein, *Buchanan*, pp. 320-321.

16. Moore, *Works*, 10: 348-349; Klein, *Buchanan*, pp. 323-324; Curtis, *Life*, 2: 224-225.

17. Moore, Works, 10: 346-348; *Senate Ex. Doc. 30* (36th cong., 1st sess., 1859-69), Klein, *Buchanan*, p. 326; Curtis, *Life*, 2: 226-227.

18. Buchanan, *Buchanan's Administration*, pp. 272-273, 267-276; Moore, *Works*, 10: 253-257; Klein, *Buchanan*, pp. 321-323.

19. McLane cited by Klein, *Buchan-*

an, p. 323; see also pp. 321–322; Moore, *Works*, 10: 353–359; Curtis, *Life*, 2: 215–222.

20. Frederick Merk, *Manifest Destiny and Mission in American History* (New York: Vintage Edition, 1966), pp. 180–201.

21. Moore, *Works*, 10: 249–252, 349–350; 11: 29. Klein, *Buchanan*, p. 324.

CHAPTER 9

1. Speech reprinted in Edwin C. Rozwenc (ed.), *The Causes of the American Civil War* (Boston: D. C. Heath and Co., 1961 edition), pp. 11–20, quotations, pp. 13, 20; Nevins, *Lincoln*, 1: 409–411.

2. Hammond cited by Nevins, *Lincoln*, 1: 412; Buchanan, *Buchanan's Administration*, pp. 57–58.

3. Klein, *Buchanan*, pp. 333–335.

4. *Life and Times of Frederick Douglass Written by Himself* (Hartford: Park Publishing Co., 1881), pp. 406–407.

5. Johannsen, *Douglas*, pp. 685–690.

6. Unionist euphoria in early fall, 1859, described by Avery O. Craven, *Coming of the Civil War* (New York: Scribner's Sons, 1942), pp. 403–407.

7. See bibliographical essay for evaluation of several of the host of books that have deified, damned, and dissected Brown. Factual details drawn from Oswald G. Villard, *John Brown, 1800–1859* (New York: A. A. Knopf, 1943 edition); Stephen B. Oates, *To Purge This Land With Blood* (New York: Harper and Row, 1970); and the verbatim proceedings of the Mason committee in Robert M. Fogelson and Richard E. Rubenstein (advisory eds.), *Mass Violence in America, Invasion at Harper's Ferry* (New York: Arno Press and New York Times, 1969).

8. Nevins, *Lincoln*, 2: 29–30.

9. Tilden G. Edelstein, "John Brown and His Friends," essay in Hugh Hawkins (ed.), *The Abolitionists* (Lexington, Mass.: D. C. Heath and Co., 1964 edition), pp. 71–83, quotation p. 76. This essay has been much shortened in the later edition.

10. Emerson and Thoreau cited by Louis Ruchames, "John Brown in the American Tradition," excerpt from Ruchames (ed.), *A John Brown Reader* (London: Abelard Schuman, 1959), reprinted in Hawkins, *Abolitionists*, p. 56. Whittier cited by Edelstein, "John Brown and His Friends," Hawkins, *Abolitionists*, p. 56. The Ruchames and Edelstein essays appear together almost in the form of a debate on pp. 55–83.

11. Parker cited by Ruchames in Hawkins, *Abolitionists*, pp. 56–57.

12. Brown cited by Nevins, *Lincoln*, 1: 214; James B. Ranck, *Albert Gallatin Brown* (New York: Appleton Century Co., 1937), pp. 197–198.

13. Moore, *Works*, 10: 339; see also 339–342; Buchanan, *Buchanan's Administration*, pp. 62–66.

14. Nevins, *Lincoln*, 2: 122.

15. Fogelson and Rubenstein (eds.), *Invasion at Harper's Ferry*. The records in the National Archives have been brilliantly summarized by Roger Bruns, "Select Committee Clamor Echoes Through a Century," *Washington Post*, Sept. 16, 1973. Bruns draws constitutional and other parallels between the Mason Committee of 1859 and the Senate Watergate Committee of 1973–74.

16. Moore, *Works*, 10: 442; see also 435–443; Curtis, *Life*, 2: 246–260; Klein, *Buchanan*, pp. 338–339; Nevins, *Lincoln*, 2: 196–199.

CHAPTER 10

1. The details of the convention appear in numerous books. Best contemporary account by an actual observer is that of Murat Halstead in William B. Hesseltine (ed.), *Three Against Lincoln* (Baton Rouge: Louisiana State University Press, 1960), pp. 3–106. Cf. Johannsen, *Douglas*, pp. 749–750; George F. Milton, *The Eve of Conflict* (Boston: Houghton-Mifflin Co., 1934), pp. 409–449; Nevins, *Lincoln*, 2: 203–228; Nichols, *Disruption*, pp. 288–322.

2. Hesseltine, *Three Against Lincoln*, p. 45; 45–46 for entire majority report. This book deals entirely with the four conventions, including that of the Republicans, and its title is very misleading.

3. Ibid., p. 47; 47–48 for entire report.

4. Payne cited by Nevins, *Lincoln*, 2: 215.

5. Yancey cited by Milton, *Eve of Conflict*, p. 435; Cf. Hesseltine, *Three Against Lincoln*, pp. 52–53; and Nevins, *Lincoln*, 2: 217.

6. Pugh cited by Milton, *Eve of Conflict*, p. 436; Hesseltine, *Three Against Lincoln*, pp. 54–55.

7. Yancey cited by Halstead in Hesseltine, *Three Against Lincoln*, p. 86.

8. Hesseltine, *Three Against Lincoln*, p. 256; 185–264 for details of entire convention; see also, Milton, *Eve of Conflict*, pp. 469–477; Nichols, *Disruption*, pp. 314–318.

9. Hesseltine, *Three Against Lincoln*, p. 271; 271–272 for entire platform.

10. Stephens cited by Gerald M. Capers, *Stephen A. Douglas* (Boston: Little, Brown and Co., 1959), p. 204.

CHAPTER 11

1. Hesseltine, *Three Against Lincoln*, pp. 121–140.

2. Basler, *Works of Lincoln*, 3: 547–548; entire speech, pp. 522–550.

3. Ibid., p. 550.

4. Ibid., 4: 10–11, 18; two versions of entire speech, pp. 2–30.

5. Ibid., p. 12; see also pp. 24–25.

6. Hesseltine, *Three Against Lincoln*, pp. 141–177; Benjamin P. Thomas, *Abraham Lincoln* (New York: Alfred A. Knopf, 1952), pp. 205–213; Nevins, *Lincoln*, 2: 229–260.

7. Bryant cited by Nevins, *Lincoln*, 2: 278.

8. Craven, *Coming of Civil War*, pp. 419–420; Nevins, *Lincoln*, 2: 279–280.

9. Nevins, *Lincoln*, 2: 279–280.

10. Keitt cited by Nevins, *Lincoln*, 2: 288.

11. Ollinger Crenshaw, *The Slave States in the Presidential Election of 1860* (Baltimore: Johns Hopkins Press, 1945); Norman A. Graebner (ed.), *Politics and the Crisis of 1860* (Urbana: University of Illinois Press, 1961); Craven, *Coming of Civil War*, pp. 422–427; Nichols, *Disruption*, pp. 357–367; Nevins, *Lincoln*, 2: 287–290.

12. Douglas cited by Milton, *Eve of Conflict*, p. 493.

13. Ibid., p. 494; cf. Johannsen, *Douglas*, pp. 777–803.

CHAPTER 12

1. "A Declaration of the Causes Which Induced the Secession of South Carolina," reprinted in Edwin C. Rozwenc (ed.), *Slavery as a Cause of the Civil War* (Boston: D. C. Heath and Co.,

1963), pp. 26–31, quotations, pp. 29, 30.

2. "Mississippi Resolutions on Secession," reprinted in Richard Hofstadter (ed.), *Ten Major Issues in American Politics* (New York: Oxford University Press, 1968), pp. 150–152, quotations, pp. 151–152.

3. Genovese, *Political Economy of Slavery*, pp. 243–270.

4. Morrow, "The Proslavery Argument Revisited," *Mississippi Valley Historical Review* 48 (June, 1961): 70–94. Also reprinted in Crowe, *Civil War and Reconstruction*, pp. 98–108.

5. William Barney, *The Road to Secession* (New York: Praeger Publishers, 1972).

6. Dwight Dumond (ed.), *Southern Editorials on Secession* (New York: The Century Co., 1931), editorials cited on pp. 41–48, 360, 384.

7. "The Tragic Southerner," from Sellers (ed.), *The Southerner as American,* reprinted in Crowe, *Civil War and Reconstruction,* pp. 81–108.

8. Barney, *Secession*, pp. 4–5. Numerous historians, including Craven, Nevins, Sellers, Dumond, Genovese, and Barney have listed wounded feelings and resentment of criticism as a factor involved in secession, but in my judgment none has emphasized it sufficiently. Craven in *Civil War in the Making* stresses it most.

9. Dumond, *Southern Editorials*, pp. 315–316.

10. Rhett cited by Nevins, *Lincoln*, 2: 334.

11. Ralph Wooster, *The Secession Conventions of the South* (Princeton: Princeton University Press, 1962).

12. U.S. Bureau of the Census, *Historical Statistics of the United States, 1789–1945* (Washington: U.S. Govt. Printing Office, 1949), p. 187. The figure is 845,410 bales, which I converted to pounds.

CHAPTER 13

1. Holt cited by Philip G. Auchampaugh, *James Buchanan and His Cabinet on the Eve of Secession* (Lancaster, Pa.; Lancaster Press, Inc., 1926), pp. 81–82.

2. Buchanan to Slidell, Jan. 29, 1861, reprinted in footnote by Curtis, *Life*, 2: 445.

3. Moore, *Works*, 11: 69; see also 70; Curtis, *Life*, 2: 355.

4. Woodward cited by Auchampaugh, *Buchanan and His Cabinet*, pp. 105–106; full text of letter pp. 102–106.

5. Ibid., p. 109.

6. Black cited by Klein, *Buchanan*, p. 359; pp. 357–390 for entire discussion.

7. Ibid., p. 360.

8. Moore, *Works*, 11: 7, 8; 7–43 for entire address.

9. Ibid., p. 10.

10. Ibid., p. 11.

11. Ibid., p. 12.

12. Ibid., pp. 13, 14, 15.

13. Ibid., pp. 16–17.

14. Madison quoted in ibid., pp. 18, 19.

15. Ibid., p. 74.

16. *Senate Committee Reports*, 288 (36th cong., 2nd sess., 1860–61). Full accounts of the committee's work in Nichols, *Disruption*, pp. 440–447; Nevins, *Lincoln*, 2: 390–405; David Potter, *Lincoln and His Party in the Secession Crisis* (New Haven: Yale University Press, 1942), pp. 171–187.

17. William E. Barringer, *A House Dividing: Lincoln as President Elect* (Springfield: The Abraham Lincoln Association, 1945), pp. 28–58; Thomas, *Abraham Lincoln*, pp. 226–237.

18. Basler, *Works of Lincoln*, 4: 141–142; Trumbull cited by Barringer,

House Dividing, pp. 36, 37; see also pp. 33–38.

19. Barringer, *House Dividing,* p. 58.
20. Ibid., pp. 196–197; Basler, *Works of Lincoln,* 4: 151–152, quotation on 152.
21. Basler, *Works of Lincoln,* 4: 160.
22. Stephens cited by Barringer, *House Dividing,* p. 212.
23. Basler, *Works of Lincoln,* 4: 172. Barringer, *House Dividing,* pp. 210–248, summarizes Lincoln's exchanges of letters and opinions in much detail.
24. Barringer, *House Dividing,* pp. 221–226; Nevins, *Lincoln,* 2: 405–409; Basler, *Works of Lincoln,* 4: 183.
25. Nevins, *Lincoln,* 2: 409–410.
26. Basler, *Works of Lincoln,* 4: 162–163.
27. Moore, *Works,* 11: 94–99, quotation p. 97.
28. Jesse L. Keene, *The Peace Convention of 1861* (Tuscaloosa: Confederate Publishing Co., 1961), p. 63.
29. Ibid., pp. 85–86.
30. Ibid., pp. 110–111.

CHAPTER 14

1. Scott's "Views" of October 29 and 30, 1861, published in the *National Intelligencer,* Jan. 18, 1861, and reprinted in Buchanan, *Buchanan's Administration,* pp. 287–290, quotations p. 289.
2. The factual story of Buchanan and the forts has been well documented by Klein, *Buchanan,* pp. 368–402; Curtis, *Life,* 2: 297–314, 365–417, 446–490; Auchampaugh, *Buchanan and His Cabinet,* pp. 149–182; Nevins, *Lincoln,* 2: 363–384; Nichols, *Disruption,* pp. 407–433, 459, 479–480. The relevant documents in Moore, *Works,* 2, strongly support Buchanan's own version in *Mr. Buchanan's Administration.* The portrait of Buchanan as a weakling in the hands of a traitorous Southern cabinet, in books like Roy Meredith, *Storm Over Sumter* (New York: Simon and Shuster, 1957), pp. 18–22, 40–41, is quite erroneous.
3. Buchanan cited by Klein, *Buchanan,* p. 358; Floyd speech in Richmond published by *New York Herald,* Jan. 17, 1861, cited by Nichols, *Disruption,* p. 381.
4. Cited by Curtis, *Life,* 2: 388–390; cf. Buchanan, *Buchanan's Administration,* pp. 166–167.
5. Moore, *Works,* 11: 56; Buchanan, *Buchanan's Administration,* pp. 267–268.
6. Moore, *Works,* 11: 56–57.
7. Ibid., pp. 60, 61; 57–65 for entire exchange.
8. Burton J. Hendrick, *Lincoln's War Cabinet* (Boston: Little, Brown and Co., 1946), pp. 237–242; cf. Nevins, *Lincoln,* 2: 358–359.
9. R. W. Wooley to Montgomery Blair, July 17, 1865, Blair MS, Library of Congress; in same collection see also Sallie H. Wooley to Abraham Lincoln, Feb. ___, 1865, and Lillie Chifelli to Montgomery Blair, Feb. 8, 1865.
10. Klein, *Buchanan,* pp. 417–419; Buchanan, *Buchanan's Administration,* pp. 168–179.
11. Moore, *Works,* 11: 71–72.
12. Buchanan cited by Klein, *Buchanan,* p. 379; see also pp. 378–380.
13. Black cited by Klein, *Buchanan,* p. 379.
14. Buchanan cited by Auchampaugh, *Buchanan and His Cabinet,* p. 159.
15. Ibid., pp. 380–381.
16. Black cited by Auchampaugh, *Buchanan and His Cabinet,* p. 110.
17. Ibid., p. 111.
18. Buchanan cited by Auchampaugh, *Buchanan and His Cabinet,* p. 163; for entire cabinet crisis see Black's account on pp. 161–165; Holt's version in Moore,

Works, 11: 84–91. Cf. Klein, *Buchanan,* pp. 380–381; Curtis, *Life,* 2: 379–391.

19. Moore, *Works,* 2: 79–80, 82, 83, 84; entire letter, 79–84.

20. Hunter cited by Auchampaugh, *Buchanan and His Cabinet,* p. 65.

21. Charles W. Elliott, *Winfield Scott* (New York: Macmillan, 1937), p. 685. Using different sources, Elliott documents Buchanan's version of his relations with Scott. Elliott also prints Scott's "Views," most of which the general himself conveniently forgot when writing his own *Memoirs of Lieut.-General Scott, LLD* (New

York: Sheldon & Co., 1864), 2: 613–630.

22. Klein, *Buchanan,* pp. 388–389; Curtis, *Life,* 2: 446–448.

23. Kate Thompson cited by Klein, *Buchanan,* p. 390; Moore, *Works,* 11: 100–101.

24. Dix cited by Nevins, *Lincoln,* 2: 384.

25. Black cited by Klein, *Buchanan,* p. 398.

26. Buchanan and Lincoln cited by Klein, *Buchanan,* p. 402.

27. Basler, *Works of Lincoln,* 4: 271; see also, p. 262–271; Thomas, *Abraham Lincoln,* pp. 245–246.

CHAPTER 15

1. Buchanan, *Buchanan's Administration,* pp. iv–v.

2. The ex-president's trials and tribulations are detailed in Klein, *Buchanan,* pp. 403–420.

3. Cited by Klein, *Buchanan,* p. 410.

4. Buchanan to Dr. Blake, Nov. 21, 1864, Moore, *Works,* 11: 377.

5. Buchanan cited by Klein, *Buchanan,* p. 426.

6. Ibid., p. 427.

Bibliograpical Essay

The controversial years of Buchanan's presidency have been analyzed and contested by a multitude of historians, but the president himself has received but little attention. His first biography, George T. Curtis, *Life of James Buchanan* (New York: Harper & Brothers, 1883), is a ponderous and poorly organized work, although it contains many valuable documents and letters. The 1926 study by Philip G. Auchampaugh, *James Buchanan and His Cabinet on the Eve of Secession* (Lancaster, Pa.: Lancaster Press, Inc.), also contains valuable source material, but is very partisan and lacking in balanced judgment, as evidenced by the author's view that John Floyd was a great secretary of war. Buchanan's one scholarly biography, however, Philip S. Klein, *President James Buchanan* (University Park: Pennsylvania State University Press, 1962), is a thorough and well-written work by a Pennsylvanian who may have been excessively generous in a few places, but clearly understood Buchanan and dealt honestly with his warts as well as his better qualities. The twelve-volume collection of Buchanan papers edited by John B. Moore, *The Works of James Buchanan* (New York: Antiquarian Press Reprint, 1960) and Buchanan's own memoir, *Mr. Buchanan's Administration on the Eve of the Rebellion* (New York: D. Appleton & Co., 1866), are indispensable and easily accessible original sources for anyone seeking to understand the character and policies of James Buchanan. A brief but valuable compilation and bibliography is Irvin J. Sloan (ed.), *James Buchanan* (Oceana Publications, 1968).

Because the Buchanan years marked the climax of several decades of sectional struggle, numerous books dealing with the background and causes of the Civil War are highly relevant to this study. A good starting point is the historiographical study by Thomas Pressly, *Americans Interpret Their Civil War* (Princeton: Princeton University Press, 1962). An excellent and highly detailed study of the Buchanan years and beyond to the beginning of the war is Allan Nevins, *The Emergence of Lincoln* (New York: Scribner's Sons, 1950). This two-volume work deals brilliantly with virtually every event of the period, although in my view his treatment of Buchanan as a weak pawn dominated by his cabinet is in error. Another outstanding book which covers the same ground is Roy F. Nichols, *The Disruption of American Democracy* (New York: Oxford Press, 1954). Several books by Avery O. Craven also add both information and profound insight. These include *Coming of the Civil War* (New York: Scribner's Sons, 1942), *The Growth of Southern Nationalism* (Austin: University of Texas Press, 1953), and *Civil War In The Making* (Baton Rouge: Louisiana State University Press, 1959), among others. Various older books by historians or contemporaries like Alexander H. Stephens, Jefferson Davis, James Ford Rhodes, Woodrow Wilson, John Draper, William E. Dodd, Henry Wilson, and others offer a variety of interpretations, but the general reader can more profitably study their ideas in anthologies like that of Pressly or Edwin C. Rozwenc (ed.), *Causes of the American Civil War* (Boston and Lexington: D. C. Heath and Co., 1961 and 1972 editions). Because of their great impact the works of Charles Beard as exemplified in *The Rise of American Civilization* (New York: Macmillan Company, 1927), and in an excerpt in the Rozwenc compilation; and Ulrich B. Phillips, *Life and Labor in the Old South* (Boston: Little, Brown and Co., 1929), and *American Negro Slavery* (Baton Rouge: Louisiana State University Press, 1966 edition) deserve special mention.

A variety of newer interpretations with regard to slavery, its impact, its profitability, and its significance in the road to war include Kenneth M. Stampp, *The Peculiar Institution* (New York: Alfred A. Knopf, 1956); Eugene Genovese, *The Political Economy of Slavery* (New York: Pantheon Books, 1961); J. C. Furnas, *Goodbye to Uncle Tom* (New York: H. Wolfe, 1956); Stanley Elkins, *Slavery: A Problem in American Institutional and Intellectual Life* (Chicago: University of Chicago Press, 1959); Charles Sellers (ed.), *The Southerner as American* (Chapel Hill: University of North Carolina Press, 1960); and William Barney, *The Road to Secession* (New York: Praeger Publishers, 1972). An often-cited article, Alfred H. Conrad and John Meyer, "The Economics of Slavery in the Ante-bellum South," *The Journal of Political Economy*, 66 (April, 1958), pioneered the use of quantitative techniques to reverse a widely shared view by proving that slavery was in fact highly profitable. This process has reached its ultimate in a recent controversial study by Robert W. Fogel and Stanley L. Engerman, *Time on the Cross* (Boston: Little, Brown and Co., 1974).

Several compilations of contemporary and historical viewpoints and essays are very valuable. Perhaps the best of these is

Charles Crowe (ed.), *Age of Civil War and Reconstruction* (Homewood, Illinois: Dorsey Press, 1966), a superb collection which has sent many students eagerly off in search of further work by authors cited. In addition to the previously cited Edwin C. Rozwenc (ed.), *The Causes of the American Civil War*, the D. C. Heath Co. of Lexington, Massachusetts, has also published Rozwenc (ed.), *Slavery as a Cause of the Civil War* (1963); Hugh Hawkins (ed.), *The Abolitionists* (1964 and 1972 editions); and Norton Garfinkle (ed.), *Lincoln and the Coming of the Civil War* (1959). Harold D. Woodman (ed.), *Slavery and the Southern Economy* (New York: Harcourt, Brace, and World, Inc., 1966), is also very useful.

The court proceedings and the opinions and decision in the Dred Scott case have been reprinted as *Report of the Decision of the Supreme Court of the United States in the Case of Dred Scott Versus Sandford* (New York: The Da Capo Press, 1970). Various books on the period have dealt with the case in different ways, but the best volume dealing entirely with it is probably Stanley Kutler (ed.), *The Dred Scott Case: Law or Politics* (Boston: Houghton Mifflin Co., 1966), which includes relevant parts of the proceedings along with contemporary praise and criticisms and the later views of several historians. Thomas Hart Benton's contemporary *Historical and Legal Examination of the Dred Scott Case* (New York: D. Appleton & Co., 1857) is still worth the attention of the serious scholar.

A starting point for the Kansas question is Roy F. Nichols, "The Kansas-Nebraska Act, A Century of Historiography," *Mississippi Valley Historical Review*, 43 (Sept., 1956). Frank H. Hodder, "Genesis of the Kansas-Nebraska Act," *Wisconsin State Historical Society Bulletin No. 60* (1912), and his protégé James C. Malin, *The Nebraska Question* (Ann Arbor: Edwards Brothers, 1953), and *John Brown and the Legend of '56* (New York: Haskell House, 1971, originally 1942), pioneered in research to show that Kansas was far more than a struggle between slavery and freedom. Paul W. Gates, *50 Million Acres* (Ithaca: Cornell University Press, 1954), stresses the conflicting land claims. The most complete monograph on actual events in Kansas is Alice Nichols, *Bleeding Kansas* (New York: Oxford Press, 1954).

Because Stephen A. Douglas and Abraham Lincoln play such major roles in the Buchanan period, their biographies are essential. Douglas has been fortunate in that various talented historians have been rescuing him from obscurity for half a century, and surely the recent massive *Stephen A. Douglas* (New York: Oxford University

211

Press, 1973) by Robert Johannsen should stand as a definitive work. Earlier and also valuable are Allen Johnson, *Stephen A. Douglas* (New York: Macmillan Co., 1908); George F. Milton, *The Eve of Conflict* (Boston: Houghton-Mifflin Co., 1934); and Gerald M. Capers, *Stephen A. Douglas* (Boston: Little, Brown and Co., 1959). Milton concentrates on the last few years and, while openly partisan, his book contains many valuable details. Capers is much briefer but he captures the essential Douglas.

A list of Lincoln titles would fill a book. Benjamin P. Thomas, *Abraham Lincoln* (New York: Alfred A. Knopf, 1952) is usually considered the best one-volume study. Lincoln can best be captured, however, by reading his own words in Roy P. Basler (ed.), *The Collected Works of Abraham Lincoln* (New Brunswick: Rutgers University Press, 1965), eight volumes plus index. Robert Johannsen has provided an accessible edition of *The Lincoln-Douglas Debates* (New York: Oxford University Press, 1965). William E. Barringer, *A House Dividing: Lincoln as President-Elect* (Springfield: The Abraham Lincoln Association, 1945), and David Potter, *Lincoln and His Party in the Secession Crisis* (New Haven: Yale University Press, 1942), provide detailed and incisive analyses of Lincoln's thinking and policies during the period between his election and inauguration. Potter and Richard N. Current, *Lincoln and the First Shot* (Philadelphia: J. B. Lippincott Co., 1963), carry the story through the attack on Fort Sumter. The Lincoln portrait in Richard Hofstadter, *The American Political Tradition and the Men Who Made It* (New York: Alfred A. Knopf, 1948), also deserves careful study, as does the previously mentioned compilation by Norton Garfinkle (ed.), *Lincoln and the Coming of the Civil War*. Don E. Fehrenbacher, *Prelude to Greatness* (Palo Alto: Stanford University Press), deals profoundly with Lincoln in the 1850s.

The controversy between Buchanan and General Scott cannot be judged fairly without studying Scott's version, but neither of Scott's biographers, Charles W. Elliott, *Winfield Scott* (New York: Macmillan Co., 1936), and Arthur D. H. Smith, *Old Fuss and Feathers; the Life and Exploits of Lt. General Winfield Scott* (New York: The Greystone Press, 1937), nor the general himself in *Memoirs of Lieut.-General Scott, LLD* (New York: Sheldon & Co., 1864), two volumes, does much for his side of the argument.

Other biographies that shed light on the period include James P. Shenton, *Robert John Walker* (New York: Columbia University Press, 1961); Glyndon Van Deusen, *William Henry Seward* (New York: Oxford Press, 1967), and *Horace Greeley* (New York: Hill and Wang, 1964 edition); David Donald, *Charles Sumner and the Coming of the Civil War* (New York: Alfred A. Knopf, 1960); Avery Craven, *Edmund Ruffin* (New York: D. Appleton & Co., 1932); Laura White, *Robert Barnwell Rhett* (New York: Century Co., 1931); Hudson Strode, *Life of Jefferson Davis* (New York: Harcourt, Brace and Co., 1955), 2 vols.; Elbert B. Smith, *Magnificent Missourian: The Life of Thomas Hart Benton* (Philadelphia: J. B. Lippincott Co., 1958); Oliver P. Chitwood, *John Tyler* (New York: Russell & Russell, Inc., 1964); James B. Ranck, *Albert Gallatin Brown* (New York: Appleton Century Co., 1937); James T. Dubois and Gertrude S. Mathews, *Galusha A. Grow* (Boston: Houghton Mifflin Co., 1917); Tilden G. Edelstein, *Strange Enthusiasm, a Life of Thomas Wentworth Higginson* (New Haven: Yale University Press, 1968); Benjamin P. Thomas and Harold M. Hyman, *Stanton: The Life and Times of Lincoln's Secretary of War* (New York: Alfred A. Knopf, 1962); John W. Dubose, *The Life and Times of William Lowndes Yancey* (New York: P. Smith, 1942); Louis M. Sears, *John Slidell* (Durham: Duke University Press, 1925); Claude M. Fuess, *The Life of Caleb Cushing* (New York: Harcourt, Brace and Co., 1923); and Burton J. Hendrick, *Lincoln's War Cabinet* (Boston: Little, Brown and Co., 1946). Another incisive memoir is *Life and Times of Frederick Douglass Written by Himself* (Hartford: Park Publishing Co., 1881). Another important printed original source is "The Correspondence of Robert Toombs, Alexander H. Stephens, and Howell Cobb," *Annual Report of the American Historical Association, 1911* (1913), II. William and Bruce Catton trace the events leading to war through the lives of Lincoln and Jefferson Davis in *Two Roads to Sumter* (New York: McGraw Hill, 1963).

Still the best of the John Brown eulogies is Oswald Garrison Villard, *John Brown, 1800–1859* (New York: Alfred A. Knopf, 1943 edition). Villard was William Lloyd Garrison's grandson. Other admirers include William E. B. Dubois, *John Brown* (New York: International Publishers, 1962 edition); David Karsner, *John Brown, Terrible Saint* (New York: Dodd, Mead & Co., 1934); Allan Keller, *Thunder at Harper's Ferry* (Englewood Cliffs: Prentice Hall, Inc., 1958); Richard J. Hinton, *John Brown and His Men* (New York: Funk and Wagnall, 1894, reprinted by Arno Press, 1968); Truman Nelson, *The Old Man: John Brown at Harper's Ferry* (New York: Holt, Rinehart and Winston, 1973); Jules Abels, *Man on Fire: John Brown* (New York: Macmillan Co., 1971); and Louis Ruchames (ed.), *A John Brown Reader* (London: Abelard-

Schuman, 1959). Benjamin Quarles (ed.), *Blacks on John Brown* (Urbana: University of Illinois Press, 1972), as the title implies, stresses Brown's personal relations with blacks, and their natural response to his efforts on their behalf. Among the Brown critics, James C. Malin, *John Brown and the Legend of Fifty-six* (New York: Haskell House, 1971 edition), emphasizes the Kansas phase of Brown's career and argues that he was a horse thief and economic opportunist; Robert Penn Warren, *John Brown, the Making of a Martyr* (New York: Payson & Clark, Ltd., 1929), writes brilliantly and lets the facts speak unfavorably for themselves; J. C. Furnas, *The Road to Harper's Ferry* (New York: William Sloane Associates, 1959), is particularly harsh on the Secret Six, and reflects the 1950s by comparing them to the supporters of Senator Joseph McCarthy; Stephen B. Oates, *To Purge This Land With Blood* (New York: Harper and Row, 1970), stresses Brown's incompetence; and Tilden G. Edelstein in the previously mentioned *Strange Enthusiasm, a Life of Thomas Wentworth Higginson* also deals with Brown's sponsors. The argument essentially involves the question of whether and when a good end justifies a violent and otherwise unjustifiable means. The side-by-side arguments of Ruchames and Edelstein in Hawkins (ed.), *The Abolitionists*, are a good summary of the philosophical controversy. Perhaps the best readily available original source is the record of the Senate investigating committee, published as Robert M. Fogelson and Richard E. Rubenstein (advisory editors), *Mass Violence in America, Invasion at Harper's Ferry* (New York: Arno Press and the New York Times, 1969). See also the provocative comparison of this committee with the Watergate Commission of 1973-74 by Roger Bruns, "Select Committee Clamor Echoes Through a Century," *Washington Post*, Sept. 16, 1973.

The background against which President Buchanan's foreign policies were enunciated and occasionally executed is well described by Frederick Merk, *Manifest Destiny and Mission in American History* (New York: Vintage Edition, 1966); Kenneth Bourne, *Britain and the Balance of Power in North America* (Berkeley: University of California Press, 1967); and J. Fred Rippy, *Latin America in World Politics* (New York: F. S. Crofts and Co., 1940). Buchanan's own statements and reports are all in Moore, *The Works of James Buchanan*. The president's near war on the Mormons is detailed in Robert R. Mullen, *The Latter-Day Saints* (Garden City: Doubleday, 1966); Nels Anderson, *Desert Saints* (Chicago: University of Chicago Press, 1942); and Stanley Hirsshon, *The Lion of*

214

the Lord (New York: Alfred A. Knopf, 1969). Cornelius Conway, *The Utah Expedition . . . by a Wagon Master of the Expedition* (originally 1858, published on microcards in 1960 by Lost Cause Press, Louisville), tells the story from a soldier's perspective.

Most of the contemporary works which helped feed the "Cold War" of the 1850s remain available to the general reader. The Frederick Law Olmsted series includes *A Journey in the Seaboard Slave States* (New York: Mason Brothers, 1856); *A Journey Through Texas* (New York: Dix, Edwards & Co., 1857); *A Journey in the Back Country* (New York: Mason Brothers, 1860); and *The Cotton Kingdom* (New York: Mason Brothers, 1861–62). Hinton Rowan Helper, *The Impending Crisis of the South and How To Meet It* (New York: A. B. Burdick, 1860) was reprinted by Collier Books in New York in 1963. Samuel M. Wolfe's refutation, *Helper's Impending Dissected* (New York: J. T. Lloyd, 1860), shows both the Southerner's indignation and his concern. George Fitzhugh's *Sociology for the South; or, The Failure of Free Society* and *Cannibals All!; or, Slaves Without Masters* (both Richmond: A. Morris, 1854 and 1857) remain the classic defense of slavery. Harvard University Press published a new edition of *Cannibals All!* in 1965. An excellent distillation of Helper and Fitzhugh is Harvey Wish, *Antebellum Writings of George Fitzhugh and Hinton Rowan Helper on Slavery* (New York: Capricorn Books, 1960). Thomas P. Kettell, *Southern Wealth and Northern Profits* (New York: George W. and John A. Wood, 1860) has been republished on microcards by Lost Cause Press, Louisville, 1966. A good overall summary is William S. Jenkins, *Pro-Slavery Thought in the Old South* (Gloucester, Mass.: P. Smith, 1960).

Perhaps the best contemporary account of the three presidential conventions in 1860 is that of Murat Halstead, a journalist whose reports have been edited and combined by William B. Hesseltine (ed.), *Three Against Lincoln* (Baton Rouge: Louisiana State University Press, 1960). Special studies of the election itself include Ollinger Crenshaw, *The Slave States in the Presidential Election of 1806* (Baltimore: Johns Hopkins Press, 1945); Norman A. Graebner (ed.), *Politics and the Crisis of 1806* (Urbana: University of Illinois Press, 1961); and the older but still useful Emerson D. Fite, *The Presidential Campaign of 1860* (New York: Macmillan Co., 1911).

The all-important question of secession is in one way or another dealt with by most of the books previously mentioned. Dwight L. Dumond, *The Secession Movement, 1860–1861* (New York: Macmillan Company, 1931), remains unsurpassed for thoroughness of research, and his *Southern Editorials on Secession* (New York: The Century Co., 1931) is still an invaluable original source. The previously mentioned newer books by Eugene Genovese, *The Political Economy of Slavery*, and William E. Barney, *The Road to Secession*, argue that a desperate need for expansion triggered secession. Charles G. Sellers in his own chapter in Sellers (ed.), *The Southerner as American*, stresses the internal psychological conflict of Southern leaders trying to reconcile slavery with the obvious contradictions of slavery. Gerald Johnson, *The Secession of the Southern States* (New York: G. P. Putnam's Sons, 1933), follows a popular rather than scholarly format, but contains some profound insights. Steven A. Channing, *Crisis of Fear and Secession in South Carolina* (New York: Simon and Schuster, 1970), brilliantly analyzes the attitudes in one state. The older book by Ulrich B. Phillips, *The Course of the South to Secession* (New York: Hill and Wang, 1964), also stresses race, pride, and fear. Clarence P. Denman, *The Secession Movement in Alabama* (Montgomery: State Department of Archives and History, 1933), contains many valuable documents and quotations. Ralph Wooster, *The Secession Conventions of the South* (Princeton: Princeton University Press, 1962), is primarily a statistical and demographic study. George H. Knoles (ed.), *The Crisis of the Union, 1860–1861* (Baton Rouge: Louisiana State University Press, 1965), presents the views of several mature and wise historians. Jesse L. Keene, *The Peace Convention of 1861* (Tuscaloosa: Confederate Publishing Company, 1961), is a detailed chronicle of the Tyler peace effort sponsored by the Virginia legislature.

Probably the best study of the Fort Sumter situation and crisis is W. A. Swanberg, *First Blood; The Story of Fort Sumter* (New York: Scribner's, 1957). Both he and Samuel W. Crawford, *The History of the Fall of Fort Sumter* (Philadelphia: S. W. Crawford, 1887), deal fairly with Buchanan. Crawford was an army surgeon at the fort. Abner Doubleday, who was also present, recorded his experiences and his anti-Southern feelings in *Reminiscences of Fort Sumter and Moultrie in 1860–61* (New York: Harper & Brothers, 1876). John S. Tilley, *Lincoln Takes Command* (Chapel Hill: University of North Carolina Press, 1941), deals primarily with Lincoln's role, as does the previously mentioned Richard N. Current, *Lincoln and the First Shot*. Roy Meredith, *Storm over Sumter* (New York: Simon and Shuster, 1957), is an exciting if unscholarly narrative, but is entirely inaccurate in its treatment of President Buchanan.

My conviction that racial prejudice rather than economic gain made both slavery and a war for its preservation possible stems in large part from my childhood and youth in the South. My belief that the same feelings in the North made Southern slavery entirely safe in 1861 is equally affected by my adult years in the North. These opinions receive strong scholarly support in Winthrop Jordan, *White Over Black: Development of American Attitudes Toward the Negro* (Chapel Hill: University of North Carolina Press, 1966); William R. Stanton, *The Leopard's Spots: Scientific Attitudes Toward Race in America, 1815–59* (Chicago: University of Chicago Press, 1960); Leon F. Litwack, *North of Slavery: The Negro in the Free States* (Chicago: University of Chicago Press, 1961); Eric Foner, *Free Soil, Free Labor, Free Men* (New York: Oxford University Press, 1970); James A. Rawley, *Race and Politics: "Bleeding Kansas" and the Coming of the Civil War* (Philadelphia: J. B. Lippincott Co., 1969); and several other previously mentioned books.

Index